BOOK OF THE TRANSCENDENCE

COSMIC HISTORY CHRONICLES

Volume VI

TIME AND THE NEW UNIVERSE OF MIND

Transmitted by Valum Votan—Jose Arguelles
Received by Red Queen—Stephanie South
"We are but the secretaries, the authors are in Eternity"

YELLOW SELF-EXISTING SEED: DEVOTION

Book of the Transcendence – Cosmic History Chronicles Volume VI
Copyright © Galactic Research Institute

 Yellow Self-Existing Seed Year (2010)

Law of Time
P R E S S

ISBN 978-0-9785924-3-1
www.lawoftime.org

Printed by Interlink Productions, Ltd., China

Original Graphics by Valum Votan (Jose Arguelles), Kin 11 and Red Queen (Stephanie South), Kin 185
Computer enhancement by Kelly Harding, Kin 240 and Jacob Wyatt, Kin 201
Book Design and Layout by Kelly Harding, Kin 240
Copy Edit by Forrest O'Farrell, Kin 140 and Jacob Wyatt, Kin 201

Dedicated

to

The Children of Tomorrow

BOOK OF THE TRANSCENDENCE
COSMIC HISTORY CHRONICLES VOLUME VI

CONTENTS

INTRODUCTION TO *BOOK OF THE TRANSCENDENCE*

This book, the sixth of the series, was born out of the need and the urgency of the time. We sense that as we approach the end of the cycle the current civilization, already experiencing deep structural problems, may face even more catastrophic breakdowns, including the possibility of a disruption of the electromagnetic grid. Should this occur, what do you do then? How do you respond? What do you need to know?

Not only is it necessary to have a grasp of rudimentary survival skills and be prepared in advance by developing an elementary garden culture, a system of alternative technologies, and simplification of our material plane habits, but also to be a worthy vessel and carrier of the new knowledge and consciousness. This would not be the first time in the history of the race that the continuity of knowledge was kept alive by a few dedicated groups of people in the face of the destruction of the old order.

In this case, however we are confronted with the breakdown of an entire global civilization, and the need to carry the seeds of an entirely new system of knowledge into the dawn of a new and purified world.

With these contingencies in mind *Volume VI, Book of the Transcendence* has been prepared. You will find this volume packed with new information, new methods, new forms of yoga or yogic discipline, new programs of information, and new practices to orient your mind and heart in the direction of full noospheric engagement. In short, this volume contains a new whole system program that can be studied, followed and applied. It is a whole system that relates the whole person to the whole planet—and then to the galaxy beyond.

It is called *Book of the Transcendence* because the whole point of intelligent existence on this planet at this time is to answer the question: how do we transcend the log-jam and biases of culture, family history, religion, politics and so forth that clog our minds and souls? Not only do we have whole catalogs of misdirected or worn-out psychic and spiritual baggage that we continue to haul around with us, but we are also enmeshed in a physically debilitating, psychically draining and ego-magnifying cybersphere. How do we get beyond the cybersphere? What does it look like on the other side of the cybersphere?

The historical cycle provided a few clues or foundational tools for the enduring science and spiritual practices that constitute the science and methods of transcendence, and which have been incorporated into the *Book of the Transcendence* as the they provide the links or continuity that take us from the cycle of transformation (history) into the cycle of Transcendence (noosphere). These links include: The system of yoga, the I Ching and the shrine of the Ka'bah in Mecca. In the *Book of the Transcendence* these spiritual foundations are renewed and expanded both in their meaning and application, so you will find for study and practice forms of Holographic and Synchrogalactic Yoga, the Cube of Knowledge, and the 128-Codon Galactic I Ching.

The premise of transcendence is, of course, wholly spiritual. The cosmological framework for the transcendence has already been established in the previous volumes of the *Cosmic History Chronicles:* Out of the divine nature the soul was manifest into the world of matter, and at a critical point of involution, the soul evolves out of matter back to the divine source. What each of us is in our deepest self is the Divine in the individual form ascending back out of our limited nature into our own proper divinity and sacred wholeness, where we become united and whole with the All.

This can be both an individual soul process and a collective evolutionary process. When the collective reaches the critical point of involution of the mass planetary soul, then a great turning point occurs, the transformation of organic matter into the direction of reaching a purely spiritual and supermental existence. *Book of the Transcendence* occurs at precisely this turning point, a guidebook with methods to practice and absorb as we aspire to receive the descent of the supermind of cosmic consciousness.

emerges is of a highly realistic exercise in pursuit and interrogation, during which the recruit must show the ability to evade capture and also to resist some incisive interrogation techniques. If he fails at any stage, then he is RTU'd.

So what do we know about the course content? In its outline it runs in roughly three stages. Firstly, the recruit is given training in evasion techniques, usually as part of his general survival training. Secondly, he and several other recruits have to conduct an evasion exercise, while being pursued by soldiers from other British Army units plus the instructors. Whether they are caught or not (the recruits have to evade until they reach a particular rendezvous) at the end of the exercise they will have to go into a Resistance to Interrogation exercise. This third section of the course is run by the Joint Services Interrogation Unit (JSIU) – responsible for interrogation training amongst all sections of the armed forces. Indeed, during the E&E the SAS recruit may find himself in a mixed team of soldiers which can include RAF and Navy pilots, another group highly desirable for an enemy unit to capture. During the Resistance to Interrogation exercise, the recruit will be exposed psychologically and physically to the type of treatment they could expect at the hands of captors, short of damaging physical torture. If they can get through a 24-48 hour period of this treatment without talking inappropriately to their interrogators, then they will have passed the E&E section of the course. Completing this section can also be the last element of CT, so the inspiration and motivation to do well is powerful. Pass this, and you could be a full member of the SAS.

We shall now look in more detail at the E&E content as it is known in the public domain, and pick up on the tips for successfully passing this element of the course. The pursuit section takes place in various wilderness locations across the UK, sometimes Exmoor, sometimes Snowdonia or the Brecon Beacons, other times up on the North York Moors.

RIGHT: Jungle locations are usually laced with waterways, and there is also plenty of wood for constructing rafts. All rafts should be tested in safe stretches of water before using them more ambitiously. They should be light enough to carry for short distances around obstacles.

PART I
TRANSCENDENCE AND EVOLUTION

CHAPTER 1

KEY TO TRANSCENDENCE

1. Every living dynamic has ever aspired to surpass itself. In this aspiration lies the key to transcendence. The need to transcend is often the function of a crisis in which we find ourselves, individually or collectively.

2. The planet has a cosmic life program apart from the external chaos and disturbances that affect the world today. At this stage in the evolutionary cycle, the biopsychic field is in a state of maximum turbulence, to such a degree that even the DNA is in a state of agitation.

3. The theater of psychic activity on this planet is interplanetary—beyond the scale of what most of us can presently imagine. The consciousness horizon that we have been operating on has been set at a low frequency and is continually lowering.

4. The average person today is so involved in technological gadgets, sporting events, movies and social networking that it is hard for most to conceive what it is to consciously function as a cosmic impulse receiver and transmitter. We have traded in the keys of higher consciousness and transcendence for online personas that have little to do with our essence.

5. To gain a wider view of cosmos it is important to develop the capacity to withdraw our mind from the chaos of the world and look down on the whole Earth from above. We must leave our conditioned world-view behind and find the thread of light within that connects us to the Divine Source.

6. The divine calls upon the human in order to realize itself. Only a few at this time can penetrate that barrier of consciousness and realize themselves as interplanetary vortex transmitter-receivers within the solar system, and ultimately in other parts of the universe.

7. The urge to transcend is a natural dynamic built into the cosmic principle of the involution and evolution of consciousness. It is the duty of those who hear the call to surrender and merge with the cosmic energies that are currently working for the liberation of the Earth.

8.   The first key to transcendence is to recognize that the external world is only a particular hologram of reality. It is a collective dream that operates purely on the third-dimensional plane and is ruled by conditioned patterns of thought and behavior with a narrow band of mental frequencies.

9.   Most people operate habitually and unconsciously according to programs inherited from family and influenced by friends, media, environment, education and geographical location. Who they think they are is actually a set of programs running in a predictable order according to different cues and stimuli that creates particular responses. This pattern plays out in self-reinforcing feedback loops. Many people believe that this pre-recorded feedback loop is who they are and what reality is. This creates a theater of events populated by programmed automatons who are run by a system of which they are largely unconscious.

10. Cosmic History contains coded keys for the development of transcendental thoughtforms that surpass the limitations of our present knowledge structures. This is all part of the interdimensional software program downloaded from higher dimensions.

11. To transcend is to go beyond the present state of conditioned being; this is the purpose of life. True fulfillment is experienced when we orient our will to a vision or purpose greater than ourselves. To fulfill this purpose we must constantly strive to become better, to expand our consciousness and lift our awareness above day-to-day concerns. We are meant to become channels of divine intelligence. In this process, it is helpful to have a system or systematic application that makes the path clear.

BOOK OF THE TRANSCENDENCE

The sixth heptad gate, coded by radial plasma Limi, opens to the Book of the Transcendence. This gate is coordinated by the archetype of the Yogi/Yogini, the exemplar whose sole purpose is to enact the possibilities of transcendence in the human form.

12. Many spiritual or psychological systems exist for this purpose, though most are referred to in an individual context (like personal transcendence as described in the majority of religious or mystical traditions). This usually means waking up to the fact that the world is living mired in confusion within a veil of ignorance, and that a path or paths exist by which we may acknowledge the illusion and the ignorance and move beyond it.

13. We are at the time of the great synthesis, when we must extract the useful nectar from historical teachings and scriptures in the process of reenvisioning and reshaping the world. We transcend

duality by recognizing the place of all paths within the whole. This defines the systems of yoga as a universally integrative template of evolving consciousness within the synchronic order.

14. Up to this point we have only been operating with a small portion of our brain capacity. We are so preoccupied by the external world that we let outside circumstances decide for us so we do not have to think. We let the government do it. We let the insurance company do it. We let the institutions do it. We let the machine do it. Our will to exertion is greatly undermined.

15. The machine maintains an unquestioned, unspoken belief system about the physical nature of reality and being. As technological speed and expansion increases, the cyber and electronic technologies impact the human mind and senses so swiftly that there is no time for social assessment of the impact. Our inner power of analytic wisdom is replaced by online avatars who can think for us.

CYBER-MATRIX

Many are caught in a routine that prioritizes the cybersphere over real life. The cybersphere is an intermediate and necessary stage in the evolution of the human species. It is the system of intelligence produced by and dependent upon the artificial electronic information technology, i.e. the Internet.

The cybersphere is a primitive shadow of the noosphere, the fourth-dimensional thinking layer of the planet. At present it is the cyber matrix that holds the entire knowledge of the present world order in place. Everyone to some degree or another is caught up in this particular world construct or matrix.

16. We are maintainers of the machine, and maintainers of the illusory order that governs us. We allow our brain power to be usurped by machine consciousness. We do not think. We play games. We watch videos. We email and text message. We do anything but think. We exhaust ourselves by trying to keep up with and maintain the machine so we do not have much energy to think.

For this reason we are kept in a narrow third-dimensional frequency using only 15 percent of our brain power.

17. We are evolving from our present human nature, mutating as a unified humanity and transforming into a new state of being. At this stage, personal transcendence is insufficient; we must strive for collective planetary transcendence. Transcend. Evolve. Mutate. Transform. These are powerful, loaded words. By evolutionary necessity—the survival of consciousness—we are now in a time of accelerated transcendence.

We must transcend conditioned thought responses in order to look at any person, place or thing and see clearly which point in Cosmic History it is reflecting.

18. We are pointed toward the noosphere, the evolving mental sheathe of our planet. This involves a major transition, transmutation or evolutionary change. This change is inevitable. We may think we have to do nothing, it will just happen. However, if we wish to transcend, we must cooperate with the higher forces. This process requires an intentional exercise of will, otherwise it cannot happen.

THE POWER OF WILL

19. Transcendence is innate to our nature. If you do not wish to stay the same, then you have to do something. If you are not satisfied, then change your patterns—try something new—something that will elevate your mind and lift your horizons. Conscious change requires you to exercise your power of will.

20. Dissatisfaction and boredom are signals to rise above your present state of consciousness; they are keys to transcendence. Align with the Divine Plan by being ruthless in an honest evaluation of yourself. In this way boredom and dissatisfaction are portals into higher awareness.

21. Our perceptions and ways of thinking are a result of the duality within our minds and the particular moment-to-moment frequency in which we are functioning. These perceptions are actually constructs of different thinking layers that permeate the galaxy in holographic bundles. We tune into specific thinking layers according to our level of consciousness, which is always fluctuating.

22. Transcendence is not only innate to our nature; it is an inherent quality of the entire cosmic fabric into which we are woven. Any process of transcendence requires a simultaneous dose of exertion and patience. If you do not exert, then you recycle the same thoughtforms and perceptions. Most people are impatient and want immediate results. Exertion and patience are the keys. If you do not exert then you are not consciously evolving.

SIX VIRTUES

Transcendental virtues are found in all Holy Scriptures. In the Buddhist tradition there are six paramitas, or transcendental virtues: Generosity, discipline, exertion, patience, meditation and wisdom. Practice of these six virtues requires surrender of self or ego which leads to transcendence.

---

23. Self-help books and programs as well as positive slogans and affirmations are symptomatic of the universal urge to transcend. Beyond the level of self-help analysis, there is a mystical urge to transcend the third-dimensional plane—to break free altogether from the suffocation of our self-reinforced feedback loops. The yogi Milarepa is an outstanding example of one who was able to tame the lower forces and transcend.

24. After a career as a black magician, Milarepa (1052-1135 AD), repented and lived and meditated in a cave for years, sustaining himself on nettle soup and astral light. Through rigorous self-discipline he transcended the physical plane and obtained supernatural powers like walking on water and flying through the air. These powers came through extreme states of exertion set forth by an irresistible mystical urge. In yogic traditions these people are called *siddhas* and their powers, *siddhis*.

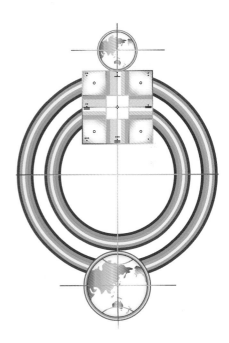

25. Once a certain state of consciousness is reached then cultivation of paranormal powers is experienced; but these powers are only side effects and not the object of practice and exertion. This is true in all cultures at different levels. There are people who exert to the point of transcendence at the physical plane to develop the siddhis. All these types of transcendence have to do with the individual transcendence.

26. By recognizing that individual life is the basic operating unit of the life of the cosmos, then we can raise our sights to collective transcendence and cosmic unification. Liberation is attained

only through ego transcendence. We transcend only when our contained belief system goes beyond automatic robotic egoic impulses.

EXPANDING OUR VISION

27. Let's now expand our lens to encompass the whole collective mind of planet Earth: the noosphere. This awareness leads us to the next stage of evolution. To understand the noosphere, we must first understand the nature of the universe and the purpose and nature of the galaxy.

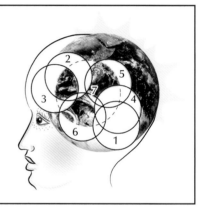

Our evolving consciousness cannot be separated from that of the whole Earth. Like the whole Earth, the human evolves through different stages of consciousness; beginning with preconscious (1), to the unconscious (2), passing through the conscious (3) and continuing conscious (4) to the superconscious (5), and subliminal conscious (6). In the process of evolution, we evolve a new perceptual organ: the holomind perceiver (7).

In Cosmic Science, these states of consciousness are specific functions of the six (+1) mental spheres. To pass through or access these phases requires persistent discipline in control of thoughts.

28. As knowledge expands so does our sphere of consciousness. One hundred forty years ago people scarcely knew that galaxies existed. Now, with the Hubble telescope and space technologies, we can view pictures of the universe and see billions of galaxies—50 billion galaxies! Yet, we cannot even comprehend our own galaxy.

29. Space is full, yet vast and empty. Each galaxy has anywhere from 10 to 50 billion stars. Try to imagine 10 billion × 50 billion stars! Many of those stars have their own planetary systems. If this is so, then how many of these planets are there that support life and consciousness and what, who and where are we?

30. This universe that the Hubble space telescope photographs is the existential dimension of cosmic reality or the manifest universe. This cosmos visible to our senses is the second or external universe.

31. The first universe is the light universe beyond our imagination—the super divine realm where the blueprint of this universe came into existence. The secondary existential universe goes through cycles of expansion and collapse. Within that secondary universe is our own inner universe of evolving consciousness—reaching for the light universe beyond.

32. There occurs from time to time a powerful moment when a physical universe comes into existence from a non-physical plane. Each new universe is "self generated" from the organizational plan of a greater non- or supra-physical universe beyond this one. Materialist science refers to the beginning of this present universe as the "big bang."

33. The existential universe that we know is in its entirety a conglomeration of billions of galaxies, and their billions upon billions of stars and untold numbers of planets. This is but one universe.

34. This universe in its entirety is an enlightenment body projected as a complex thoughtform. The thought construct that formed the universe is still present, alive and evolving. The present chaos and disorder of our small planet has little to do with this thought construct. We must work to comprehend the whole, then we will understand that all of our bickering and wars mean nothing.

35. This universe entity is the evolutionary projection of the light body of God. This light body is the first universe, a complex entity whose beams of thought whisper as spinning spools; each spinning spool is a galaxy and each galaxy is a gigantic thought molecule.

36. Our galaxy is such a thought molecule, a spinning spool 100,000 light years in diameter. We can get a close-up of one little sector of this galaxy and see our solar system—this is an unimaginably vast process that we are involved in.

37. The acceleration of the process of knowledge and technology has brought us to this point of self-reflection where we can get a side view of our galaxy. Think of our galaxy as a galactic being composed of a cosmic thought molecule: The form and structure of a mental entity of the universe, a living being.

Untold numbers of beings just like us in parallel universes are now reading these words and coming to terms with this existential reality.

Tune into this.

17

38. The stars are thought atoms. Around many of the stars different planets go spinning like electrons. In some planets there is life that evolves in all sorts of different forms or structures, such as the planet we find ourselves on.

39. The universe is a luminous and omniscient mental organization. It is the universal thoughtform of the nature of the light universe. How many world systems are there that have biospheric electrons such as Earth now evolved to the present stage as we see here? These planetary electrons seem to be a complex geochemical dynamic meant to sustain thought or a mental layer of the universal order. What is this going to become?

THE HUMAN IS MEANT TO EVOLVE INTO A HOLONOMIC ENERGY CAPACITATOR AND ACTIVATOR, WORKING AS A VITAL COMPONENT IN THE WHOLE SYSTEM OF THE PLANET.

40. The human being is simultaneously a nanospeck and, as a whole, a self-reflective subatomic quantum of intelligence. Nonetheless we—or our collective mind, at least—can conceive of the whole thing. This is an amazing power. Are we like those transistorized micro-nanochips into which numerous complex functions have been programmed?

41. Our mind has the capacity to step outside of the universe and conceive of the whole. This shows that as a subatomic self-reflective intelligence we have a bit of feedback to coordinate with the local star system. This total planetary feedback system is the noosphere.

42. This local star system can be thought of as the thought atom within which we are revolving and evolving. The planet is an electron or little magnetic nanocore of the evolvement of the self-reflective quantum—the human. This electron rotates around the star or thought nucleus.

43. The planetary orbits form a part of the whole etheric stellar body. This body is defined by the resonant waves created by the planetary orbits. To participate wholly in this process—of the planetary self-reflective quantum—we have to vibrate in a state of unified resonance with the rest of the electron we are revolving on. This then places us in resonance with the thought molecule that we are involved in, evolving within, and revolving around. This unified resonance, when realized, is the planetary noosphere.

44. Our mission as reflective transistorized subatomic quanta of intelligence is to unify into a single thought reflex. Right now we are passing through a state of disorganization that creates chaos for the electron that we are revolving on. The star requires a unified orbital field of intelligence to attain a state of higher resonance. We are all in the process of evolution.

45. There are early stages of stellar evolution and there are later stages. We are currently, as a species, at a stage where there is disunification without transcendence. Without unification, there can be no transcendence. The next step is to unify the species and transcend to the level of identification with the structural resonance of the Planet as a whole system. This is what is meant by a "single thought reflex," or noosphere.

46. To attain the power of transcendence is to cultivate the ability to bypass ego and switch into your higher self in any moment (much like Clark Kent going into the phone booth and coming out as Superman). How do we escape the babble of the cybersphere and go upstairs to the higher state?

47. As long as there are political institutions and organizations that affirm the reality of arbitrary boundaries there can be no real unification, just empty structures with egos at the helm. The planetary whole itself—trees, birds, water, atmosphere—is ego free. This is the meaning of transcendence in a planetary context.

48. When the planetary consciousness has attained this ego-free state, then its resonant frequency aligns with all life, and harmony becomes augmented as feedback from the Sun. At this stage, coordinated thought molecules increase frequency and the whole system of the Sun moves to a higher harmony of resonance. In this lies the value and purpose of the noosphere as the medium of collective human transcendence.

We are rapidly accelerating toward the supreme unification of planetary consciousness.

49. The system of yoga from the Hindu tradition is the most prevalent on the planet; its systems of psychophysical integration are a necessary prerequisite for universal transcendence. Yoga is the purest, most well-defined system of spiritual unification, making it the most practical basis of the collective transcendence.

50. We are members of the galaxy, the galaxy being a constituent building block of this universe, the thought projection of the light universe beyond. Within this vast web, building on the foundation of yoga, we acquire new methods and techniques to raise our frequency into resonance with our core essence.

51. Among these new methods is what we refer to as *Synchronotron*, the method consistent with the star masters to affect collective planetary transcendence. This system can first be entered through the gate of the seven chakras in a method of *Synchrogalactic Yoga* (see Chapters 4 and 5). This system gives us steps to create our own ladder to climb up, lifting our perceptions with every step. In this sense yoga is a universal spiritual practice that forms a path of transcendence from one state to another.

52. Though we are involved in a collective transcendence, none of us can raise the consciousness of another. Each of us has to work out his/her own destiny. We can proceed up the steps as quickly as we choose, leaving the stage of history and entering the technicolor reality of the noosphere.

CHAPTER 2

YOGA—FOUNDATION OF COSMIC EVOLUTION

One who has his mind self-absorbed through Yoga, and who has the vision of sameness everywhere, sees his Self existing in everything, and everything in his Self.
                                                                        —*Bhagavad Gita 6.29*

Discard all thoughts that weaken you.
                                    —*Swami Vivekananda*

1. Yoga is the art of cosmic existence, or how we live as cosmic beings. Advance into the next evolutionary stage, homo noosphericus, requires a collective exertion that is yogic in nature.

2. We are at a time when knowledge is being renewed. We are being called to turn inward, away from the virtual cyber-world into the vast realm of our own mind—the ultimate supercomputer. Here, we must learn to harness this enormous energy and potential that we currently project outward, and use it to construct an inner architectural landscape for the good of all.

3. To practice yoga is to reconnect with universal consciousness. This process penetrates artificial layers of conditioned mind in an unwinding or unveiling process that little by little allows true being to emerge. Exertion is the key; it is the mechanism that propels us toward a state of transcendence pushing us ever nearer the godhead.

4. We are all linked to an underlying essence of consciousness. The purpose of yoga is to return to this essence in accordance with the cycles of nature by bringing the body under control of the mind. We think we need wires or satellites to send electricity and transmit information, but Nature needs no wires to send Her currents. Once we learn this we will no longer be enslaved to matter. We will be buddhas, organizing the universe through our minds. To accomplish this, it is necessary to assume some type of yogic process or discipline.

5. Yoga is the most pervasive system in Indian philosophy and spiritual traditions. In the Western world and much of the far

Eastern, there are yoga studios in just about every sizable town and community. There are also numerous books and magazines on the subject of yoga. The yoga phenomenon is so pervasive that it has become a form of popular culture. Why is this so and what does it signify?

6. Yoga means union and is related to the word yoke. More specifically, yoga means union with the divine. This assumes that we have a divine nature or essence and that there is a Supreme Being, a Creator of the universe, an Absolute Reality.

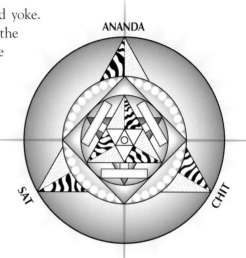

7. Seeking union implies that a separation has occurred. This separation brings a longing to reunite with the divine source, which is a fundamental premise of most spiritual traditions. In Hindu spirituality, yoga is the central method of practice.

8. Every aspect of our daily life embodies a divine gesture, if we are awake in the moment to see. Every moment of existence is a play of divine consciousness or awakening. Yoga practice enhances the quality of existence within our body/mind allowing us to increasingly recognize the divine within each moment. This quality of existence takes into account breathing, postures, movement, mind training, sound and visual techniques.

Sat-Chit-Ananda is a Sanskrit word for God or Eternal Being. Yoga is a path that takes us from unconscious, unrestrained animal appetites to conscious and superconscious states of refined being and superbeing: Sat (being), Chit (mind/consciousness), and Ananda (bliss). Bliss, divine rapture and self-realization are the normative conditions in the next stage of evolution.

9. When yoga was developed in India, a clear distinction was made between yoga for householders and yoga for sannyasins or forest dwellers. The option was given to, either, lead the life of a householder and then at the end of life responsibility, become a sannyasin; or become a sannyasin early on and renounce worldly life.

10. Those who chose to live and practice in remote locations such as forest or mountain retreats, meditating for long hours, moons or years in caves, are the ones who demonstrated the possibilities of superhuman or supermental forms of evolution. Now there are fewer sannyasins.

INDIA
Non-eater to be studied
AHMEDABAD. Prahlad Jani, who has not eaten food or drunk water for 74 years of his 82-year-old life, will be kept under observation by a wing of the Indian defence ministry for 15 days. The Defence Institute of Physiology and Allied Science wants to understand if this process can be replicated in others.
    Jani grew up in the Mehsana district in Gujarat. He claims to have been blessed by a goddess at the age of eight. He says he has gone several decades without food or water because of a hole in his palate. Drops of water filter through this hole, he says, sustaining him.
    Jani, who spends his time meditating, praying and giving blessings.

11. Yoga practitioners today constitute the full spectrum of lifestyles, from the forest yogini down to the common householder. Some yogis even wear watches and carry cell phones. Many people in Western cities practice yoga during their lunch breaks, after work, or on weekends. The key point is that anyone can practice yoga, and at any time in the life cycle.

YOGIC FORMS

12. Hatha Yoga is the most well-known form of yoga in the Western world. Many people mistakenly believe that Hatha Yoga is yoga, but it is merely the branch of yoga dedicated to the physical body. Conditioning and strengthening the body alone does not ensure spiritual evolution or expansion of consciousness. Yoga is a philosophy, system or way of life that covers many forms and techniques, as well as stages of a universal process of spiritual development.

SIX TYPES OF YOGA

There are six principle types of yoga in the Hindu system:

1. Hatha Yoga (primarily focuses on body, asanas and pranayams).
2. Mantra Yoga (chanting and study of absorption of vibrations as path of liberation).
3. Raja Yoga (pure meditation/total subjugation of lower nature).
4. Bhakti Yoga (devotion/prayer as path to liberation).
5. Karma Yoga (work/service to attain liberation).
6. Jnana Yoga (spiritual attainment through mastery of knowledge and awareness—also known as the yoga of knowledge or mind).

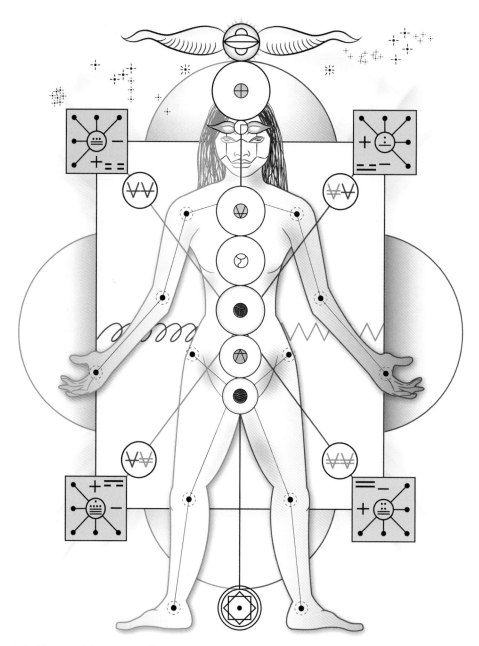

Biopsychic Chips and Supermental Descent
We practice yoga to realize ourselves as synchronized biopsychic chips unified with many other synchronized chips. The point is to create an amalgamated field that will be met by the supermental descent at a particular moment in time. This collective effort will result in advancement into the next evolutionary stage of consciousness. This is the thought or purpose behind the study and practice of yoga.

13. Yoga, in one form or another, has been around as long as human existence. The roots of yoga are closely derived from shamanic techniques of assuming the nagual or spirit animal. This is done by holding particular physical postures, such as the crouching tiger or cobra asana, while simultaneously practicing breath techniques.

14. By holding a particular animal pose, the shaman is able to channel specific levels of energy and attunement that facilitates cosmic alignment. Animals contain a continuous identity between their essence and outer form. They do not deviate from what they are. They are always aligned with themselves.

15. While animals consistently maintain integrity of essence and form, humans tend to separate themselves from their true essence. Practicing asanas or different body positions combined with conscious breathing helps us to regain integrity of form with essence. This is key in the mastery of the asana as defined by the system of Hatha Yoga.

YOGA—NOT JUST FROM INDIA

Different forms of yoga exist throughout most cultures—most notably in the Chinese system of Taoism and martial arts or body arts. These are akin to yoga; especially so with Tai Chi Chuan and traditional Hatha Yoga, which have both developed exercises that coordinate breath with movement of the body in order to develop a concentrated mind. While prana is essential as a subtle energy in yoga, similarly, chi, the vital force, is integrated into the Taoist tradition of form, movement and breath control.

ASHTANGA YOGA AND PATANJALI

By dedicated practice of the various aspects of yoga impurities are destroyed; the crown of wisdom radiates in glory.

—Patanjali, Yoga Aphorisms, 11.28

16. Patanjali, a spiritual master who lived somewhere between 500 and 200 BC, systematized yoga as we know it into "Ashtanga Yoga" or eight-limbed yoga. This is a form of Raja Yoga based on the system of Samkhya, a rigorous analysis of mind and perceptions developed in the late Vedic period.

17. Patanjali compiled these ancient yogic teachings into a series of aphorisms around 2600 years ago. This was the time of the Buddha and about four centuries before the great era of philosophers in

India. The mental conditions we live in today are not the same as the consciousness of the rishis and the Vedic seers of 2000 to 4000 years ago. This is important to keep in mind when studying and practicing yoga.

18. We live in another time—a time of speeded up machine artificiality which leads to increased mental conflict, anxiety and agitation. There is no resemblance between this time and the time before machines and artificial lights to dim the wonders of the night time sky. In essence, yoga is the transmission of a state of consciousness from a time when the world mind was far less contaminated.

19. When we practice yoga today, maybe we are fortunate to live in the forest, maybe it does not matter. Even if we live in a forest, we are still psychically connected to the planetary mind stream and, most likely, to the cybersphere. Our job as conscious humans is to uncover and bring to light the divine or sacred order from beneath the profanity that has embraced the world at the end of the historical cycle.

KALI YUGA AND EXTERNALIZATION OF CONSCIOUSNESS

The Kali Yuga began in 3102 BC with the disincarnation of Krishna, eleven years after 3113 BC. At this point we emerge from the battleground and realize that all the wars and conflicts of the Kali Yuga have been to test the collective human body/mind and bring it to a certain state (where we are now).

At present, we have the opportunity to see how clever we can be, as exemplified by computer engineers. We have seen how high we can jump at the Olympics; we have sent a man to the Moon and robots to Mars; we have cloned animals, tampered with the weather and genetically modified food; and we have created enough nuclear weapons to destroy the world several times over. This is the externalization of consciousness; testing the bounds of the physical realm. Yet we have not solved the problem of human poverty, nor can we keep from destroying the biosphere.

We are now at the threshold of another Sat Yuga or Golden Age. This will transpire through our collective exertion, which opens us as a species to the descent of the supermental force.

There is a higher entity called the Supreme Soul, who is the indestructible, eternal Lord that enters the world and supports it
—Bhagavad Gita, 15:17

EIGHT LIMBS OF YOGA

In his culminating work, the *Yoga Aphorisms,* Patanjali describes the eight limbs of yoga for the ascension of the Kingdom of Heaven within: Yama, Niyama, Asana, Pranayama, Pratyahara, Dharani, Dhyana, and Samadhi. The first four are the four outer limbs and the last four are the four inner limbs.

Yama

Restraint or correct moral practice of truth. Non-violence. Non-stealing. Refrain from greed. Non-killing. Truthfulness.

Niyama

Inner discipline and outer conduct. Cleanliness. Austerity. Study and self-surrender. Inner purification. Exertion. Remember the one Supreme Creator. Control ego.

One whose mind is deluded with egotism thinks, "I am the doer." Yoga system says we are instruments of the divine. For this reason we strive to purify and evolve the body. When Ramakrishna was asked how to attain happiness he said to accept that you are a machine operated by God. This is at the root Niyama; taming ego and surrendering lower impulses through processes of inner and outer purification.

Asana

Body positions/postures. Physical exercises. Disciplining, toning, and strengthen the body. Disciplining mind by attaining control of body and breath.

Asanas include different positions and locks within the body that can be practiced at any time throughout the day no matter what activity you are engaged in. Some traditions say there are 84 asanas. Some yoga systems teach that there are 33 primary asanas, others teach that there are only five.

Pranayama

Breath control. Respiration. Life. Vitality. Prana means breath; Yama means to extend and interrupt the breath.

Pranayama deals with the activation of the inner body through conscious respiration. Pranayams activate the energy body by intaking oxygen through disciplined techniques.

Practice breathing: Inhale four counts, hold four counts, breath out four counts and hold four counts. This simple exercise attunes us to a cosmic process. As you inhale think of the karma of the world. When you hold your breath transmute negative karma and exhale toxins from body transmuting them to light. Retain breath again attaining a state of absolute quiet identification or union with the universal process.

These are the four outer limbs.

Pratyahara

Detaching or withdrawing mind from senses. Training mind to master senses. Withdrawing habitual responses to conditioned sensory input.

Pratyahara—the ability of attaching or detaching the mind from the senses—means "gathering towards." How do we free the mind from the voice of the senses? When we blindly succumb to the whims of our senses then we are no more than mindless machines. How do we stop being a machine operated by the external world and return to being a machine operated by God? To do this we must learn to submit to a higher will and not respond to every conditioned sensory input. This is the essence of Pratyahara.

If the mind were disciplined then people would not do foolish things that they later regret. This is the training of the mind—to make it so strong that the senses have no control over it nor do the opinions of others. This is the mastery of the external and internal nature, the ability not to be influenced by the thoughtforms of others.

Dharani

Concentration. Focus. Ability to fix the mind on a certain point, thought or sound to the exclusion of all other input.

In order to practice Dharani it is helpful to know your mission in life. Then you will have a focus to base your one-pointed practice on. From time to time, shut your mind to outside influences or opinions. Set aside a time when you will not be distracted. If you can really concentrate, the mind will focus: Sustain the mental focus on one dot or one sound allowing nothing else to interfere. This develops concentration, the ability to keep your mind in one place for an extended duration. The method of concentration is also applied to the Hatha Yoga asanas when holding a bodily position. If your mind starts to wander then you will lose your balance.

Dhyana

Uninterrupted meditation. Unbroken current of mindfulness.

In Dhyana practice we see how thoughts arise and dissolve. If a thought arises, do not examine it, just let it go. Experience how ceaseless the process of thoughts may be. Practice not chasing every thought that arises. Observe how your mind begins to calm as less and less thoughts arise.

Dhyana teaches us to experience the essence of ourselves and of reality. This leads into the final stage of the eight limbs, or samadhi, which means union or integration. Dhyana comes only after your mind is able to remain in a state of concentration for a prolonged duration. When this power is cultivated then it is easy to focus purely on a plane of inner contemplation, which brings us to samadhi.

Samadhi

Uninterrupted Dhyana. Cessation of thought. Attainment of union with space, akasha or the universal plane of existence.

Swami Vivekananda explains samadhi this way: "If the mind can first concentrate upon an object, and then is able to continue in the concentration for a length of time, and then, by continued concentration, can dwell only on the internal part of the perception, of which the object was the effect, or gross part, everything comes under its control. This meditative state is the highest state of existence: samadhi."

Samadhi is the superconscious state arrived at after following the other steps of yoga. This forms the foundation for the yogic way of life. Informative samadhi occurs effortlessly when telepathic networks of the universe become evident at the periphery of consciousness. Information may spontaneously fall into your mind. This is where so-called channeled information or revelation comes from.

These are the four inner limbs.

20. Patanjali says that yoga, union with God, is possible only by stilling the restlessness of the heart. He enumerates five obstacles to be cautious of when practicing yoga (*Yoga Sutras* 11.3): *avidya* (ignorance, individual delusion), *asmita* (ego, the body-identified state of the soul), *raga* (attachment, attraction to what one likes), *dvesha* (aversion, dislikes), *abhinivesha* (body attachment).

21. In his book, *The Second Coming of Christ,* Indian yogi, Paramahansa Yogananda, describes Patanjali as a great sage and illustrates how his teachings are similar to that of Jesus. Yogananda describes Jesus as a great yoga master and compares his teachings in the Sermon on the Mount to the foundational steps of yama and niyama. Yogananda compares the Lord's Prayer as given by Jesus, with the ancient sacred scriptures of India as epitomized by the Bhagavad Gita. Yogananda breaks down the prayer into four distinct parts, the first three of which he compares with the systems of Jnana, Karma and Bhakti yoga.

Our Father which art in heaven, hallowed be thy name. Thy kingdom come. Thy will be done in earth, as it is in heaven. Give us this day our daily bread. And forgive us our debts as we forgive our debtors. And lead us not into temptation, but deliver us from evil. For thine is the kingdom, and the power and the glory forever. Amen. (Matthew 6:9 – 13)

YOGA OF THE LORD'S PRAYER

1. *Our Father which art in heaven, hallowed be thy name. Thy kingdom come.* (Demonstrates Jnana yoga—union with the infinite through wisdom. Realization of spirit as the only reality. Refers to the Creator (Father) of transcendental consciousness and to His eternal creation (kingdom). This is an example of truth realization of ultimate wisdom—Jnana Yoga).

2. *Thy will be done in earth, as it is in heaven. Give us this day our daily bread. And forgive us our debts as we forgive our debtors.* (Demonstrates Karma yoga—union with the infinite through right action. The key word is "will." Signifies that the holy creative vibration will be brought to earth via Divine Will. Bread refers to cosmic energy which sustains all life. "Forgive" expresses karmic law of cause and effect. This is Karma Yoga—through right action and selfless work we receive divine sustenance and union).

3. *And lead us not into temptation, but deliver us from evil.* (Demonstrates Bhakti yoga—union with the infinite through divine love. Surrender, prayer and devotion to God helps us stay on the right path and diverts us from temptation).

4. *For thine is the kingdom, and the power and the glory forever. Amen.* (Illustrates the power of the Infinite Spirit and the underlying unity of the universal experience of God realized by Jesus, Buddha, Muhammad, Krishna, Moses, Abraham and all other illumined prophets. Amen is similar to Aum. All things are one within this cosmic vibration).

SRI AUROBINDO AND YOGA

22. The high purpose of the realized yogis and spiritual masters has always been sustained by samadhi. This is not a static achievement but a dynamic one. At the closing of history, the samadhi opens to an evolutionary transformation. This is the contribution of the last great sage and yogi of this tradition: Sri Aurobindo, a contemporary of Yogananda.

23. While synthesizing the entirety of yogic tradition Aurobindo clearly saw that humanity was in a process of cosmically ordained transformation. He presented a revolutionary vision of yoga and foresaw the next stage of human evolution as the supermental descent of the supermind.

24. Sri Aurobindo perceived that the human is now at a transitory stage going from individual consciousness to higher collective consciousness and finally to the supermental mind. He believed in the transformation and spiritualization of the physical body and saw no dualism between body, mind, soul and consciousness.

25. In Aurobindo's philosophy, the body, spirit and mind are one integrated vehicle of a continuously self-transformative process, ascending into ever more subtle vibrations of light. He emphasizes that as we make the effort to etherealize the body by lifting ourselves into higher states of mind and consciousness, we will be met—at a certain point—by a supramental descent that will begin a new order of being beyond mind. In his book, *Synthesis of Yoga*, Sri Aurobindo emphasizes three types of yoga.

   1) **Yoga of divine works**. This is a form of Karma Yoga, where we dedicate our service to the Supreme One. This is the process of continuing remembrance.

   2) **Yoga of divine love.** This is a form of Bhakti Yoga, where everything we do becomes an expression of the principle of divine love and compassion. We are not living just for ourselves, but we devote everything to the Supreme One. Everything is an act of love. In this yoga, we continuously surrender the lower self by embracing and dedicating all of our actions to the whole of humanity. This type of yoga is exemplified by Indian teacher, Ammachi, also known as the "hugging saint."

   3) **Yoga of integral knowledge and self-perfection**. This is a form of Jnana Yoga, where we are continuously rising to ever-greater refinements of knowledge and being: mental, supermental and supramental. The attainment of these states of knowledge comes about through a process of continuous self-perfection, the very method of spiritual evolution.

26. As life in its early stages evolves into a human or intelligence phase, it develops mind and consciousness. The final process of this development is what Aurobindo refers to as the "Yoga of Self-Perfection"—the full embodiment of Higher Mind and being. This is the ultimate expression of the process of yoga as the foundation for cosmic evolution. This yogic process activates and evolves the noosphere. What Aurobindo refers to as the "descent of the supermind" coincides with the transformative appearance of the noosphere, the planetary mind.

SUPERMENTAL CONSCIOUSNESS

27. In *Integral Yoga*, Sri Aurobindo makes clear that just as there is a stage of matter before life, there is life after mind and consciousness. This is the supermental state, and beyond that is the supramental. This climax of the latter state is the source of the descent of different revelations of divine information. This implies that in the universe there are stages of evolution and consciousness far beyond what we can currently conceive.

FULFILLMENT OF THE EVOLUTIONARY JOURNEY

In the process of life and creation, we advance from a beginning state of electron plasma to crystallization into matter. Matter then goes through a natural state of refinement and becomes life. When matter becomes life it develops an unconscious mental faculty that evolves into mind. However, this is a limited conditioned mind that learns through ignorance, ever aspiring to a higher state. This next stage is the supermind or truth consciousness and occurs through a supermental descent.

---

28. As mind advances to the supermental it inevitably engages levels of intelligence and self-perfection that constitute a vast unified domain of evolved life in numerous other world systems: Cosmic civilization. There is an incredibly vast cosmic civilization that has its own levels and grades of evolution. At this cosmic state of evolution, we are supramental beings that have gone beyond the entitization of individual self. This is what the Dynamics of Time refers to as the hyperorganic and subliminal states of consciousness where finally the body itself has been transmuted into light.

29. The stage of the Earth human occurs at 13.7 billion years into the current cosmic cycle. The human is passing from the state where consciousness has been operating in a preconscious or unconscious manner. The struggle of the human being at this stage is to remain conscious and develop discipline of both body and mind to rise to the stage of continuing consciousness, the supermental descent.

30. As we advance on the inner planes, we recognize that there are hierarchies of intelligence beyond us. There are higher intelligences that create crop circles through supermental techniques of telepathic inscription at long distances. We are also capable of this. Higher beings are showing us that this is a potentiality for us as well.

31. We can create crop circles just as we can create a circuit board or computer chip. The emphasis is now on the yoga of self-perfection—the self evolving into a perfect state of union with God and with other selves as a collective called the noosphere or the descent of the supermind. This is the process of self-synchronization.

32. In the life of the noosphere, everything will be considered yoga. Asanas, pranayama,

Image source: www.cropcircleconnector.com

dhyana, mudra, mantra, mandala and synchronotronics all combine to create a spectrum of higher consciousness through disciplined activity. This is the purpose of *Synchrogalactic Yoga* as introduced in Chapters 4 and 5.

33. By synchronizing body, mind and spirit, we become an integrated noospheric chip. This is a yogic process of total integration. In this process we become synchronized with cosmic forces and parallel universes. This is an unfolding stage that we are now entering.

> *Note: We honor and give thanks to all yogic transmissions that have been handed down from the stone ages to the present. Because of the dedicated practice of the yogi/yoginis we have a sense of knowledge that connects with higher cosmic consciousness, allowing us to become instruments channeling higher cosmic voices that can be heard at this time as we enter the next evolutionary stage of planetary consciousness: the noosphere.*

CHAPTER 3

MIND AND THE MENTAL SPHERES

When we begin to explore the vast capacity of our mind and how to consciously operate and direct it, then our perception of reality shifts; we can actually change the movie that is playing in our mind.

1. As the foundation for cosmic evolution, yoga is a psychology of the integration of ourselves with the divine. In this integration it is important that we understand how our mind functions. The unlimited possibilities of universal being—superconscious and continuing conscious—are our birthright and should be reclaimed as our normal waking state.

2. Many people know and talk about mind. Whole schools of thought and systems go to great lengths to define and describe the mind. In Buddhist philosophy the first step in understanding mind is to recognize that mind is the source of all suffering (samsara). In learning how to work with and control the thought waves of the mind, we may learn how our mind functions and rise to a different perception.

3. Materialist philosophers say there is no mind apart from brain. What is mind? What is brain? What is consciousness? Mind is first and foremost a medium for channelling different types and levels of energy and consciousness; it is a link that connects the invisible 4-D world with the manifest 3-D world. To harness the energies of the mind and ground them into the physical (brain) it is helpful to have a working system.

4. According to the original text, *Introduction to Cosmic Science*, mind consists of six electronic spheres located in the brain. The center of each sphere is made up of *analphas* or electrical fluids that give rise to thinking. (Analphas are external or imaginally conceived impressions that create thoughtforms).

5. Cosmic Science describes thought as an analphic engraving in a series. Thinking is the inbuilt human capacity to receive information and to deliberate or examine information to determine what, if any, kind of logical construct might arise and what the implications of these logical constructs might be.

6 + 1 MENTAL SPHERES

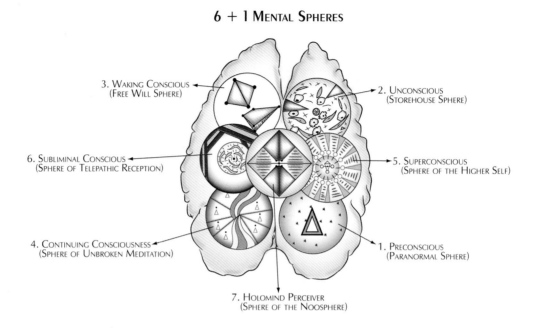

3. WAKING CONSCIOUS
(FREE WILL SPHERE)

2. UNCONSCIOUS
(STOREHOUSE SPHERE)

6. SUBLIMINAL CONSCIOUS
(SPHERE OF TELEPATHIC RECEPTION)

5. SUPERCONSCIOUS
(SPHERE OF THE HIGHER SELF)

4. CONTINUING CONSCIOUSNESS
(SPHERE OF UNBROKEN MEDITATION)

1. PRECONSCIOUS
(PARANORMAL SPHERE)

7. HOLOMIND PERCEIVER
(SPHERE OF THE NOOSPHERE)

6. Each mental sphere holds specific capacities of memory and information that accommodates different thinking layers, or dimensions of reality. The six (+1) mental spheres include: preconscious, unconscious, conscious, continuing conscious, superconscious, subliminal conscious and the holomind perceiver.

7. The primary purpose of working with the mental spheres is to learn who and what we are, how our mind functions and the capability of our mind.

COSMIC PSYCHOLOGY

8. As we describe the different mental spheres, a cosmic psychology is implicit. Cosmic psychology is the evolutionary psychology of consciousness based on the belief that cosmos is filled with mind. The idea of psychology as the science of consciousness was first put forth by earlier psychologists and philosophers such as Bertrand Russell, Edward B. Titchener, and James Ward.

9. Cosmic psychology leads us to increasing levels of superconscious and metaconscious functioning through a process of introspection and self-study. Cosmic psychology also focuses on the cultivation of a new mental perceptual organ, the *holomind perceiver* (the seventh mental sphere).

SIX MENTAL SPHERES
AND THE PRINCIPLES OF COSMIC PSYCHOLOGY

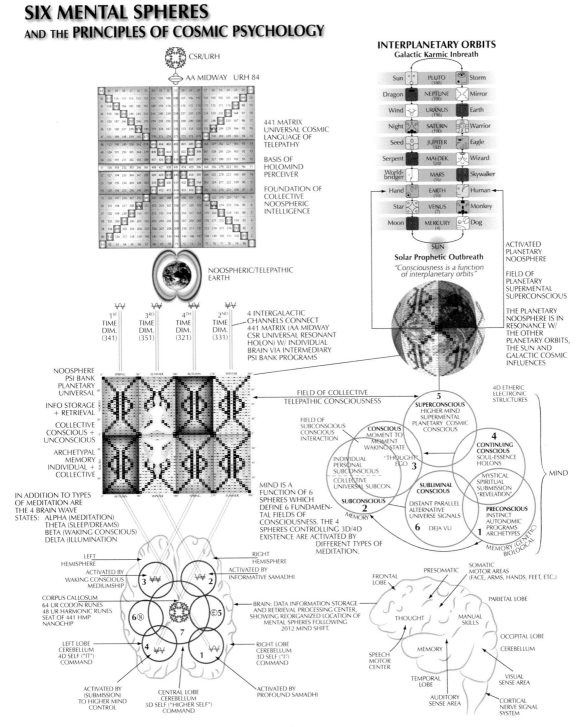

CSR/URH

AA MIDWAY   URH 84

441 MATRIX
UNIVERSAL COSMIC
LANGUAGE OF
TELEPATHY

BASIS OF
HOLOMIND
PERCEIVER

FOUNDATION OF
COLLECTIVE
NOOSPHERIC
INTELLIGENCE

NOOSPHERIC/TELEPATHIC
EARTH

1ST TIME DIM. (341)
3RD TIME DIM. (351)
4TH TIME DIM. (321)
2ND TIME DIM. (331)

4 INTERGALACTIC
CHANNELS CONNECT
441 MATRIX (AA MIDWAY
CSR UNIVERSAL RESONANT
HOLON) W/ INDIVIDUAL
BRAIN VIA INTERMEDIARY
PSI BANK PROGRAMS

NOOSPHERE
PSI BANK
PLANETARY
UNIVERSAL

INFO STORAGE
+ RETRIEVAL

COLLECTIVE
CONSCIOUS +
UNCONSCIOUS

ARCHETYPAL
MEMORY
INDIVIDUAL +
COLLECTIVE

IN ADDITION TO TYPES
OF MEDITATION ARE
THE 4 BRAIN WAVE
STATES: ALPHA (MEDITATION)
THETA (SLEEP/DREAMS)
BETA (WAKING CONSCIOUS)
DELTA (ILLUMINATION)

LEFT
HEMISPHERE
ACTIVATED BY
WAKING CONSCIOUS
MEDIUMSHIP

RIGHT
HEMISPHERE
ACTIVATED BY
INFORMATIVE SAMADHI

CORPUS CALLOSUM
64 UR CODON RUNES
48 UR HARMONIC RUNES
SEAT OF 441 HMP
NANOCHIP

LEFT LOBE
CEREBELLUM
4D SELF ("IT")
COMMAND

RIGHT LOBE
CEREBELLUM
3D SELF ("I")
COMMAND

ACTIVATED BY
(SUBMISSION)
TO HIGHER MIND
CONTROL

CENTRAL LOBE
CEREBELLUM
5D SELF ("HIGHER SELF")
COMMAND

ACTIVATED BY
PROFOUND SAMADHI

BRAIN: DATA INFORMATION STORAGE
AND RETRIEVAL PROCESSING CENTER,
SHOWING REORGANIZED LOCATION OF
MENTAL SPHERES FOLLOWING
2012 MIND SHIFT.

FIELD OF COLLECTIVE
TELEPATHIC CONSCIOUSNESS

FIELD OF
SUBCONSCIOUS
CONSCIOUS
INTERACTION

CONSCIOUS
MOMENT TO
MOMENT
WAKING STATE

"THOUGHT"
EGO

INDIVIDUAL
PERSONAL
SUBCONSCIOUS

COLLECTIVE
UNIVERSAL SUBCON.

SUBCONSCIOUS
MEMORY

5 SUPERCONSCIOUS
HIGHER MIND
SUPERMENTAL
PLANETARY COSMIC
CONSCIOUS

4 CONTINUING
CONSCIOUS
SOUL-ESSENCE
HOLONS

MYSTICAL
SPIRITUAL
SUBMISSION
"REVELATION"

3

SUBLIMINAL
CONSCIOUS

DISTANT PARALLEL
ALTERNATIVE
UNIVERSE SIGNALS

6 DEJA VU

PRECONSCIOUS
INSTINCT
AUTONOMIC
PROGRAMS
ARCHETYPES

1

MEMORY (GENETIC)
BIOLOGICAL

MIND IS A
FUNCTION OF 6
SPHERES WHICH
DEFINE 6 FUNDAMEN-
TAL FIELDS OF
CONSCIOUSNESS. THE 4
SPHERES CONTROLLING 3D/4D
EXISTENCE ARE ACTIVATED BY
DIFFERENT TYPES OF
MEDITATION.

MIND

4D ETHERIC
ELECTRONIC
STRUCTURES

INTERPLANETARY ORBITS
Galactic Karmic Inbreath

Sun	PLUTO (388)	Storm
Dragon	NEPTUNE (300)	Mirror
Wind	URANUS (196)	Earth
Night	SATURN (100)	Warrior
Seed	JUPITER (52)	Eagle
Serpent	MALDEK (28)	Wizard
World-bridger	MARS (16)	Skywalker
Hand	EARTH (10)	Human
Star	VENUS (7)	Monkey
Moon	MERCURY (4)	Dog

SUN

Solar Prophetic Outbreath
*"Consciousness is a function
of interplanetary orbits"*

ACTIVATED
PLANETARY
NOOSPHERE

FIELD OF
PLANETARY
SUPERMENTAL
SUPERCONSCIOUS

THE PLANETARY
NOOSPHERE IS IN
RESONANCE W/
THE OTHER
PLANETARY ORBITS,
THE SUN AND
GALACTIC COSMIC
INFLUENCES

FRONTAL
LOBE

PRESOMATIC

SOMATIC
MOTOR AREAS
(FACE, ARMS, HANDS, FEET, ETC.)

PARIETAL LOBE

THOUGHT

MANUAL
SKILLS

OCCIPITAL LOBE

CEREBELLUM

SPEECH
MOTOR
CENTER

MEMORY

TEMPORAL
LOBE

AUDITORY
SENSE AREA

VISUAL
SENSE AREA

CORTICAL
NERVE SIGNAL
SYSTEM

37

The holomind perceiver establishes radial consciousness to help us integrate and/or override the dualistic bias of binary consciousness.

10. In the thinking layers of the cosmos, the multi-faceted mind correlates to different spheres located in the brain. Mind controls brain; brain grounds mind. In this regard, brain is the computer or hardware and mind, with its mental spheres, is the software. These six (+1) mental spheres are both independent from and can be located in the brain. The brain is a wireless receiver or antenna with the capacity to tune into any number of vibration stations.

HUMAN THINKING

Presently, human thinking is no different from that of a computer. The average human is a composite of unconsciously orchestrated conditioned reflexes—chains of analphs set to shoot off on cue according to primitive binary on/off intelligence. These analphs are imprisoned by the ego. To tune into the cosmic thinking layers, the human must first identify these conditioned thoughtforms through mindfulness practice. Once these disempowering thoughtforms are brought to consciousness they can be dissolved and released; only then is it possible with conscious intentionality to activate and realize each of the six (+1) mental spheres.

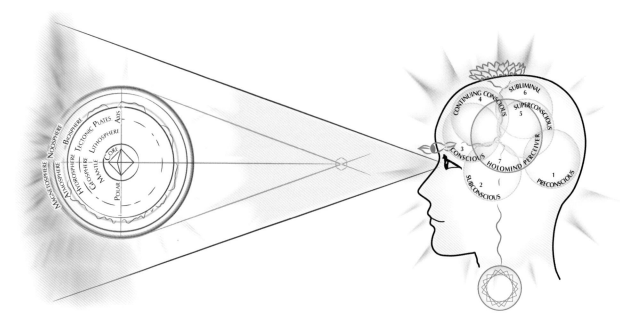

Study of the six (+1) mental spheres allows us new ways of perceiving and linking our daily experiences with the larger unfolding of the cosmic plan.

11. Cosmic psychology works in tandem with Cosmic Science to explore how the brain works and how the mind evolves a personality from the workings of the brain. Are we using our minds effectively? How do we activate the dormant parts of our brain? Why do humans behave the way they do? What are the steps of further integrating our human psyche, individually and collectively, into the natural cosmic order of planetary consciousness? This is the purpose of cosmic psychology, which is actually a cosmocentric cosmology.

12. The mental spheres are largely dormant fourth-dimensional structures that, when activated, facilitate and interconnect brain and noosphere with interdimensional, cosmic and intergalactic channels. When we tune into these channels, our mind unfolds into different thinking layers of the universe.

13. The nature of internal and external messages we receive changes in proportion with the consciousness we attain. How do we apply the mental spheres to evolve ourselves into a regenerated superbeing? Let's take a look at the potentialities that are contained within each of the six (+1) mental spheres.

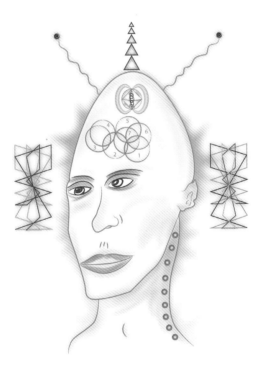

The mental spheres allow us to link interdimensional information and hook up to the wireless cosmic internet in order to retrieve knowledge for the evolution of the planet.

39

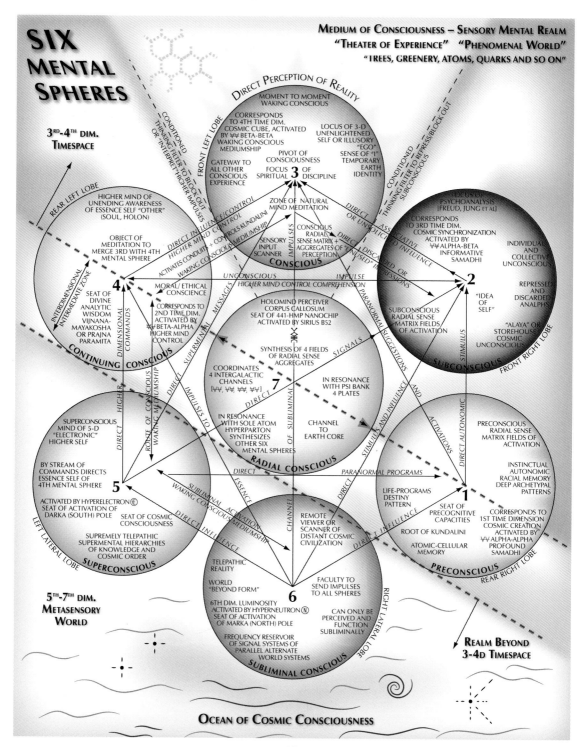

SIX MENTAL SPHERES

MEDIUM OF CONSCIOUSNESS – SENSORY MENTAL REALM
"THEATER OF EXPERIENCE" "PHENOMENAL WORLD"
"TREES, GREENERY, ATOMS, QUARKS AND SO ON"

3RD-4TH DIM. TIMESPACE

5TH-7TH DIM. METASENSORY WORLD

REALM BEYOND 3-4D TIMESPACE

OCEAN OF COSMIC CONSCIOUSNESS

First Mental Sphere: Preconscious
(Paranormal Sphere)

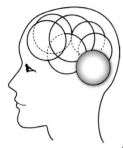

This sphere contains karmic patterns, past life dormant analphs, racial archetypal memory and all other primal instinctual programs and autonomic functions. This mental sphere serves as the resonance chamber of the physical body where paranormal faculties are developed, stored and out-sourced. This sphere is the producer of parapsychological phenomena and paranormal activity. It is the main storehouse of untapped psychic energy.

Paranormal phenomena includes but is not limited to: clairvoyance, clairaudience, invisibility, interdimensional communication, levitation, bilocation, materialization, mediumship, premonition or precognition and retrocognition, as described in *CHC Vol. I*, p. 202-203. Paranormal powers are referred to by yogis as *siddhis*. Although these powers exist as evolutionary potentialities they are not the purpose of evolution. Within the noosphere, paranormal functioning is the norm. This is just a matter of flipping the switch—and the switch, as we shall see, is in the corpus callosum.

This first mental sphere is also the place of precognition, similar to resonant attunement. Resonant attunement occurs at a precognitive level, bypassing logical linear cause and effect. Crystals are an example of a preconscious form structure of time. As a transduction medium and a communicative or informational conductor, a crystal can be used to transfer preconscious instinctual energy into subliminal telepathy.

Evolutive activity is directed and channelled through the preconscious sphere by the third- and fourth-dimensional being/holon. This is achieved through states of profound samadhi that activate evolutive programs stored in the preconscious. The preconscious is also directly linked to the psi bank's evolutionary timing programs.

The first mental sphere controls the three lobes of the cerebellum, each with a different function. The central lobe receives orders from the 5-D higher self, the left lobe from the 4-D self, and the right lobe from the 3-D self. So, not only are there six mental spheres with their different consciousness functions, but there is also a triad of dimensional selves that all together create a cosmic blueprint for the unfolding of being.

Certain mediums of the past required enormous energy to create psychic effects. Why? Because they had not prepared their body/mind to come to full capacity and so their system burned out quickly. This is also true of gifted "channels" such as poets, painters, performers and rock artists (see *CHC Vol. III*).

FUNCTION OF PRECONSCIOUS IN RELATION TO OTHER MENTAL SPHERES

- Preconscious is the autonomic stimulus to patterns of the unconscious (second mental sphere).
- Employed by the higher self (fourth and fifth mental spheres) to send orders and commands to the waking conscious (third mental sphere).
- Assists continuing conscious (fourth mental sphere) with instinctual program flashes during time of crisis or problem solving.
- Receives psychic input from superconscious (fifth mental sphere) and subliminal conscious (sixth mental sphere).
- Reformulated by Holomind Perceiver (seventh mental sphere). When reformulated, the preconscious (first mental sphere) functions as an intergalactic channel for the alpha-alpha hyperplasma. At this stage, the preconscious sphere receives electroplasmic analphic configurations accessed through states of profound samadhi (to be reimprinted in the right lobe of the cerebellum).

SECOND MENTAL SPHERE: SUB- OR UNCONSCIOUS
(STOREHOUSE SPHERE)

This sphere contains conditioned and acquired thought reflexes. It also contains material that was once conscious, but is now repressed; it is the basis of "conditioned mind." Every perception and experience is recorded, but only a fraction is registered into our conscious awareness. The remaining impressions are filed into the unconscious mind. This mental sphere is the repository of rejected conscious stimuli, and of automatically derived complexes perceived as reality.

The unconscious sphere contains fears, phantoms/ghosts, past life memories, lower emotions, traumatic experience and repressed emotion. Input that comes to us is often filtered through this mental sphere and can become distorted if left unexamined. Many beliefs by which we operate our life by were formed within the unconscious.

This unconscious sphere creates polarity of consciousness or psychic knots that, when released, free tremendous psychic energy. The conditioned patterns that lie within the unconscious must be consciously recognized and transcended in order that we may tap the psychic wellspring of the preconscious.

The unconscious mind is the main topic of psychoanalysis as formulated by Sigmund Freud. Freud considered the unconscious as the storehouse of instinctual patterns, psychic actions, and all neurotic habits and tendencies. The Law of Time states that instinct is unconscious telepathy, whether distorted as neurosis or not.

Buried prejudices and predispositions that confirm preconceptions reside in the unconscious sphere. A preconception is an assumption made according to unexamined conditioning rather than direct perception or logic. The unconscious is merely latent consciousness. Is the unconscious merely that which we are averse to being consciously aware of?

According to Cosmic Science, the second mental sphere functions as the residual area or receptacle of selective impulses that are rejected by the electro-conductive (behavioral) genetic template. On Earth, this template is known as the 64-unit DNA code and contains the information program for all life possibilities and planetary unfolding. This process concerns an aspect of biopsychic functioning hitherto unknown (see Chapter 11, *Galactic DNA*).

When psycho-sensory impressions come to us, they are filtered through the 64 unit rune code located in the upper forepart of the corpus callosum. Information that corresponds to our present consciousness is accepted and integrated into our waking consciousness, while the rest of the impressions are filed into the unconscious.

Some people refuse to examine the contents of their unconscious and so accept, as fact, the messages from their unconscious. It is within this sphere that fundamentalism takes root, whether religious or some other inherited and unquestioned belief structure. For example, if inherited religious knowledge exceeds learned knowledge then religious messages will be rotely repeated over and over again.

Analphs (thoughtforms) are produced, engraved and stored in the unconscious (second mental sphere). This corresponds in Buddhism to *alaya*, "storehouse" consciousness and also to Carl Jung's "collective unconscious." Jung determined that the collective unconscious was the

---

FUNCTION OF SUB OR UNCONSCIOUS IN RELATION TO OTHER MENTAL SPHERES

- Stimulated automatically by the preconscious (first mental sphere) as well as by constant input from discarded conscious (third mental sphere) impressions.
- Provides spontaneous "suggestion" to the conscious (third mental sphere). The conscious (third mental sphere) is shaped through unconscious selection of analphs (thoughtforms). These analphs are brought forward as "interpreters" of conscious mental sphere impressions that are not discarded. Also functions as storage and retrieval system for conscious mental functions to be used as needed, i.e. "I am in Mexico. Need to retrieve Spanish language."
- Experienced as impulses to the continuing consciousness (fourth mental sphere). Through higher mind control of the continuing conscious (fourth mental sphere), "interpreter analphs" that break into the conscious (third mental sphere) can be deflected or integrated into a composite higher mental perception.
- Provides the superconscious (fifth mental sphere) with certain unused or conscientiously stored analphs as structures or components of superconscious universal constructs.
- Receives direct signals and impulses from subliminal conscious (sixth mental sphere); often in the form of "telegrams" that activate dormant analphs, understood as intuition or intuitive knowledge.
- Reorganized by the holomind perceiver (seventh mental sphere). When reorganized the unconscious (second mental sphere) is sorted through and realigned according to a hierarchy of "new" perceptions, like a research library fitted to the specific persona.

deepest level of the human psyche that serves as the repository of inherited psychic structures and archetypal experiences. All karmas—results of previous actions—reside in seed state within the collective unconscious.

As the collective unconscious, the second mental sphere is in resonance with the psi bank, the storage and retrieval system of the unconscious as a total planetary mind.

THIRD MENTAL SPHERE: WAKING CONSCIOUS (FREE WILL SPHERE)

This sphere perceives and contains fleeting and moment-to-moment awareness, also known as the "scanner". It is responsive to immediate external stimuli and is meant to stabilize ordinary consciousness into cosmic awareness.

The term "conscious" or "consciousness" has long been used in Eastern philosophy and religion, but the idea of it in Western philosophy is quite recent. Rene Descartes (1596-1650) was the first Western philosopher credited for using the word "conscious" (*conscienta*), though the word is traced to Cicero who defined consciousness in terms of law or moral conscience; as "the knowledge that a witness has of the deed of someone else." In this sense, conscious literally means "with knowledge of".

John Locke also wrote of consciousness in 1690 in his *Essays on Human Understanding*, which he defined as "the perception of what passes in a man's own mind." Also Samuel Johnson's *Dictionary*, 1755, defines conscious as "endowed with the power of knowing one's own thoughts and actions." This sphere is what meditation practice intends to keep clear.

According to Cosmic Science the third mental sphere—waking consciousness—gives commands to the etheric body system, including the chakras and central nerve centers. This is the control center of the third dimension, also known as the "free will" sphere. Lucidity of this sphere accommodates discriminating intelligence.

The powers of free will and analytical discrimination are programmed into this sphere in precise patterns of consciousness. These patterns of connection are woven together based on the stitching of the psi bank, a mechanism unknown to most people. These patterns contain weavings of the past and future and can be mapped through the system of the synchronic order.

The four levels of brainwaves are generated within this sphere and are experienced by the three higher spheres (4-6). While the alpha state characterizes meditation, and the theta state characterizes sleep and dreams, the beta state is the "normal" waking consciousness that occurs discontinuously and with interruptions from theta states. The Delta state is rare and represents the total illuminating consciousness of avatars—"Buddha mind."

The third mental sphere is also the locus of ego. Unless ego is realized as a transient non-reality usurping reason for its own cause, there can be no evolutionary advancement into the fourth mental sphere. Those who are too egocentric cannot cross the threshold from conscious to continuing consciousness. As well meaning as they may be, their attention span is short, saying one thing one day and forgetting it the next. These are people who are not yet ready to hear about what is happening in the totality.

FUNCTION OF WAKING CONSCIOUS IN RELATION TO OTHER MENTAL SPHERES
• Influenced by impressions from all mental spheres. These impressions penetrate into waking consciousness; this is recognized through intuition, insight, etc. Because this mental sphere is the waking conscious scanner, when it is in a state of heightened awareness it is receptive to input from any of the other spheres of consciousness, especially the second, fifth and sixth. In fact, this is what is meant by the notion "waking conscious mediumship."
• Controlled by the preconscious (first mental sphere) through set autonomic/biological patterns that determine or inhibit the conscious program. This operating conscious program is summarized by the ego as illusion of false permanent self (circumstantial persona).
• Controlled by the unconscious (second mental sphere) through any number of set patterns of unconscious programs. The autonomic functions also give rise to some idea of permanent self and consequently to ego as illusion of false permanent self (circumstantial persona). These programs are engendered by any number of conscious stimuli affecting and distorting the quality and nature of the conscious mind, third mental sphere, and intensify sense of ego.
• *Affected by mental spheres 4 - 7.* It is disciplined by the 4th mental sphere, as ordinary (cosmic) awareness meant to be medium of telepathic projective images. Gives commands to etheric body system (chakras, subtle currents). When this awareness discipline is consciously exerted it is known as "natural mind meditation" intended to aid in the recognition of unconscious programs and illusory ego.
• Receives signals or commands from superconscious (fifth mental sphere) and subliminal conscious (sixth mental sphere). This occurs only when the third mental sphere is in a clear waking condition, free of unconscious thoughts from second mental sphere or even subliminal sixth mental sphere. In samadhi, it is normal to receive subliminal impulses from the sixth mental sphere.
• When the seventh mental sphere is activated it will cause the third mental sphere to be in a permanent condition of waking conscious mediumship, the 3D "radar scanner."

FOURTH MENTAL SPHERE: CONTINUING CONSCIOUSNESS (SPHERE OF UNBROKEN MEDITATION)

This sphere is the seat of the 4-D etheric "Other", the soul mind that responds to the 5-D Higher Self. This is the sphere where you merge with nature, flowers, trees, rivers, mountains; where you feel communion with the All.

Continuing consciousness is the ability to maintain direct awareness of a specific mental structure for a prolonged duration in order to establish and extend realization of the whole. This is done

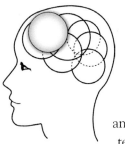

through conscious concentration. Concentration (Dharani) means centering your mind on a fixed idea and thinking consciously or unconsciously upon it for a prolonged period so that it becomes part of your waking consciousness. This is the application of dharani and the basis of dhyani, meditation, as well as samadhi.

This is the sphere where higher states of consciousness are *maintained,* and that experiences original wakefulness, samadhi and divine contact, as well as telepathic receptivity. This is the normal mind-state of the fourth-dimensional essence self.

The third-dimensional self can engage its own beta-beta (conscious mediumship) and alpha-alpha (profound meditation) states, becoming absorbed into the fourth-dimensional continuing consciousness. This is known as profound meditation, samadhi or stabilizing the intrinsic, unceasing self-existing wakefulness, or *rigpa* (true self-essence). This means when mind becomes stabilized through meditation then it enters its own innate state of non-meditation. In its essence, meditation is only a means. Mystical experiences within the realm of continuing consciousness evolve toward becoming telepathically collective rather than individualistic.

This mental sphere functions solely with the fourth-dimensional "Other," *the soul or essence self that responds to the higher self and influences the third mental sphere with spiritual learning.* The brainwaves function parallel to the third sphere, with the exception that the beta and alpha states may be prolonged. Basically we are dealing with a samadhi-like condition that is normal for this mental sphere.

As the ability to concentrate for a prolonged duration on a single object or thoughtform, continuing consciousness wields a great expansive power that opens us to parallel universes. Parallel universes are accessed through continuing consciousness which defines an amplitude of awareness.

The *Dynamics of Time* defines parallel universes as co-existent thought moments to whatever thought-moments we may be experiencing. Parallel universes are actually a function of subliminal consciousness (sixth mental sphere). It is the samadhi-like states of the fourth mental sphere that open us to the sixth mental sphere.

Continuing consciousness is the state when ordinary awareness is stabilized into (fourth- and fifth-dimensional) cosmic awareness. This state is created through meditation that enters the GAP (space between thoughts) for a prolonged duration. This also relates to Dhyana—uninterrupted flow of mindfulness—as described in the eight limbs of yoga.

As perceived by the third mental sphere (3-D mind), this GAP is usually a mere flicker at best—a break in the continuum of thought. The point of meditation is to stabilize the GAP into a continuum of awareness. In this GAP (4-D mind), the self-existing universal awareness—continuing consciousness—can be applied to project telepathic images.

Continuing consciousness is the first step into cosmic or superconsciousness or being conscious every moment without falling into fear states, conceptual errors, negligence or forgetfulness. This sphere is the medium of telepathic projective images. It is the seat of the beta-alpha hyperplasma and contributes to the experience of "higher mind control".

The codes of the Law of Time help us maintain continuing consciousness in the 13:20 frequency. Once we get to this level we can develop cosmic consciousness as explored in Chapter 4, *Synchrogalactic Yoga*.

FUNCTION OF CONTINUING CONSCIOUS IN RELATION TO OTHER MENTAL SPHERES

- Medium where the three lower spheres, beginning with preconscious, cease to have control. In this sphere, unconscious states or analphs are perceived in an objective manner that comprehends their value from a perspective of higher consciousness.
- Directs and manages third-dimensional affairs (third mental sphere) as higher conscious mind control, and experience of spiritualized awareness.
- Mediates impulses of the fifth and sixth mental spheres. Also mediates the impulse of the third mental sphere when it is awakened and stabilized through meditation.
- Reformulated by the seventh mental sphere, the holomind perceiver, as unceasing continuity of "higher mind control." The fourth-dimensional holon or essence self of the fourth mental sphere is continuously operating by command of the fifth-dimensional higher self (or selves).

FIFTH MENTAL SPHERE: SUPERCONSCIOUS
(SPHERE OF THE HIGHER SELF)

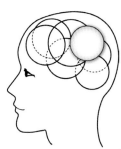

This is the sphere of the fifth-dimensional Higher Self. It is the receiver station for telepathic mind programs from higher-dimensional hierarchies. It is the seat of cosmic consciousness that is activated by natural mind meditation. While continuing consciousness organizes the third/fourth dimension of timespace, the superconscious operates at a metaconscious level beyond the timespace program.

Superconscious functions become operative only when telepathic continuing conscious has been stabilized as "normal" consciousness. At this stage the universe has been reformulated within you.

The fifth mental sphere functions with the fourth-dimensional "Other," carrying the engravings of strong (fourth-dimensional) impressions. It is meant to direct the third and fourth mental spheres. The effective conscious functioning of these three spheres (3, 4 and 5) grounds the triadic self in the plane of higher operating reality. Each of the higher dimensions includes qualities of the lower dimensions.

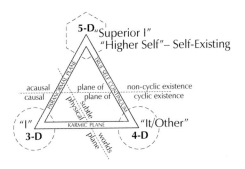

Superconscious is a virtually omniscient state of mind. It contains the capacity for radar sensitivity of the whole field of reality. This is based on the ability to establish a collectively unified hyperorganic telepathic sense field that thinks thoughts such as: "I am the planet and the planet is thinking this thought." At this stage it is realized that it is *all of we* who think this thought.

This sphere is increasingly activated by the advent of the noosphere—descent of the supermind—and is characterized by total holistic perception. This perception incorporates continuing conscious (fourth mental sphere) within itself to expand into the universal mentation waves of the fifth-dimensional higher self. Mentation waves are thought currents of cosmic consciousness that are spread throughout the universe.

FUNCTION OF SUPERCONSCIOUS IN RELATION TO OTHER MENTAL SPHERES

- Transmits signals to the preconscious (first mental sphere) which are absorbed and released as certain paranormal powers or qualities.
- Serves as a higher mental organizer for the unconscious (second mental sphere), arranging it into hierarchies of intelligence and archetypal modalities that are accessible through the waking conscious mind (third mental sphere).
- Directs waking conscious (third mental sphere) by either direct commands or directives, or indirectly through continuing conscious (fourth mental sphere) programs of spiritual life discipline.
- Directs continuing conscious (fourth mental sphere) by downloading specific supermental programs of advanced conduct and higher modes of perception for advancing spiritual enlightenment.
- Influenced by subliminal consciousness (sixth mental sphere), from which it receives specifically directed subliminal messages regarding alternative universe programs. These messages are of the same nature as those that the superconscious (fifth mental sphere) is actively engaged in.
- Affected by the holomind perceiver (seventh mental sphere), which enhances its holographic radar perceptual capacity through radialized mental programs. This allows the superconscious (fifth mental sphere) to function as a kind of quadraphonic higher consciousness telepathic cosmic consciousness "sound system."

SIXTH MENTAL SPHERE: SUBLIMINAL CONSCIOUS
(SPHERE OF TELEPATHIC RECEPTION)

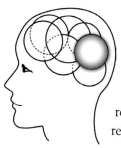

This is the sphere of parapsychic supermental access. Subliminal means "below threshold", that is, the subliminal sphere is the sphere or plane of mind that processes signals and thought frequencies beyond the metasensory threshold of the biological organism. Along with the second mental sphere, this mental sphere is affected and can be imprinted by positive affirmations, repetitive suggestions, autosuggestion, hypnosis and subliminal messaging for reprogramming conventional third-dimensional mental programs.

This sphere is the seat of the telepathic scanning system and reception of interdimensional programs. Subliminal means you are operating independent of past and future (this is how people can contact entities on different planes of existence or in different galaxies). Since subliminal consciousness is independent of past and future, it can be tuned into at the conscious level by stilling and attuning to the peripheral "noise".

This mental sphere contains subliminal suggestive impulses that affect third-dimensional functions as "intuitive flashes." These flashes of insight are often telepathic transmissions from remote points of supermental cosmic civilization trying to establish "contact." These contacts leave impressions in the sixth mental sphere, which may be transmitted or transduced in any number of ways, including ear-ringing, subliminal or hypnogogic imagery, sounds or voices.

The subliminal conscious is also the place of déjà vu. This is experienced as an event or flicker that occurs in our mind but is generally not immediately accessible to our third-dimensional consciousness. Most people experience déjà vu as a fleeting sensation of another time or place that is strangely familiar, though it is difficult to define, *but feels like you have been here (or there) before.* As soon as we try to recall the déjà vu experience with our 3-D mind it vanishes much like a dream. This experience exists in another sphere or plane incomprehensible by our 3-D mind. Déjà vu can occur at anytime, often while you are attending to seemingly mundane chores.

The subliminal conscious is the mental sphere that receives impulses from alternative universes. It is in the subliminal conscious where the knowledge of parallel universes or other galactic brains lies. All fourth-dimensional tools and codes of time are derived from subliminal information. Certain types of visionary experiences, hallucinations or psychotropic substance-induced experiences also tap into this subliminal sphere.

FUNCTION OF SUBLIMINAL CONSCIOUS IN RELATION TO OTHER MENTAL SPHERES

- Transmits direct impulses to the first, second, and fourth mental spheres. In the first and second mental sphere these impulses are either stored or perceived as peripheral conscious flashes or messages in the conscious (third mental sphere). In the fourth mental sphere, these impulses are quickly comprehended by the soul essence self and applied as spiritually enhancing information from higher or parallel dimensions.
- Informs superconscious (fifth mental sphere) with direct command from higher dimensions of alternative hierarchies.
- Mediates between superconscious (fifth mental sphere) and holomind perceiver (seventh mental sphere).
- Provides a repository of alternative universe possibilities for radial conscious of the holomind perceiver (seventh mental sphere).

Seventh Mental Sphere: Holomind Perceiver (HMP)
(Sphere of the Noosphere)

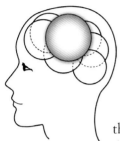

The holomind perceiver is the evolving organ: the noospheric sensing device. It is localized in the central corpus callosum of the Higher Self and telepathically engraved on the corpus callosum of the 3-D and 4-D Self. This is the seat of the soul memories, the akashic records, the life summarization of all experiences.

Noospheric programs of collective telepathic consciousness are accessed through the holomind perceiver. This seventh mental sphere is also the elevated locus of the "true self", rigpa—wisdom self—union of awareness and mind/space.

All mental spheres are unified or accessed from this sphere. It is the locus of the interdimensional shift that elevates the consciousness from egoic to noospheric levels.

This seventh mental sphere opens us into an entirely new and cosmic reality. It is the site of the UR runes, the DNA cosmogenetic behavioral codes, the fourth-dimensional timing matrices, and the 441 *Synchronotron* matrix. It is also the site of the fourth-dimensional psychocultural programs and the holoneme of the psi bank grid, meaning it holds the hologram of the total perceived and imperceptible planetary reality.

When fully activated, it radializes the psycho-sensory perceptual apparatus according to the four simultaneously-existing outer time dimensions. This means both perceiving all at once, from preconscious to continuing conscious, whatever we experience, as well as experiencing everything from the perspective of a 360 degree sensory panorama.

Study of and meditation on the holomind perceiver prepares the mind to open to the galactic dimension and receive an entirely new base of knowledge and perception.

Function of Holomind Perceiver in Relation to Other Mental Spheres
• Affects all mental spheres and reformulates them to function according to radialized hierarchies of information organization (see Chapter 13).
• Note: The planetary noosphere receives impressions from and is accessed by **homo noosphericus** through the seventh mental sphere. The homo noosphericus, through its evolved enlargement of perceptions and chakra activations, can access the noosphere/psi bank, arousing the AC and CA Manitous, receiving impressions of the akashic records.

This is merely a brief review of the vast nature of the mental spheres, and the means and purpose of their activation in order to stimulate or advance into increasing orders of cosmic psychology.

The mental spheres are formed outwardly by the heptocubic plasmatic quantos, based on the seven-part division of 51.428571 degrees.

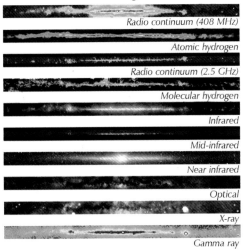

THE MILKY WAY AT DIFFERENT WAVELENGTHS

Different wavelength readings correspond to different galactic mental layers. All wavelength frequencies are functions of the Master Code 441, Foundation of Mind and Cosmic Order.

Radio continuum (408 MHz)
Atomic hydrogen
Radio continuum (2.5 GHz)
Molecular hydrogen
Infrared
Mid-infrared
Near infrared
Optical
X-ray
Gamma ray

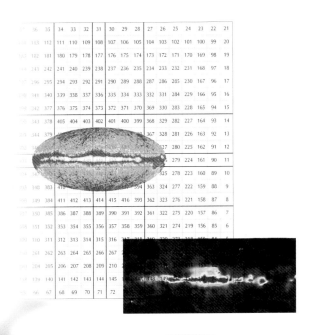

36	35	34	33	32	31	30	29	28	27	26	25	24	23	22	21
113	112	111	110	109	108	107	106	105	104	103	102	101	100	99	20
182	181	180	179	178	177	176	175	174	173	172	171	170	169	98	19
	242	241	240	239	238	237	236	235	234	233	232	231	168	97	18
	296	295	294	293	292	291	290	289	288	287	286	285	230	167	96	17
	341	340	339	338	337	336	335	334	333	332	331	284	229	166	95	16
	342	377	376	375	374	373	372	371	370	369	330	283	228	165	94	15
	343	378	405	404	403	402	401	400	399	368	329	282	227	164	93	14
	344	379								367	328	281	226	163	92	13
										327	280	225	162	91	12
											279	224	161	90	11
	347									325	278	223	160	89	10
	348	383	410					394	363	324	277	222	159	88	9
	349	384	411	412	413	414	415	416	393	362	323	276	221	158	87	8
	350	385	386	387	388	389	390	391	392	361	322	275	220	157	86	7
	351	352	353	354	355	356	357	358	359	360	321	274	219	156	85	6
	310	311	312	313	314	315	316								
	261	262	263	264	265	266	267								
	204	205	206	207	208	209	210								
	139	140	141	142	143	144	145								
	66	67	68	69	70	71	72								

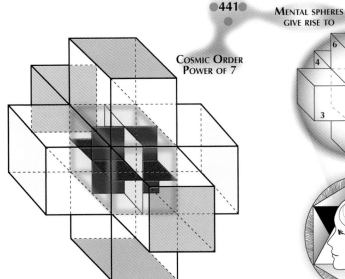

441

COSMIC ORDER
POWER OF 7

MENTAL SPHERES
GIVE RISE TO

HEPTOCUBIC
PLASMATIC STRUCTURE
OF MIND

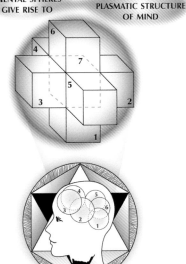

HEPTOCUBIC STRUCTURE

Transcendental Soul Consciousness: Means by which Higher Self incarnates in supermental descent [see: *noogenesis*]. Heptocubic structure is the essence function of the Cubic Power of 7; emanated by 441 ($=7^2 \times 3^2$); 6 (+1) mental spheres; function of 441 Design Template.

PART II
YOGA AND COSMIC ELECTRICITY

CHAPTER 4

SYNCHROGALACTIC YOGA

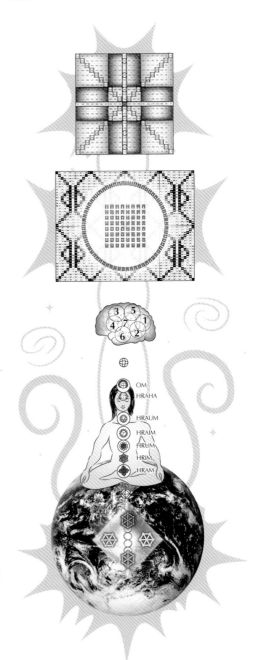

1. Synchrogalactic Yoga is a system of inner discovery and self-research that unites traditional yoga practices with the synchronic order. The system of Synchrogalactic Yoga provides the template or matrix for realizing the supermental superhuman within ourselves.

2. True knowledge is based on experience of both the external and internal worlds. It is easy to concentrate on sensory objects as the mind naturally goes outward. It is inner concentration that we are concerned with. The external world is merely the projection of the inner or subtle worlds. The external world is the effect; the internal world is the cause.

3. The power of mind is unlimited. The system of yoga equips us with the means of observing and interacting with internal states of consciousness primarily by learning how to concentrate, operate and focus the mind.

4. The practice of Synchrogalactic Yoga helps us purify our mind and transmute our psychophysical structure by changing the vibration of our thought cells so that we become a medium of transformation embodying a superconscious level of reality.

UNDERSTANDING THE SYSTEM

5. Synchrogalactic Yoga is most closely aligned with Jnana, Raja and Kundalini Yoga. In this chapter, we will focus on the system of Synchrogalactic Yoga which is followed by the practices in the next chapter. The entry point to Synchrogalactic Yoga is through the seven chakras.

6. When we awaken our chakras, our mind and consciousness go through systematic changes, heightening our perceptions, releasing blocked energies, strengthening our magnetic field, and tuning us into higher frequencies. Before we begin the practices, let's review some basic tenets of Kundalini Yoga.

SAHASRARA

> *You must leave your limitations and use all methods to raise your consciousness. If you understand kundalini, you understand the whole universe. It is your existence. It is the power in you through which you make your mind expand.*
> —*Yogi Bhajan*

AJNA

7. Kundalini Yoga is part of the tantric system that focuses on expanding and broadening consciousness by releasing contracted forces within the physical body. Through yogic practice the body relaxes and consciousness is released into a liberating force that unlocks the dormant powers of mind.

VISUDDHA

ANAHATA

8. The spinal column is the capacitor of the internalized electromagnetic field, with a positive and negative terminal. The nadis are the channels that carry pranic energies to and from the spinal column or central channel. Ayurveda mentions 72,000 nadis. The Law of Time teaches that the 72,000 nadis are on either side of the body for a total of 144,000.

MANIPURA

9. The sense organs and chakras operate by three main nadis: Ida, Pingala and Sushumna, that begin at the Muladhara or root chakra. The system of Kundalini Yoga tells us that those who are able to master the nadis enter the highest states of consciousness and attain full command of their bodies and minds, thereby attracting the power of the siddhis (perfections).

SVADHISTHANA

MULADHARA

10. Vital energy is channeled through the chakras or wheels, the psychophysical centers that are aligned at the central channel *Sushumna*. Sushumna is the passage through the center of the spinal column. In most people this passage is closed. Through yogic practice we can open this channel and reach states of continuing and superconscious.

> *By seven successive steps the soul escapes into cosmic consciousness. In its conscious upward passage through the seven opened chakras, the soul travels the highway to the infinite, the true path by which the soul must retrace its course to reunite with God.*
> —*Paramahansa Yogananda*

11. Chakras are strung along the Sushumna channel in the form of lotuses and/or wheels. These chakras begin at the base of the spine with the Muladhara (root), then Svadhisthana (secret center),

Manipura (solar plexus), Anahata (heart), Visuddha (throat), Ajna (third eye) and Sahasrara (crown). Around the chakras are two other channels: the solar channel, Pingala (right) and the lunar channel, Ida (left). Pingala conducts life-force and Ida conducts consciousness.

EVER-BLOOMING FLOWER OF COSMIC CONSCIOUSNESS

FAULTLESS SINGLE EYE OF WISDOM

SUPERMENTAL POWER OF COMMUNICATION

HEART OF ENLIGHTENMENT MIND OF GOD

HIGHWAY TO THE GALACTIC CORE

THE SECRET SACRED POWER OF SEX

COSMIC VIBRATORY ROOT

THREE MAIN NADIS AND FULLY ACTIVATED CHAKRAS

12. These two channels feed the two hemispheres of the brain which control all bodily systems. Ida and Pingala function according to natural cycles by the law of alternation. However, at this time these flows are disrupted in most humans due to living in an artificial civilization out of harmony with nature and natural time. The imbalance of these two flows manifests as the mental and physical imbalances that we see in the world today.

13. The purpose of yoga and breath control is to balance these energies by consciously realigning them with the cycles of nature. Like the two strands of DNA, the Ida and Pingala alternate from right to left of the Sushumna at each succeeding chakra, until they meet at the third eye where they unite and form a subtle knot: "My lineage is the union of intrinsic awareness and the ultimate sphere …" This is the affirmation for radial plasma, Gamma, located in the third eye or Ajna chakra.

14. From the third eye, the Ida and Pingala channels then terminate in the left and right nostrils, while the Sushumna continues upward to the crown chakra. Only when the Ida and Pingala come into proper balance does the Sushumna channel awaken from the root to the crown.

15. Within the Sushumna nadi is the *Brahma nadi* or the void channel that connects the Brahmarandhra, a cavity between the two hemispheres of the brain (corpus callosum) located in the crown chakra, Sahasrara. This is precisely the location of the *holomind perceiver*, the newly evolved sense organ.

THREE MAIN NADIS

The system of Kundalini Yoga utilizes channels called *nadis* to activate different energies. Ida, Pingala and Sushumna are the three main nadis in yogic tradition. Nadi comes from the Sanskrit word meaning "movement." In the *Rig Veda*, the most ancient Hindu scripture, the word nadi means "stream." When harmony is attained between these two, then the third nadi, *Sushumna*, is awakened. Through yoga practice and control of the breath, the nadis—the streams that carry vital energies—are purified and disciplined leading the mind to expanded awareness.

AC/CA TIMING CIRCUITS

16. According to the Law of Time, there are two primary circuits of consciousness that serve as cosmic memory templates: the Aboriginal Continuity (AC) and the Cosmic Awareness (CA) circuits. These two circuits process information that can be activated through yogic practices and are essential to understanding the system of Synchrogalactic Yoga.

17. The Aboriginal Continuity current contains the primary codes of enlightened conduct. It also corresponds to innate psychomental forms, internal sensations and the sense organs themselves. The AC represents information flow from future to present. It weaves the original matrix from which history arises.

18. Cosmic Awareness accounts for history and represents analytical methods, articulating specific action modes built upon models of past acquired behavior and knowledge. The CA contains the cumulative cultural forms and, eventually, the civilizational sense fields inclusive of the planetary environment.

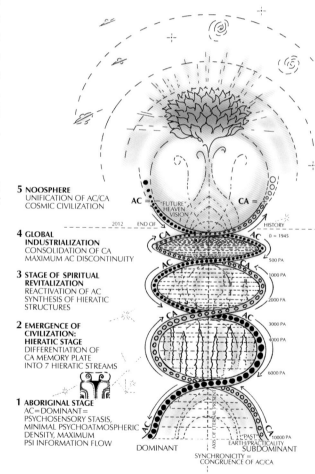

5 NOOSPHERE
UNIFICATION OF AC/CA
COSMIC CIVILIZATION

4 GLOBAL INDUSTRIALIZATION
CONSOLIDATION OF CA
MAXIMUM AC DISCONTINUITY

3 STAGE OF SPIRITUAL REVITALIZATION
REACTIVATION OF AC
SYNTHESIS OF HIERATIC
STRUCTURES

2 EMERGENCE OF CIVILIZATION: HIERATIC STAGE
DIFFERENTIATION OF
CA MEMORY PLATE
INTO 7 HIERATIC STREAMS

1 ABORIGINAL STAGE
AC=DOMINANT =
PSYCHOSENSORY STASIS,
MINIMAL PSYCHOATMOSPHERIC
DENSITY, MAXIMUM
PSI INFORMATION FLOW

AC/CA CIRCUITS
AND SPIRITUAL EVOLUTION OF PLANET EARTH

The CA current represents the information flow from past to present. While AC is intuitive, innate knowledge, CA is learned, acquired knowledge, which ultimately expands into a state of pure cosmic awareness.

19. However, this Cosmic Awareness has been covered over by artificial time and replaced by Civilizational Advance, manifesting as worldly power and acquisition, with the highest priority given to technological advancement and the proliferation of materialist values and belief systems.

EFFECTS OF AC/CA DISCONNECTION

The sum effect of the AC/CA deviation from the biosphere norm is twofold: the crystallization of artificial constructs ultimately undermines biological functions and aborts instinctual intelligence from becoming intelligently conscious; this results in a simultaneous condition of sensory overload and sensory deprivation within the individual organism of the deviant species as a whole.

—*Dynamics of Time, 8.5*

"THE TWO SIDES OF THE GALACTIC BRAIN"
Aboriginal Continuity — Cosmic Awareness

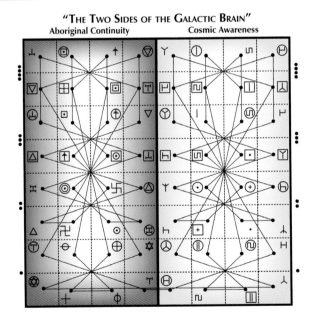

20. Like the Ida and Pingala, the AC/CA currents form the root of the DNA double helix pattern, spinning up through the central column of the etheric body. Currently the AC is separated from the CA function. This separation is exacerbated by living in artificial time apart from nature's cycles. It is the purpose of the Law of Time to reestablish balance between the AC and CA currents through methods of yoga.

21. The AC/CA structure holds together the two sides of the galactic brain or galactic field of intelligence holonomically registered as the noosphere. It also constitutes the regulating mechanism of the psi bank, which coordinates the noosphere as a supermental organism. This will be further elucidated in Chapter 6, *Holographic Yoga*, and also the Appendix: *Galactic I Ching*.

THE MAGIC 33

In Synchrogalactic Yoga the conscious movement of breath into the body is directed toward and correlated with the spine and central nervous system. The spinal column consists of 33 divisions, or 33 esoteric joints that can also be allocated with the seven chakras. According to Cosmic Science, there are 33 secret chambers in the Great Pyramid of Ra in Egypt, three of which contain information about Cosmic Science (5th chamber, 11th chamber and 13th chamber). 33 is the number of the initiate.

How to Begin

22. It is recommended to begin Synchrogalactic Yoga with a complementary practice of Hatha Yoga (asana and pranayams). The word hatha has two syllables, *ha* (sun) and *tha* (moon). Bodily postures combined with deep, rhythmic breathing help us to release physical and psychic blockages while at the same time cultivating a flexible biohomeostasis, bringing different aspects of ourselves into greater cosmic alignment. We want to create a fluid continuum where exertion and discipline of both body and mind become one fluid seamless whole.

23. Pranayams or correct breathing calms our thought-currents, relaxes our body and opens us into higher forms of meditation. Our rate of breath is inseparable from our state of mind. If we want to calm our mind, then we first slow our breath. The mind follows the breath and the body follows the mind. Along with asanas and pranayams, a vegetarian diet high in plant foods is strongly recommended not only for the body, but for the Planet.

24. Find a program that works for you when cultivating the body-mind: Asanas, mudras, pranayams, martial arts, dancing, etc, cleansing, and fasting for the mental/emotional body; meditation, visualization, artistic expressions and/or telepathic exercise for the mental body.

HYPERORGANIC EVOLUTION

In Kundalini Yoga, the main key is to balance the Ida and Pingala channels so that the life-force can rise from root to crown unimpeded by obstacles. The Law of Time introduces a new stage of evolution: hyperorganic evolution. This refers to the ability of the human to utilize the sense organs as points of energy emission and consciousness. This means that the sense organs get telepathically extended outward, which results in natural phenomena such as clairvoyance and clairaudience.

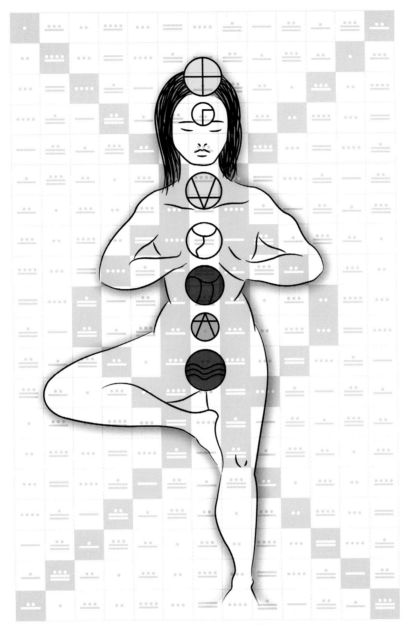

YOGA AND TIME TRAVEL

The practice of yoga, generically understood, is a prerequisite for any consideration of time travel. Time travel is the function of an AC-CA integrated biopsychic circuit internal body sensation which can be uniformly experienced and consolidated into a single focused energy directive or form.

—Dynamics of Time, 8.9

OPENING THE CHAKRAS

25. Within the body, the AC/CA currents are etherically aligned with the Ida and Pingala currents. The function of the AC/CA currents is dependent on the activation of the chakra generators and radial plasmas. The chakras are energy vortices within the body that can be thought of as transmutation chambers. They are conductors of electromagnetic energy and control centers for the transformation of etheric and subtle energies.

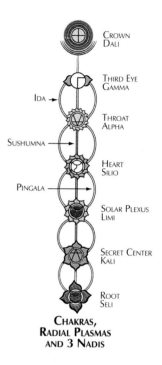

CROWN
DALI

THIRD EYE
GAMMA

IDA

THROAT
ALPHA

SUSHUMNA

HEART
SILIO

PINGALA

SOLAR PLEXUS
LIMI

SECRET CENTER
KALI

ROOT
SELI

**CHAKRAS,
RADIAL PLASMAS
AND 3 NADIS**

26. Energy from higher or subtle dimensions is brought into the physical dimension through these seven energy vortices. Through the chakras, physical energy can also be transmuted into higher forms or stages of consciousness, such as continuing and superconscious.

27. The chakras, as psychic centers, are psychoactive energy generators fed by streams of prana. Prana is the life-force energy, both of the physical and astral worlds. Within the prana lie the seven radial plasmas, each with its own qualities and powers. Once consciously breathed in, these plasmas may be directed to different chakras where they provide the energetic psychotelepathic fuel. Each of the seven centers is a receiver for one each of the seven radial plasmas.

28. The first step in Synchrogalactic Yoga is to activate each of the chakras making them powerful, purified receivers and transmitters of cosmic energy. We want to raise each chakra from the level of unconscious, to conscious, continuing conscious and superconscious levels of operation through a consistent series of practices and meditations. We first awaken these chakras within ourselves and then transfer our consciousness into awakening the chakras of the Earth.

29. The chakras can be thought of as switches that we turn on. When we switch them on then the light streams in purifying our perceptions and thinking. When the chakras inside the Planet are switched on then shadows dissolve and a new world is revealed (see Chapter 6, *Holographic Yoga*).

30. The five principle chakras are: *root, solar plexus, heart, throat* and *crown*. These focus on the integration of the three bodies: Nirmanakaya (physical/third-dimensional body), Sambogakaya (radiant soul essence/fourth-dimensional body) and Dharmakaya (electronic higher self/fifth-dimensional body).

31. The two minor chakras—secret center and third eye—focalize on transcendental functions of being. The third eye is associated with inner vision, intuition and wisdom and the secret center is associated with sex and life-force or kundalini. These two minor chakras are connected by the kundalini third eye wisdom channel (capacitates paranormal powers). The unification of these two chakras holds the purposive function of sex as an evolutionary process.

32. Above and below the seven chakras we introduce two new chakras: the root of root (Earth core) and crown of crown (noosphere). These are planetary centers of cosmic information transmission-reception (noosphere) and reception-transmission (Earth core). Through these two new chakras we extend our intelligence circuits through the solar/planetary intelligence dynamic. This encompasses the entire orbital system governed by the Sun, known as the interplanetary solar noosphere.

CHAKRAS AND THREE BODIES

The three bodies: physical, emotional and mental, are suspended on the central axis of the chakra system. The root main chakras govern from the bottom of the physical body, root, to the top of the mental body, crown. The center of the mental body is the third eye, and the center of the physical body is the secret center. The center of the emotional body is the heart that extends to the throat chakra for its expressive ability, and to the solar plexus chakra where emotional energy is received and transmitted.

ACTIVATING THE RADIAL PLASMAS

33. After opening the chakras comes the activation of the radial plasmas for constructing the inner temple or etheric body. The radial plasmas are micro quanta electrical charges, each with unique characteristics. The seven plasmas create the primary micro quanta electric building blocks of universal structures, such as atoms.

34. With their capacity for instantaneous transmission, radial plasmas also function as storage units, information banks, and telepathic message units. In their conductivity and instantaneous information-bearing capacity, the radial plasmas occur naturally throughout the universe.

PRANA AND COSMIC SCIENCE

Prana is the cosmic energy that sustains all life. It is defined by Cosmic Science as "electric vidico quanta of the type Kemio as an existential biological quanta." Kemio is one of the six types of electricities in the cosmos and relates to static distension. Quanta refers to the minimal logical detectable quantity of energy of space-time. In other words, prana is a type of dynamic cosmic electricity that establishes the electronic charges that give life, both to the physical and astral worlds.

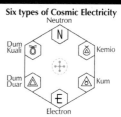

Six types of Cosmic Electricity

Neutron — N
Dum Kuali — Kemio
Dum Duar — Kum
Electron — E

     Kemio combined with the electricity type *Kum* (static) makes up *Kappa*, one of twelve electronic lines of force. The electronic lines of force are the sub-sub-sub atomic electrical flows of partons. These twelve types of electricity flow through everything in the universe, causing all atoms, molecules, planetary bodies and stellar bodies to be in a continuous spinning motion. Kappa doubled creates radial plasma *Kali* (see *CHC, Vol. II*).

35. Plasmas are the constituent components of prana or chi. According to Cosmic Science, activation of this prana or dynamic electricity calms down the processes of cariocinesis (aging) and mitosis (cell splitting). In order to delay the process of cariocinesis, it is recommended to walk with naked feet early in the morning so that the vritris (etheric soles of feet) have direct contact with the Earth.

36. Prana from the Earth enters through the vritris, which serve as receivers and transmitters of fastenic lines of force that feed the chakras. (Fastenic lines of force is what generates the auric field). If one meditates afterwards the results are even better. Regular massage of hand vritris (palms) is also recommended.

SEVEN RADIAL PLASMAS

"Within the prana, or the vital breath, are the different primary plasmas, known as the seven radial plasmas ... Once consciously breathed in, these plasmas may be directed to different chakras, where they provide the energetic psychotelepathic fuel."

— *CHC, Vol. I*

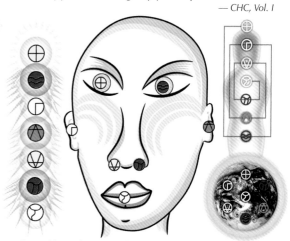

37. Prana is a function of a holonomic feedback system of the generation and recirculation of cosmic electricity. First, the raw plasmic/pranic energy is breathed in and absorbed by the chakras—as plasmic psychoelectronic generators, the chakras then transmute the radial plasmas into fastenic lines of force utilizing double parton sequences.

Shanmukhi Mudra means "the closing of 7 gates." These 7 gates refer to the 7 facial openings or 7 doors to outer perception. To close these doors is to enter the inner domain, which is key in the practice of Synchrogalactic Yoga.

38. These fastenic lines of force are then secreted by the body to create the aura. The

more consciously this process is participated in, the stronger and more spectral the aura will become and the more it will attract high vibration, plasma and prana (see *CHC, Vol. II*).

39. The air that we breathe is filled with prana. When prana is deeply inhaled it charges all of the etheric bodies, creating a feeling of lightness or weightlessness within the physical body. The ultimate goal of activating the chakras and radial plasmas is to purify and synchronize the electromagnetic field of the human brain with the electromagnetic field of the Earth.

PURPOSES OF SYNCHROGALACTIC YOGA

- To lift the lower mind into higher wisdom (realization of the supermental superhuman).
- To purify the physical/emotional body by learning to attune to pure being (5-D entity).
- To imprint radial patterns in order to grasp different levels of information simultaneously.
- To engrave new planetary programs that are beneficial to all.
- To attain cellular transmutation into a body of radiance, leading to systematic states of superconsciousness.
- To coordinate the third-dimensional being with the fourth-dimensional being—the physical body with the etheric body. The etheric body is the mantle or vehicle of the soul.
- To become integral chips or units who create the foundation of the next stage of evolution: planetary solar consciousness.

MUDRAS, MANTRAS AND MANDALA

40. Note that Synchrogalactic Yoga also incorporates a set of mudras, mantras and mandala. Mudras are gestures that create a sense of one's own being as an instrument or vehicle of cosmic forces or energies that take particular forms and give a particular cosmic sense of ritual, turning body gesture into symbolic language.

41. Mantra focuses on primordial sound vibration, the primary dimension of universal coordination. The universe is made of sound, or different musical notes, tones and resonances. Some forms of yoga are "sound yoga"—*sabdayoga*—which is an offshoot of the Sikh religion. This focuses on liberating the mind by tuning into the inner cosmic sound. Anyone can hear this. There is vast and subtle texture of sound that can be heard when the mind is empty.

42. The seven solar mantras attune the biopsychic apparatus to the solar frequencies of the coming solar age. Chanting the seven

SEVEN SOLAR SYLLABLES OF SYNCHROGALACTIC YOGA

OM — Sahasrara (Crown) – Dali

HRAHA — Ajna (Third eye) – Gamma

HRAUM — Visuddha (Throat) – Alpha

HRAIM — Anahata (Heart) – Silio

HRUM — Manipura (Solar Plexus) – Alpha

HRIM — Svadhisthana (Secret Center) – Kali

HRAM — Muladhara (Root) – Seli

solar mantras opens the seven solar gates (Solar Yoga was first brought through in the modern age by Yogacharya Janakiraman).

43. When you chant these syllables, listen to the sound while visualizing the different chakras and plasmas. These can be chanted from the bottom moving upward, in a clear strong voice. Mantra means "mind protecting", and when recited purifies the mind of lesser thoughts. This is a powerful experience to practice the mantras and engineer your own auditory matrix and system of cosmic sounds.

44. Mandalas or yantras—the visual sound—are forms that help concentrate the mind. Mandalas represent symbolic or integrated geometric structures focused into different forms. The geometry of the universe is condensed into different mandalas or yantras and you learn to identify your body and mind with these different structures. This is the visual part.

DESCRIPTIONS OF THE PRACTICES

45. Before any practice it is suggested to memorize the symbol and functions of both the traditional chakras and the radial plasmas. You can practice drawing and coloring the symbols as shown in the diagram, and meditating on each of the symbols until you become familiar with them.

SENSORY QUANTUM

DALI / Target
THERMIC

SELI / Flow
LUMINIC

GAMMA / Pacify
LUMINIC-THERMIC

CATALYTIC AGENT

KALI / Establish
STATIC-DISTENSION

TELEPATHIC QUANTUM

ALPHA / Release
DOUBLE-EXTENDED
ELECTRON

LIMI / Purify
MENTAL ELECTRON

SILIO / Discharge
MENTAL ELECTRON
NEUTRON

46. The radial plasmas can be envisioned as the motor within each of the chakras. The radial plasmas are made of heat, light, electronic partons and electronic lines of force. All together the plasmas establish two hyperquanta: sensory (Dali, Seli, Gamma) and telepathic (Alpha, Limi and Silio).

47. The following are a set of practices to increase focus and concentration in order to penetrate into higher realms. You can begin practice immediately. The best time to practice is before sunrise or in the evening around sunset. It is recommended to practice one exercise a day according to the daily radial plasma.

48. Before practicing, read through all of the practices so that you have a whole vision of the system. We will work on four levels: 1) **Traditional chakras**; 2) **Radial plasmas**; 3) **Mental spheres**; 4) **Heptad gates.** Keep in mind that every form, sound and color has a different frequency. When

these frequencies are overlaid then we have the experience of synesthesia. This is the future of yogic activity.

49. In brief, the nature and purpose of these four levels is as follows:

The first level, meditating the chakras, is a basic introductory level that serves as a bridge to the new practices. Meditating on traditional forms of the seven chakras transforms consciousness by inwardly awakening the etheric/psychic centers. Here, we also introduce two new chakras: root of root and crown of crown.

The second level, activating the radial plasmas, awakens the seven electronic lines of force, both in our body and on the planet. Plasmas are electronically charged subatomic particles that saturate the universe with electricity, electrical flows, electromagnetic fields and radial lines of force. The purpose of this practice is to learn how to direct plasma, cultivate our electromagnetic field and recognize ourselves and the planet as a purely electronic entity. This will help us to develop higher mind control.

The third level, engaging the mental spheres, familiarizes us with the six (+1) mental spheres of consciousness as introduced in Chapter 3. Through this practice, we habituate ourselves to the different states and capacities of mind that the soul journeys through. The soul, the mind and consciousness are part of one continuum, each with different levels and functions. Study of the six (+1) mental spheres teaches us about the nature of mind as it relates to the interactive telepathic fields of the universe.

The fourth level, opening the heptad gates, is an advanced level that integrates the first three levels and introduces us to the seven solar mantras and the seven gates of the holomind perceiver, the basis of the 441 matrix practice. This level is also meant to introduce us to the system of *Synchronotron,* the yoga of unification of the higher mind with the science of time as practiced by the star masters. It is the yoga of the nine star gates of Sirius. This will be further elucidated in *CHC Vol. VII: Book of the Cube.*

CHAPTER 5

SYNCHROGALACTIC YOGA II: THE PRACTICES

Synchrogalactic Yoga is a scientific process of self-synchronization that activates our etheric body according to the supermental codes of cosmic consciousness. Through the practices of Synchrogalactic Yoga, we open our inner awareness to different forms of yoga combined with the synchronic order and how to integrate the yogic way of being into everyday life. All yoga is for the purpose of self-realization.

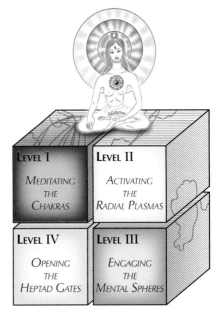

The synchronic codes of time create the context and matrix of meaning to understand our inner explorations and experiences. Through application and meditation of these codes, the body and mind become synchronized with the universal order as coordinated by the 13:20 timing frequency. This system facilitates self-synchronization, where the human mind and soul experience unification at a noospheric, planetary level. This will radically alter our self-perception and perception of the universe.

SYNCHROGALACTIC YOGA

Through the process of self-synchronization, we begin to experience many other selves who are also synchronizing to this state. It is this union of synchronized selves within the planetary circuit board that creates the planetary field of consciousness.

Herein are presented the basic practices of Synchrogalactic Yoga as four levels: 1) Meditating the Chakras; 2) Activating the Radial Plasmas; 3) Engaging the Mental Spheres; and 4) Opening the Heptad Gates.

These practices are synchronized with the 13 Moon, 28-day calendar cycle, creating four seven day cycles per moon (28 days). The seven-day cycle is coded by the seven radial plasmas: Dali, Seli, Gamma, Kali, Alpha, Limi and Silio.

Day One: DALI

OM   108

Level 1: Meditating the Sahasrara (Crown) Chakra

Sit in a comfortable meditative posture. Keep your spine erect and body relaxed. With the body completely still, practice a few moments of natural mind meditation. Once the mind is sufficiently clear, direct your attention to your crown or Sahasrara chakra. Make it as clear and pristine as possible, glistening and sparkling with vibrant energy. When it is pure and translucent, floating just above the top of your head, allow it to dissolve and transform itself into a thousand-petalled violet lotus.

Concentrate on this area inside of your crown chakra. This is the doorway to cosmic consciousness. This center contains the dormant capacity for total enlightenment. Yogic scriptures say that the Sahasrara chakra is the seat of the self-luminous soul or *chitta*, the essence of mind.

This chakra is governed by the feminine principle or Shakti Goddess *Maha Shakti* (Union). When this center is finally awakened the activities of the mind cease and merge into the light of illumination. This is the source of cosmic enlightenment.

Feel the textures of light/heat, warmth and nurturance balancing your pineal gland and cerebral cortex, bringing all of your chakras into harmony. Your entire glandular system is pacified and bathed in the warmth of this divine light. In this chakra lies our capacity to tune into and even take on different qualities or stages of being. This is the place used by mediums to channel information.

By awakening our crown chakra we become clear light oracles of planetary divination; to divine is to know directly by mind.

Sahasrara affirmation: *May the pure light universe infuse our soul's journey, that the planetary noosphere may become the crown of pure radiance!*

Level 2: Activating Radial Plasma: Dali

Dali
Crown

Breathe deeply through your nostrils and allow your awareness to flow up your nose and into your crown chakra. Bring your awareness to the inner Dali plasma at the center of the chakra. Visualize the yellow symbol radiating healing charges of heat.

Repeat the following while focusing on your crown chakra: "My father is intrinsic awareness, I feel the heat." Feel this heat power ignite at your crown chakra, blazing as your innate self-existing awareness free from conceptualization.

Cover your left nostril with your left thumb and breathe slowly and deeply three times in and out through your right nostril. Flash onto the Dali plasma and feel the heat of intrinsic awareness emanating out of your crown chakra. Now cover your right nostril with your right thumb and repeat, focusing all of your attention to your crown chakra, Dali plasma. Feel this heat move from your crown chakra down your spinal column and into your limbs, permeating your entire being. Your crown chakra is flooded with radiant warmth that connects you to the realm of cosmic consciousness. Give yourself to the process as if nothing else mattered.

Dali is the first state of the three-part primary sensory quantum. A sensory quantum is the first stage building block of sensory experience.

Level 3: Engaging the First Mental Sphere (Preconscious)

Profound samadhi activates first mental sphere.

Visualize the first mental sphere (preconscious) in the brain, located in and covering the right rear lobe and cerebellum. This sphere is the resonant chamber of the physical body and governs the right rear lobe of the brain.

By means of the preconscious, the evolutive activity of the third- and fourth-dimensional beings are programmed. This sphere corresponds to the first time dimension: *Cosmic creation*. It is activated by profound samadhi which penetrates to the deepest layers of the preconscious. This is the sphere where the primal codes of cosmic creation are situated.

Cosmic creation refers to mastery of the cosmic forces. This comes about through the self-creation of the energy of space. Here, we are no longer the victim of conditioned reality, thoughts and patterns. We have freed ourselves from the claims of the false self. Here we are creating ourselves and reality anew by embodying the five virtues: Remembrance, discipline, exertion, patience and compassion.

To experience and activate this mental sphere exert in natural mind meditation expanding the duration of the GAP—the space between thoughts.

NATURAL MIND MEDITATION

Sit still, with spine erect. Keep eyes slightly open looking toward the floor. Feel your intrinsic dignity in this posture. In this position, watch your breath. Breathe normally. As you become aware of your thoughts just label them "thinking", and as you exhale, dissolve the thoughts. It matters not the nature or content of the thoughts, just dissolve them. At that very moment, just as the thought dissolves, lies the GAP between thoughts. It is this GAP that you want to become familiar with and cultivate. It is the seed of natural mind and the key to your true, authentic self. Practice this each day and note the subtle shifts in your perceptions and attitudes.

LEVEL 4: OPENING THE FIRST HEPTAD GATE (108)

ALPHA-ALPHA

We begin this practice by introducing the seven solar mantras that open the seven solar gates (see previous chapter). For this chakra, the mantra is **OM**.

First visualize the violet thousand-petaled lotus **Sahasrara** chakra with the **yellow Dali** plasma superimposed over it at your crown. Hold this visualization and feel the two intermingle as you chant the sacred letter **OM** as long as your breath can sustain it (*Patanjali says that OM is the word that manifests God*). OM is the universal symbol for primordial sound vibration.

Locate Heptad Gate **108** and the **Alpha-Alpha** symbol on the 441 holomind perceiver. Its matrix location is V11:H2, second circuit, 7th time dimension: vertical time cosmic command descending. Now locate it in your body at the base of your skull (see graphic at the end of this chapter).

Visualize the **Alpha-Alpha** hyperplasma above the **yellow Dali** in your **crown** chakra. Take the **Alpha-Alpha** into the **first** mental sphere in the **first** time dimension (**cosmic creation**) where it activates the **preconscious mind** as **profound samadhi**. Here is the intergalactic channel (BMU 341) through which the **Alpha-Alpha** hyperplasma is secreted into the brain.

From the **first** mental sphere, mentally direct the **Alpha-Alpha** hyperplasma to the **crown** chakra and impress it above the **Dali** seal. Hold this with four alternate nostril breaths (four times in and out through each nostril), followed by one deep breath through both nostrils.

Descend down the central column (spine), secreting this red electric **Alpha-Alpha** hyperplasma into all 144,000 etheric fibers of the astral body. Practice the **breath of fire,** rapid shallow breathing through the nose, transmuting any blockages or obscurations into streams of crystal clear **profound samadhi** spreading throughout your entire nervous system.

Spectral, electric red Alpha-Alpha vibrates subtle activating force into all etheric fibers. Ascend back up central channel and leave **Dali** at the **crown** chakra. Return your consciousness to the first mental sphere, then close and seal the Heptad Gate at the base of your skull. Relax and breathe slowly and deeply at least 13 times.

 Harmonic UR rune 84: *Galactic Life Whole Becomes Medium of Transmission.*

For additional practice: Locate Heptad Gate 108 on the Hunab Ku 21. Note that it corresponds to the Primal Force, Ancient of Days, Galactatron, Queen of the Throne; G/K Neptune, Bode Number 300. Study the connections (see graphic at the end of this chapter).

Day Two: SELI

HRAM 291

Level 1: Meditating the Muladhara (Root) Chakra

Sit in a comfortable meditative posture. Keep your spine erect and body relaxed. With the body completely still, practice a few moments of natural mind meditation. Once the mind is sufficiently clear, direct your attention to your root or Muladhara chakra. Make it as clear and pristine as possible, glistening and sparkling with vibrant energy. When it is pure and translucent, pulsing at your root, allow it to dissolve and transform itself into a four-petalled red lotus.

Concentrate on this area inside of your root chakra. This is a key chakra in Kundalini Yoga where the awakening of the vital force begins; it is also the conjunction of 72,000 pairs of nerve endings in the body.

In Samkhya philosophy, Muladhara is understood as *moola prakriti*, the transcendental basis of physical nature. This is the base from which the three main psychic channels or nadis emerge and flow up the spinal cord: Ida (mental force), left; Pingala (vital force), right; and Sushumna (spiritual force), center.

This chakra is governed by the feminine principle or Shakti Goddess *Dakini* (Security). The physical body zone of psychic activation extends from the root chakra to the solar plexus. Emotional information from the solar plexus comes into the physical body at the root. At its base level this chakra deals with security and survival—the basic instincts.

This chakra also serves as a storage center for much unconscious energy including "lower" emotions such as guilt and other psychic complexes. With the awakening of this chakra, we proceed from the unconscious to the conscious.

Muladhara affirmation: *May the highest yogic force within the planetary consciousness direct all manifestation to its fulfillment!*

LEVEL 2: ACTIVATING RADIAL PLASMA: SELI

**SELI
ROOT**

Breathe deeply through your nostrils and allow your awareness to flow down from your nose and into your root chakra. Bring your awareness to the inner Seli plasma at the center of the chakra. Visualize the red symbol radiating streams of white light. This plasma accounts for the intensity of inner light.

Repeat the following while focusing on your root chakra: "My mother is the ultimate sphere, I see the light." Feel this sphere of light as the perfect form at your root chakra. This quality of perfection is the actual nature of reality.

Cover your left nostril with your left thumb and breathe slowly and deeply three times in and out through your right nostril. Flash onto the Seli plasma and feel the light of the ultimate sphere emanating out of the root chakra. Now cover your right nostril with your right thumb and repeat the three breaths, focusing all of your attention to your root chakra, Seli plasma. Feel this luminosity (light) emanate from your root chakra, moving up your spinal column to your crown chakra and then permeating your body to the tips of your fingers and toes. Feel your entire body flooded with this radiant light, grounding you into the Earth and extending upward to the crown of cosmic consciousness.

Feel the emanations of flowing streams of light clearing and releasing any blockages in your system. The Great Mother energy nurtures the root of your being, the base or seat of the kundalini force. Kundalini (life-force) energy is released from the root, activating the secret center and opening the inner wisdom channel of the third eye.

Seli is the second stage of the three-part primary sensory quantum. A sensory quantum is the first stage building block of sensory experience.

LEVEL 3: ENGAGING THE SECOND MENTAL SPHERE (SUB- OR UNCONSCIOUS)

Informative samadhi activates second mental sphere.

Visualize the second mental sphere (sub- or unconscious) in the brain and centered in the optic nerve, encompassing the pineal gland and corpus callosum. This mental sphere governs the right front hemisphere.

This sphere contains every perception and life experience that was not consciously registered or that is filtered out of your day-to-day conscious mind (third mental sphere). What people think of as their personality is primarily based on their own evaluation of their reactions to a set of circumstances. Everyone experiences a different set and order of life circumstances and is given an equal opportunity of responding consciously or unconsciously and/or positively or negatively.

This sphere corresponds to the third time dimension: *Cosmic synchronization*. Cosmic synchronization refers to mastery of the synchronic order: Self-creation through time. Here, we impress the codes of the synchronic order, embedding them into our subconscious.

The second mental sphere is activated as informative samadhi. Cultivation of unbroken meditative awareness allows us to access information previously out of range of our waking conscious. Knowledge of the Law of Time lies dormant in this mental sphere. The Law of Time makes conscious what was previously unconscious. According to the Law of Time all life possesses unconscious energy

This mental sphere is activated by cultivating states of peripheral awareness, both through meditation and by contemplation of the Law of Time: Time as the evolution of consciousness.

If our day to day experience remains unconscious of the Law of Time, then when an experience occurs in our timespace, we will not be aware of the opportunity for heightened consciousness that is being presented to us. However, if we are conscious of the Law of Time, then our experiences become triggers that enter us into higher consciousness.

LEVEL 4: OPENING THE SECOND HEPTAD GATE (291)

ALPHA-BETA

Visualize the red four-petaled lotus **Muladhara** chakra with the **red Seli** plasma superimposed over it at your root. Hold this visualization and feel the two intermingle as you chant the sacred letter **HRAM** as long as your breath can sustain it.

Locate Heptad Gate **291** and the **Alpha-Beta** symbol on the 441 holomind perceiver. Its matrix location is V11:H5, fifth circuit, 7th time dimension, vertical time cosmic command descending. Now locate it in your body at the middle back of your skull, halfway between base and crown (see graphic at the end of this chapter).

Visualize the **Alpha-Beta** hyperplasma above the **red Seli** in your **root** chakra. Take the **Alpha-Beta** into the **second** mental sphere in the **third** time dimension (**cosmic synchronization**) where it activates the **subconscious** as **informative samadhi**. Here is the intergalactic channel (BMU 351) through which the **Alpha-Beta** hyperplasma is secreted into the front, right hemisphere of the brain.

From the **second** mental sphere, mentally direct the **Alpha-Beta** hyperplasma to the **root** chakra and impress it above the **Seli** seal. Hold this with four alternate nostril breaths (four times in and out through each nostril), followed by one breath through both nostrils.

Ascend up the central column (spine), secreting this **Alpha-Beta** hyperplasma into all 144,000 etheric fibers of the astral body. Practice the **breath of fire,** rapid shallow breathing through the nose, transmuting any blockages or obscurations into streams of crystal clear **informative samadhi** spreading throughout your entire nervous system.

Spectral, electric red and blue Alpha-Beta vibrates subtle activating force into all etheric fibers. Descend back down central channel and leave **Seli** at the **root** chakra. Ascend back up central channel and return your consciousness to the second mental sphere, then close and seal the Heptad Gate at the middle of the back of your skull. Relax and breathe slowly and deeply at least 13 times.

Harmonic UR rune 88: *Galactic Life Whole Realized as Cosmic Consciousness.*

For additional practice: Locate Heptad Gate 291 on the Hunab Ku 21. Note that it corresponds to the Avatar, Accomplisher of Knowledge, the Exemplar; G/K Earth, Bode Number 10. Study all of the connections (see graphic at the end of this chapter).

Day Three: GAMMA

HRAHA   144

Level 1: Meditating the Ajna (Third Eye) Chakra

Sit in a comfortable meditative posture. Keep your spine erect and body relaxed. With the body completely still, practice a few moments of natural mind meditation. Once the mind is sufficiently clear, direct your attention to your third eye or Ajna chakra. Make it as clear and pristine as possible, glistening and sparkling with vibrant energy. When it is pure and translucent, pulsing at your brow, allow it to dissolve and transform itself into a two-petalled indigo lotus.

Concentrate on this area inside of your third eye chakra. Concentration on this chakra awakens the pineal gland, opening our inner vision to the receptivity of cosmic forces; this is the doorway to the astral and psychic dimensions of consciousness.

The word "ajna" is derived from the Sanskrit root which means "to know, obey or follow." Literally, ajna means "command" or "the monitoring center." It is also sometimes referred to as the chakra of the mind or the eye of wisdom. The Ajna chakra is the point where the three main nadis (Ida, Pingala and Sushumna) merge into one stream of consciousness and flow up to the crown center.

To awaken the Ajna chakra requires discipline and persistent concentration. Visualize a dot of light and stay focused on the single point of light to cultivate your inner vision. The purpose of this action is to pacify the lower emotions, open the inner vision, and sustain concentration. Cultivation of the Ajna chakra lifts us to a level of continuing consciousness, creating the possibility for mind-to-mind communication or telepathy.

This chakra is governed by the feminine principle or Shakti Goddess *Hakini* (Insight). It holds the key to intuition, or sixth sense—direct attunement or attaining divine knowledge directly without the aid of the senses—what is traditionally called "gnosis."

When this center is finally awakened the body becomes flooded with bliss light radiance that illuminates all you set your mind on. You are creating a light transmission antennae from the inside out so that the higher intelligence may connect with you. Once sufficiently disciplined, your inner vision can be directed to any one of your other chakras to retrieve information, impressions, stored memories and/or insights. It is through the Ajna chakra that we may see the hidden essence of the world of appearance: past, future and present at once. When the mind is purified, then the other chakras naturally awaken.

Ajna affirmation: *May we be granted galactic vision to transform all matter into the purifying radiance of the higher dream!*

LEVEL 2: ACTIVATING RADIAL PLASMA: GAMMA

**GAMMA
THIRD EYE**

Breathe deeply through your nostrils and allow your awareness to flow up your nose and into your third eye chakra. Bring your awareness to the inner Gamma plasma at the center of the chakra. Visualize the white symbol radiating out to all points of the universe with peaceful equanimity and equalization of light and heat charges.

Repeat the following while focusing on your third eye: "My lineage is the union of intrinsic awareness and the ultimate sphere, I attain the power of peace." Allow yourself to feel the merging of light (perfect radiant form) and heat (intrinsic awareness) within the third eye. Feel the inherent perfection and innate self-liberation of peace that always exists in the present moment.

To discover the lineage of heat and light cover your left nostril with your left thumb and breathe deeply three times in and out through your right nostril. First, flash onto the yellow Dali plasma at your crown chakra and feel the heat of intrinsic awareness emanating from this center. Now, cover your right nostril with your right thumb and breathe deeply three times in and out of your left nostril. Flash onto the luminous red Seli plasma at your root chakra and feel the soothing flow of the radiating sphere of light. Contemplate the mystery of light and heat.

Now merge the heat from the crown and light from the root together in your third eye, white Gamma plasma. Feel the pulsing union of this intrinsic awareness (heat) and ultimate sphere (light). Your entire body and glandular system is pacified and bathed in the warmth of this divine mother/father light.

With sufficient concentration and practice, the thermic energy from both the crown chakra as well as the exterior higher-dimensional light universe floods into the third eye and fills the physical and astral nervous system with radiant insight, reinstating our clairvoyant birthright.

Gamma is the third stage that completes the three-part primary sensory quantum. A sensory quantum is the first stage building block of sensory experience.

LEVEL 3: ENGAGING THE THIRD MENTAL SPHERE (WAKING CONSCIOUS)

Waking conscious mediumship activates third mental sphere.

Visualize the third mental sphere (waking conscious) located in the brain at the anterior portion of the right cerebral hemisphere above the right eye. This mental sphere generally functions solely with the third-dimensional self, but in a state of wakefulness it operates at the beta level governing the left front cerebral hemisphere.

The third mental sphere is the medium of thought, decision and moment-to-moment awareness. Becoming conscious means to question everything back to its source. True knowledge begins first with curiosity, a desire to *know*. This desire to *know* creates the space for intelligent questions to arise. With these questions comes the desire to know the answer. The feedback received varies according to the quality of the question.

This mental sphere governs the power of free will; it is intended to be disciplined by the exercise of will on behalf of a spiritually coordinated purpose. When this is achieved, then the eye of wisdom opens and gnosis becomes possible.

This sphere also corresponds to the fourth time dimension: *Cosmic cube.* Cosmic cube refers to the highest level of cosmic mastery entering us into higher mental design processes of co-creation. The most direct way to activate this level of awareness is by practicing tuning the third eye to the Supreme Being; shining, full of light, pure, perfect and free of obscurations. Keep the mind fixed for as long as possible on this formless One; the Creator of all Knowledge and Intelligence. Allow your mind to merge with all of creation.

The ability to have one-pointed consciousness is the key to *waking conscious mediumship.* When the mind is concentrated at this point then comes the transcendence of individual *unconsciousness* into collective planetary *consciousness.*

LEVEL 4: OPENING THE THIRD HEPTAD GATE (144)

BETA-BETA

Visualize the indigo two-petaled lotus **Ajna** chakra with the **white Gamma** plasma superimposed over it at your brow. Hold this visualization and feel the two intermingle as you chant the sacred letter **HRAHA** as long as your breath can sustain it.

Locate Heptad Gate **144** and the **Beta-Beta** symbol on the 441 holomind perceiver. Its matrix location is V11:H20, second circuit, 8th time dimension, vertical time cosmic command ascending. Now locate it in your body at the front of your skull, at the brow (see graphic at the end of this chapter).

Visualize the **Beta-Beta** hyperplasma above the **white Gamma** in your **third eye** chakra. Take the Beta-Beta into the **third** mental sphere in the **fourth** time dimension (**cosmic cube**) where it activates the **conscious** mind as **waking mediumship**. Here is the intergalactic channel (BMU 321) through which the **Beta-Beta** hyperplasma is secreted into the front, left hemisphere of the brain.

From the **third** mental sphere, mentally direct the **Beta-Beta** hyperplasma to the **third eye** chakra and impress it above the **Gamma** seal. Hold this with four alternate nostril breaths (four times in and out through each nostril), followed by one breath through both nostrils.

Descend down the central column (spine), secreting this **Beta-Beta** hyperplasma into all 144,000 etheric fibers of the astral body. Practice the **breath of fire,** rapid shallow breathing through the nose, transmuting any blockages or obscurations into streams of crystal clear **waking conscious mediumship** spreading throughout your entire nervous system.

Spectral, electric blue Beta-Beta vibrates subtle activating force into all etheric fibers. Ascend back up central channel and leave **Gamma** at the **third eye** chakra. Return your consciousness to the third mental sphere, then close and seal the Heptad Gate at your third eye. Relax and breathe slowly and deeply at least 13 times.

Harmonic UR rune 91: *Galactic Art Whole Defines Space.*

For additional practice: Locate Heptad Gate 144 on the Hunab Ku 21. Note that it corresponds to the High Priestess, Spirit Essence, Urania, Lady of the Winds; G/K Uranus, Bode Number 196. Study all of the connections (see graphic at the end of this chapter).

Day Four: KALI

HRIM 315

Level 1: Meditating the Svadhisthana (Secret Center) Chakra

Sit in a comfortable meditative posture. Keep your spine erect and body relaxed. With the body completely still, practice a few moments of natural mind meditation. Once the mind is sufficiently clear, direct your attention to your secret center or Svadhisthana chakra. Make it as clear and pristine as possible, glistening and sparkling with vibrant energy. When it is pure and translucent, pulsing at your secret center, allow it to dissolve and transform itself into an orange six-petalled lotus.

Concentrate on this area inside of your secret center chakra. This is the seat of sexual awareness and holds a supremely powerful energy. This is also the seat of body consciousness.

In yogic tradition, the Svadhisthana is known as the substratum or basis of individual human consciousness. It is the container of all karmas, impressions, past lives and previous experience, or the unconscious, as it pertains specifically to the formation of the earthly personality or circumstantial persona.

This chakra is governed by the feminine principle or Shakti Goddess *Rakini* (Sexuality). This is the place that stores the most psychic blockages and karma—the collective karma of the unconscious. We want to awaken the secret center in order to open our inner vision to the receptivity of cosmic electricity.

When this center is finally awakened the body becomes flooded with cosmic electricity that connects all other chakras. This is the area to transmute and re-channel the powerful sexual, or kundalini energy into a higher form of electricity. The energy stored in this chakra can be used to vitalize the different levels of being.

Svadhisthana affirmation: *May the supramental forces gather their electroplasmic structures of spiritual evolution and release them into the noosphere!*

Level 2: Activating Radial Plasma: Kali

Kali
Secret Center

Breathe deeply through your nostrils and allow your awareness to flow up your nose and down into your secret center chakra. Bring your awareness to the inner Kali plasma at the center of the chakra. Visualize the blue symbol radiating streams of white light.

Feel the Kali plasma gathering in the secret center, accounting for the quality of intensified light-heat, which is also associated with the sexual, or kundalini energy.

Repeat the following while focusing on your secret center: "My name is the glorious lotus-born, I catalyze the light-heat within." Feel within yourself this light-heat, the self-generated electricity that arises from a condition of immaculate purity.

Cover your left nostril with your left thumb and breathe deeply three times in and out through your right nostril. Flash onto the Kali plasma and feel the intensified light-heat emanating out of the secret center chakra. Now cover your right nostril with your right thumb and repeat the three breaths. Focus on the Kali plasma and feel this intrinsic light-heat awareness pulsing from your secret center chakra into your entire being. Feel the flowing streams of light and heat catalyzing your entire system into ever more subtle spirals of radiance. This powerful energy emanates from your secret center chakra, activating, circulating and invigorating all other chakras. You are the glorious lotus-born, born from Father Heat and Mother Light.

Kali plasma is the link between the three light-heat sensory plasmas and the three telepathic plasmas. It is the catalytic agent between the thermic/luminic sensory quantum and the subatomic telepathic quantum.

LEVEL 3: ENGAGING THE FOURTH MENTAL SPHERE (CONTINUING CONSCIOUS)

Higher mind control activates fourth mental sphere.

Visualize the fourth mental sphere (continuing conscious) located in the brain above the left eye in the left cerebral hemisphere. This mental sphere controls and governs the rear left hemisphere.

Continuing consciousness is the ability to maintain a conscious thoughtform in succession over a long, unbroken period of time. In terms of Cosmic Science, continuing consciousness is the ability of the 4-D "Other" to maintain direct communication with the 5-D "Higher Self" and to continue to establish and extend realization of the whole to the 3-D "self".

This sphere corresponds to the second time dimension: *Cosmic ascension.* Cosmic ascension refers to the mastery of higher powers of telepathic perception and projection. This means we can perceive ourselves anywhere in the universe and project to those places as necessary.

To cultivate continuing consciousness choose a thought, mental structure or series of numbers to focus on. You might also practice maintaining projective geometries, like an icosahedron or dodecahedron. Concentrate and fill your mind entirely with this inner perception or mental construct—keep it filled with this thought. The moment that any other thought tries to enter the mind displace it immediately with the thought-construct upon which you are concentrating.

Continue until you acquire the skill of being able to concentrate on anything for as long as you wish, or until it appears before you in hallucinatory clarity. Persistent training in control of your thought-world prepares you for supermental descent of consciousness. Analyze every thought that arises. If a thought is not constructive or harmonious, let it go immediately. Do this as often as necessary until it becomes second nature. When you attain this capacity you will experience higher mind control: you are no longer the doer or the thinker, but the higher self has intervened.

Level 4: Opening the Fourth Heptad Gate (315)

Beta-Alpha

Visualize the orange six-petaled lotus **Svadhisthana** chakra with the **blue Kali** plasma superimposed over it at your sacral area. Hold this visualization and feel the two intermingle as you chant the sacred letter **HRIM** as long as your breath can sustain it.

Locate Heptad Gate **315** and the **Beta-Alpha** symbol on the 441 holomind perceiver. Its matrix location is V11:H17, fifth circuit, 8th time dimension, vertical time cosmic command ascending. Now locate it in your body at the top of your forehead, just above the third eye (see graphic at the end of this chapter).

Visualize the **Beta-Alpha** hyperplasma above the **blue Kali** in your **secret center** chakra. Take the **Beta-Alpha** into the **fourth** mental sphere in the **second** time dimension (**cosmic ascension**) where it activates **continuing conscious** as **higher mind control**. Here is the intergalactic channel (BMU 331) through which the **Beta-Alpha** hyperplasma is secreted into the rear left hemisphere of the brain.

From the **fourth** mental sphere, mentally direct the **Beta-Alpha** hyperplasma to the **secret center** chakra and impress it above the **Kali** seal. Hold this with four alternate nostril breaths (four times in and out through each nostril), followed by one breath through both nostrils.

Ascend up the central column (spine), secreting this **Beta-Alpha** hyperplasma into all 144,000 etheric fibers of the astral body. Practice the **breath of fire,** rapid shallow breathing through the nose, transmuting any blockages or obscurations into streams of crystal clear **higher mind control** spreading through your entire nervous system.

Spectral, electric blue and red Beta-Alpha vibrates subtle activating force into all etheric fibers. Descend back down central channel and leave **Kali** at the **secret center** chakra. Ascend back up central channel and return your consciousness to the fourth mental sphere, then close and seal the Heptad Gate at the top front of your skull. Relax and breathe slowly and deeply at least 13 times.

 Harmonic UR rune 95: *Galactic Art Whole Becomes Meditation of Reality.*

For additional practice: Locate Heptad Gate 315 on the Hunab Ku 21. Note that it corresponds to the Prophet, the Renewer of Culture, World Teacher; S/P Mars, Bode Number 16. Study all of the connections (see graphic at the end of this chapter).

DAY FIVE: ALPHA

HRAUM 414

LEVEL 1: MEDITATING THE VISHUDDHA (THROAT) CHAKRA

Sit in a comfortable meditative posture. Keep your spine erect and body relaxed. With the body completely still, practice a few moments of natural mind meditation. Once the mind is sufficiently clear, direct your attention to your throat or Vishuddha chakra. Make it as clear and pristine as possible, glistening and sparkling with vibrant energy. When it is pure and translucent, radiating from your throat, allow it to dissolve and transform itself into a blue sixteen-petalled lotus.

Concentrate on this area inside of your throat chakra. This center contains the will to communicate and to extend oneself to others in patterns of informative thought and behavior.

The Vishuddha chakra is the channel of communication bringing the fourth dimension through to the third dimension. This deals both with the mental and emotional bodies and is the center for artistic expression and communicating intelligence derived from the higher mental spheres (5th and 6th).

The Vishuddha chakra is known by some yogic traditions as the chakra of spiritual rebirth, and in Kundalini yoga as the "fountain of youth", the place where spontaneous physical rejuvenation begins. To activate the Vishuddha chakra you may recite prayers, sing devotional songs or practice mantra. Chant "Ahhh" seven times to open the throat chakra.

This chakra is governed by the feminine principle or Shakti Goddess *Shakini* (Knowledge). The Vishuddha is also the center of purification and discrimination and the locus of vijnana, or divine analytical wisdom. By focusing our attention on this chakra, we can discriminate between messages from the higher mind from messages of ego.

This Vishuddha chakra is related with *Nada Yoga*, or the branch of kundalini yoga concerned with sound vibration (Vishuddha and Muladhara are considered to be the two basic centers of vibration). The Muladhara chakra corresponds to the cosmic vibratory root, while the Vishuddha chakra is the receiver of the higher harmonics of the music of the spheres. When this chakra reaches its highest state, sounds emitted take on magical qualities that change the space of the listener through vibration. This chakra can also be utilized as a receiving station to tune into the thoughts and feelings of people both far and near.

This is the supermental reception center of thought-waves and transmissions which discriminates then directs messages to the appropriate chakra. As this chakra awakens, we can begin to direct the energies of the body from the lower to the higher chakras, reconnecting our expression as higher resonant channels of the cosmos.

Note: The nerve channel in the throat is also associated with *kurma nadi*, the tortoise nadi. When this nadi is awakened the practitioner is able to completely overcome the desire and necessity for food and drink. (This has been demonstrated by many yogis, particularly in India. Examples of such yogis/yoginis can be found in *Autobiography of a Yogi*, by Sri Paramahansa Yogananda).

Vishuddha affirmation: *May the vision of the star elders of the great councils of light and wisdom speak through me so that all may ascend to sublime grace!*

LEVEL 2: ACTIVATING RADIAL PLASMA: ALPHA

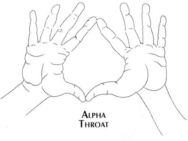

ALPHA
THROAT

Breathe deeply through your nostrils and allow your awareness to flow up your nose and down into your throat chakra. Bring your awareness to the inner Alpha plasma at the center of the chakra. Visualize the yellow symbol radiating luminous streams of white light.

Feel the electrical vibration of the Alpha plasma gathered in the throat center. This center activates the double-extended electrical charge, which is in telepathic resonance with the South Pole. Repeat the following while focusing on your throat chakra: "My country is the unborn ultimate sphere, I release the double-extended electron at the South Pole." Unborn refers to the unconditional indestructible state that pervades the entire universe from beginningless beginning to endless end. Feel your consciousness align with Universal consciousness as your vibration raises to the frequency of the new Earth. All knots and obscurations dissolve from your mental stream as you merge into the great ocean of superconscious universal mind.

Cover your left nostril with your left thumb and breathe deeply three times in and out through your right nostril. Flash onto the Alpha plasma and feel the light streaming in from the Universal Mind purifying your throat chakra, and cleansing all of your communication channels. Now cover your right nostril with your right thumb and repeat the three breaths, focusing all of your attention on the throat chakra. Your throat chakra emanates sound enlivening and resonating healing vibrations to all of the other chakras. You are the creator of the new stories, the teller of the new tales.

Alpha plasma charge is the first stage of the three-part telepathic quantum. At the center of Alpha feel the integrated charges of the sensory quanta: Dali, Seli, and Gamma, transmuted by Kali into the Alpha telepathic charge. Then by extending your mind telepathically to the south of the Planet, release the double-extended electron at the South Pole.

Level 3: Engaging the Fifth Mental Sphere (Superconscious)

Hyperelectronic superconscious activates fifth mental sphere.

Visualize the fifth mental sphere (superconscious) situated in the brain above the left ear in the left cerebral hemisphere. This is the seat of the fifth-dimensional higher self and functions with the fourth-dimensional "Other". This mental sphere governs and activates the right lateral hemispheres midway between right ear and right temple where it sends paranormal impulses to the first mental sphere: preconscious.

Superconsciousness lies behind the veil of waking consciousness. It is sometimes referred to as cosmic consciousness or Christ consciousness; the self-existing consciousness bliss that transcends creation. The quality of our thoughts and attention is key to harnessing these superconscious powers.

Our thoughts are electronic lines of force that release into the atmosphere and create specific effects according to the strength of the thought. To embody a superconscious state of mind requires persistent and attentive concentration and devotion to meditation practice.

This sphere corresponds to the fifth time dimension, the radial time of the superconscious fifth-dimensional Higher Self. It is characterized by an electrical hyper-clarity that is definitely not "of this world." This sphere is increasingly activated with the advent of the noosphere, and is characterized by total holistic perception. Incorporating the continuing conscious of the fourth mental sphere, the superconscious expands into the mentation waves of the fifth-dimensional higher self. A "mentation" wave is a configuration of telepathic potentialities, independent of language, and based on whole orders of supermental precepts intrinsic to non-egoic knowing. To cultivate a superconscious mind, meditate the whole Earth as a single organism held together by a universal thought-field.

WHOLE EARTH MEDITATION

Visualize yourself right where you are. Notice the space that you are in, whether it be inside or outside. Now lift out of the environment you find yourself in and look down on it from above. Lift out further and see the entire street or area that you are in. Now expand out and lift higher and higher into space. From space, view the Earth as a single luminous blue mandala. See the Earth from all angles. See it as a planetary orb, a wheel spinning in space with an essential value, its dharma or truth. The dharma or capacity of Earth is its capacity to sustain life.

Visualize the whole of life on Earth, from the animals, to the plants, to the humans down onto the insects and plankton. See it all as one whole system. The whole of the life on the Earth is the biosphere, or the sphere of life that covers the surface of the Earth like a film or vibrant mantle that is ever in motion. Really visualize how all of the different life forms and processes are one unity on this shining blue orb.

Now let your mind penetrate beneath the surface of the Earth. Feel the spherical layers of sediment and crystalline rock. Go to the core and find the massive iron crystal octahedron. Feel this crystal core as a dynamic radio receiver elongated in the direction of each of its magnetic poles. Place yourself in meditation at the very center of that crystal radio receiver. Who is the Earth receiving? What is the Earth broadcasting? Where is the Earth receiving? What messages is Earth giving you right now?

Note: Application of advanced pure meditation techniques are necessary to unify with universal cosmic space. Telepathic supernormative thoughtforms are always coming from the fifth mental sphere, the superconscious.

LEVEL 4: OPENING THE FIFTH HEPTAD GATE (414)

HYPERELECTRON

Visualize the blue sixteen-petaled lotus **Vishuddha** chakra with the **yellow Alpha** plasma superimposed over it at your throat. Hold this visualization and feel the two intermingle as you chant the sacred letter HRAUM as long as your breath can sustain it.

Locate Heptad Gate **414** and the **Hyperelectron** symbol on the 441 holomind perceiver. Its matrix location is V11:H14, eighth circuit, 9th time dimension, inner core time. Now locate it in your body at front, center top of your skull (see graphic at the end of this chapter).

Visualize the **Hyperelectron with the spiraling red Kuali force field** above the **yellow Alpha** in your **throat** chakra. Take the **Hyperelectron** into the **fifth** mental sphere in the **fifth** time dimension (red Kuali electrothermic force field H11:V1-7, right-handed time) where it activates the **superconscious** as **hyperelectronic superconscious** informing **mental spheres one and two.**

From the **fifth** mental sphere, mentally direct the **black Hyperelectron** to the **throat** chakra and impress it above the **Alpha** seal. Hold this with four alternate nostril breaths (four times in and out through each nostril), followed by one breath through both nostrils.

Descend down the central column (spine), secreting the **Hyperelectron** (red kuali force field) into all 144,000 etheric fibers of the astral body. Practice the **breath of fire,** rapid shallow breathing through the nose, transmuting any blockages or obscurations into streams of crystal clear **hyperelectronic superconscious** spreading through your entire nervous system.

The black Hyperelectron with spectral, electric red Kuali force field vibrates subtle activating electronic force into all etheric fibers. Descend back down central channel and leave **Alpha** at the **throat** chakra. Return your consciousness to the fifth mental sphere, then close and seal the Heptad Gate at the front top-center of your skull. Relax and breathe slowly and deeply at least 13 times.

 Harmonic UR rune 90: *Galactic Art Whole Defined by Time.*

For additional practice: Locate Heptad Gate 414 on the Hunab Ku 21. Note that it corresponds to the Enlightened One, the Bringer of the Higher Truth, the Renewer of Life, Holder of the Timespace Wisdom; G/K Pluto, Bode Number 388. Study all of the connections (see graphic at the end of this chapter).

DAY SIX: LIMI

HRUM   402

LEVEL 1: MEDITATING THE MANIPURA (SOLAR PLEXUS) CHAKRA

Sit in a comfortable meditative posture. Keep your spine erect and body relaxed. With the body completely still, practice a few moments of natural mind meditation. Once the mind is sufficiently clear, direct your attention to your solar plexus or Manipura chakra. Make it as clear and pristine as possible, glistening and sparkling with vibrant energy. When it is pure and translucent, radiating from your solar plexus, allow it to dissolve and transform itself into a yellow ten-petalled lotus.

Concentrate on this area inside your solar plexus. The solar plexus is considered the second brain and the central storehouse of prana. The energy stored in this chakra can be used to connect us both individually and as a planet, through the Sun, to the galactic core, Hunab Ku. In the Tibetan tradition this chakra is known as *mani padma*, or "jeweled lotus." This is the point where all 72,000 nerve endings (on each side of the body) meet, for a total of 144,000 nerve endings.

This chakra is governed by the feminine principle or Shakti Goddess *Lakini* (Authority). This chakra center is also associated with willpower, and power in general; it is the place of empowerment and disempowerment, judgment and identity. The solar plexus is the processing chamber of the instinctual/ intuitive energy and emotional intelligence. This energy is transferred to the heart chakra where the transduction of emotional energy is experienced as the "intelligence of the heart."

Meditation on the Manipura chakra leads to knowledge of the entire physical and subtle body system. When this center is purified and awakened, then it is possible to reconnect (via the etheric "highway" of the *kuxan suum* or cosmic umbilical cord) to the center of the galaxy, Hunab Ku. When this reconnection takes place the body becomes disease-free and luminous, and consciousness does not fall back into a lower state.

This chakra is often compared to the heat and the power of the Sun, radiating and distributing pranic energy throughout the entire human system. To awaken this chakra, breathe slowly into the solar plexus and feel the expansion and contraction of the navel as you breathe in and out through the naval. Breathe in, hold and suck the stomach in, then push it out when you exhale. Do this several times focusing on the purification of the abdominal area.

From this center feel the kuxan suum as the etheric fiber that flows directly to the center of the galaxy, making the solar plexus chakra a vital information receptacle. The kuxan suum connects the planetary circuit with the solar and galactic circuits.

Through an effort of imaginal will, we can direct our astral body through the reflective membrane of the planetary field into the Sun and then ultimately to the galactic core. This is the area allowing us to transmute and override primitive lower emotions by opening to receive the influx of higher cosmic energy. It is important to visualize the kuxan suum as a luminous etheric thread extending from the solar plexus to the center of the galaxy. This establishes us in the galactic order of reality.

Manipura affirmation: *May our perceptions be organized into a cosmic whole that we may all become one with the radialized order of the Primal Source!*

Level 2: Activating Radial Plasma: Limi

Limi
Solar Plexus

Breathe deeply through both your nostrils and allow your awareness to flow up your nose and down into your solar plexus chakra. Bring your awareness to the inner Limi plasma at the center of the chakra. Visualize the red symbol radiating luminous streams of white light.

Feel the Limi plasma vibrating, electrically gathered in the solar plexus, accounting for the mental electron electrical charge, which is in telepathic resonance with the North Pole.

Repeat the following while focusing on your solar plexus chakra: "I consume dualistic thoughts as food, I purify the mental-electron at the North Pole." Feel all conditioned thoughts dissolve in the light of intrinsic awareness.

Cover your left nostril with your left thumb and breathe deeply three times in and out through your right nostril. Flash onto the Limi plasma and feel the galactic connection out of the solar plexus. Now cover the right nostril with the right thumb and repeat the three breaths. Focus all of your attention to your solar plexus chakra, Limi plasma, and feel into the galactic reality being pulsed, breathed and radiated from your solar plexus chakra into the world.

Feel the Limi plasma gathered in the solar plexus accounting for the mental electron charge in telepathic resonance with the North Pole. The Limi charge is the second of three plasmas to form the telepathic quantum. This is the second telepathic plasma where you take the sensory quantum transmutations and breathe them out into the world through your solar plexus, emanating stabilizing vibrations to the astral and emotional bodies, soothing the rest of the chakras.

At the center of Limi feel the integrated charges of the sensory quanta: Dali, Seli, and Gamma, transmuted by Kali and the Alpha telepathic charge which initiates the telepathic quanta. Then by extending your mind telepathically to the north of the Planet, place the mental electron at the North Pole and purify it.

Level 3: Engaging the Sixth Mental Sphere (Subliminal Conscious)

Hyperneutronic subliminal consciousness activates sixth mental sphere.

Visualize the sixth mental sphere (subliminal conscious) located in the brain above the right ear in the right cerebral hemisphere. This sphere governs and controls the left lateral hemisphere. (Note how 5th and 6th mental spheres govern parts of the brain opposite their locus, exhibiting together a type of crossover polarity).

Subliminal means you are operating independent of past and future; this is how people can contact different entities on different planes of existence. Since subliminal consciousness is independent of past and future, you can tune into it at the conscious level, suspending all conditioned thought-programs. This mental sphere functions with the third-dimensional "self," storing impressions which are then transmuted into subliminal patterns of communication.

The sixth mental sphere allows us access to the parapsychic, supramental realm. This is the seat of the telepathic scanning system and interdimensional programs. To experience this, relax and focus your breath awareness on the psychic passages between the root, solar plexus and throat centers. Feel the upward circulation of energy and visualize yourself as a cosmic antenna for higher intelligence. Open yourself to become a telepathic receptor of higher mind capable of transmitting and receiving subliminal messages.

This intention, maintained through undistracted, non-conceptual meditative awareness, activates higher mind telepathic receptivity. This can also be realized and cultivated through dreamtime.

Note that this mental sphere contains subliminal suggestive impulses that affect third-dimensional functions as "intuitive flashes" (but which may actually be telepathic transmissions from remote points of supermental cosmic civilization trying to establish "contact"). These contacts leave impressions in the sixth mental sphere, which may be transmitted or transduced in any number of ways, which include ear-ringing, subliminal or hypnogogic imagery, déjà vu's, etc.

LEVEL 4: OPENING THE SIXTH HEPTAD GATE (402)

HYPERNEUTRON

Visualize the yellow ten-petaled lotus **Manipura** chakra with the **red Limi** plasma superimposed over it at your solar plexus. Hold this visualization and feel the two intermingle as you chant the sacred letter **HRUM** as long as your breath can sustain it.

Locate Heptad Gate **402** and the **Hyperneutron** symbol on the 441 holomind perceiver. Its matrix location is V11:H8, eighth circuit, 9th time dimension, inner core time. Now locate it in your body at the back, top center of your skull (see graphic at the end of this chapter).

Visualize the **Hyperneutron with the rectilinear blue Duar force field** above the red Limi in your **solar plexus** chakra. Take the **Hyperneutron** into the **sixth** mental sphere in the **sixth** time dimension (blue Duar electroluminic force field H11:V15-21, left-handed time) where it activates the **subliminal conscious** as **hyperneutronic subliminal conscious** informing **mental spheres three and four.**

From the **sixth** mental sphere, mentally direct the **Hyperneutron** to the solar plexus chakra and impress it above the **Limi** seal. Hold this with four alternate nostril breaths (four times in and out through each nostril), followed by one breath through both nostrils.

Ascend up the central column (spine), secreting the **Hyperneutron** (blue duar force field) into all 144,000 etheric fibers of the astral body. Practice the **breath of fire,** rapid shallow breathing through the nose, transmuting any blockages or obscurations into streams of crystal clear **hyperneutronic subliminal consciousness** spreading through your entire nervous system.

The black Hyperneutron with spectral, electric blue Duar force field vibrates subtle activating neutronic force into all etheric fibers. Descend back down the central channel and leave **Limi** at the **solar plexus** chakra. Return your consciousness to the sixth mental sphere, then close and seal the Heptad Gate at the back top-side of your skull. Relax and breathe slowly and deeply at least 13 times.

 Harmonic UR rune 81: *Radiogenesis Establishes Galactic Life Whole.*

For additional practice: Locate Heptad Gate 402 on the Hunab Ku 21. Note that it corresponds to the Yogi/Yogini, the Meditation Master, Holder of the Transcendental Wisdom; S/P Neptune, Bode Number 300. Study all of the connections (see graphic at the end of this chapter).

DAY SEVEN: SILIO

HRAIM 441

LEVEL 1: MEDITATING THE ANAHATA (HEART) CHAKRA

Sit in a comfortable meditative posture. Keep your spine erect and body relaxed. With the body completely still, practice a few moments of natural mind meditation. Once the mind is sufficiently clear, direct your attention to your heart or Anahata chakra. Make it as clear and pristine as possible, glistening and sparkling with vibrant energy. When it is pure and translucent, radiating from your heart, allow it to dissolve and transform itself into a green twelve-petalled lotus.

Concentrate on this area inside of your heart chakra. The heart is the main transducer of energy and is also an organ of knowing; it is the key to developing clairsentience—divine sense of touch—and also the place where "gnosis", direct knowledge of the supreme reality, occurs.

This Anahata chakra is governed by the feminine principle or Shakti Goddess *Kakini* (Devotion). This chakra serves as the seat of the memory of God through devotion, or *bodhichitta*, the mind of the aspiration to enlightenment. This area contains the transcendental programs that transform biological survival issues into forms of selfless compassion.

The heart energy is fed by the secret center, the seat of life-force energy. The heart chakra contains all impulses of innate being or essence nature. At this center comes the input from both the physical and mental bodies. The heart is like a mirror: if the input is unclear and distorted then so is the feedback. To activate the heart essence, body and mind must be purified. The heart center balances male/female (yin/yang) energies through pure unconditional love and cultivation of the higher emotional body.

To awaken the heart chakra, think of someone that you love deeply. Feel your heart open, emanating warmth and light. Now stay with this feeling and expand it until it becomes love for all beings. Allow this quality of love-bliss to circulate from your heart center to the rest of your body. Extend love and forgiveness toward yourself and to everyone on the Planet.

Feel the electromagnetic energy radiate from your heart. Feel your love and gratitude cradling the whole Earth and all of life. When the Anahata center is fully awakened, the body is transmuted by higher emotions and the heart chakra floods the subtle body with divine love; this flow of vital energy is the love of God.

Yogis say this chakra can be awakened simply through repetition of a syllable or mantra until it becomes the spontaneous form of your conscious awareness. This chakra is awakened in accordance with the degree of our love and devotion to the Creator, or Higher Self—the divine consciousness of All That Is.

Anahata affirmation: *May the abundance of the galactic power of the higher dream generate forever the compassionate heart of cosmic love!*

Level 2: Activating Radial Plasma: Silio

Silio Heart

Breathe deeply through your nostrils and allow your awareness to flow up your nose and down into your heart chakra. Bring your awareness to the inner Silio plasma at the center of the chakra. Visualize the white symbol radiating luminous streams of white light.

Feel the Silio plasma gathered in the heart chakra discharging waves of unconditional love throughout the planet. Within this spiritual heart energy feel the mental electron-neutron charge telepathically in resonance with the center of the Earth.

Repeat the following while focusing on your heart chakra: "My role is to accomplish the actions of the Buddha, I discharge the mental electron-neutron at the center of the Earth." The Buddha is the enlightened mind. This potential exists in all beings. It is also known as the bodhichitta, or mind of enlightenment.

Feel this love enlightenment energy within your heart. Keep expanding this beautiful energy from your chest so that it sweeps powerfully through the planet bringing an end to all suffering. Feel love and light pulsing out, wave after wave, for the healing of all afflictions, all the hungry souls, the sick and the weary—healing them all with positive self-enlightening heart impulses. With this visualization, you may wish to chant the Buddhist Heart Sutra (Prajnaparamita): *Gate Gate Paragate Parasamgate Bodhi Svaha* (gone, gone, gone, beyond, gone totally beyond, all hail the Enlightened One).

Cover your left nostril with your left thumb and breathe deeply three times in and out through your right nostril. Flash onto the Silio plasma and feel the new world of higher spiritual emotions vibrating and emanating out of the heart chakra. Now cover your right nostril with your right thumb and repeat the three breaths. Focus all of your attention to your heart chakra, Silio plasma, and draw in with your breath the new enlightened reality—then release, breathing pure love through your heart chakra into the world, emanating stabilizing vibrations to the astral and emotional body, soothing the rest of the chakras.

The Silio charge completes the telepathic quantum and also completes the seven-part time atom. At the center of Silio, feel the integrated charges of the sensory quantum: Dali, Seli, and Gamma, transmuted by Kali and joined to the telepathic quantum, Alpha and Limi. Then by extending your mind telepathically to the Earth's core, discharge the mental electron-neutron at the center of the Earth.

Note: One sensory quantum joined by the catalytic plasma to one telepathic quantum makes one time atom. There are four time atoms per 28-day moon stored at the center of the Earth as one Master Time Molecule (for full instructions see 7:7::7:7 Telektonon Revelation).

LEVEL 3: ENGAGING THE SEVENTH MENTAL SPHERE (HOLOMIND PERCEIVER)

Visualize the seventh mental sphere (holomind perceiver) located in the central corpus callosum of the higher self and projected onto the corpus callosum of the 3-D and 4-D Self. This is the new perceptual organ allowing us to access the noospheric programs inclusive of the akashic register. This seventh mental sphere is also the seat of your "true self" or rigpa (wisdom self). All mental spheres are unified by and accessed through the seventh mental sphere.

The holomind perceiver is an evolving organ, the noospheric sensing device opening us to an entirely new cosmic reality. As the site and generator of the UR runes, the fourth-dimensional timing matrices and the 441 Synchronotron Matrix, the holomind perceiver contains the fourth-dimensional psychocultural programs and the holoneme of the psi bank grid, meaning that it holds the hologram of the total perceived planetary reality.

Study of and meditation on the holomind perceiver prepares the mind to open to the galactic dimension and receive an entirely new base of knowledge and perception. The holomind perceiver is activated through diligent application and study of Cosmic History and the disciplined application of the 441 matrix codes as they are regulated by the synchronic order.

Note: Cosmic thoughts are referred to as "mentation" waves, formulated as the correct laws of thought, and are a function of the holomind perceiver. A "mentation" wave is a configuration of telepathic potentialities, independent of language, and based on whole orders of supermental precepts, intrinsic to non-egoic knowing. The mentation waves are a function of the holomind perceiver and operate at the central core, radiating out to the different mental spheres as is needed. This is how the noosphere is established.

Level 4: Opening the Seventh Heptad Gate (441)

**Sirius B52
Element 113**

Visualize the green twelve-petaled lotus **Anahata** chakra with the **white Silio** plasma and the **etheric blue Sirius Beta 52/Element 113** superimposed over it at your heart. Hold this visualization and feel the three intermingle as you chant the sacred letter **HRAIM** as long as your breath can sustain it.

Locate Heptad Gate **441** and the **etheric blue Sirius Beta 52/Element 113** signature on the 441 holomind perceiver. Its matrix location is V11:H11, eleventh circuit, 9th time dimension, inner core time. Now locate it in your body at the top center of your skull (see graphic at the end of this chapter).

Visualize the **Sirius Beta 52/Element 113** above the **white Silio** in your **heart** chakra. Take the **Sirius B52** into the **seventh** mental sphere in the **ninth** time dimension (inner core time) where it activates **hyperplasmic enlightenment** as **hyperelectronic superconscious** informing mental spheres one and two as well as the **hyperneutronic subliminal conscious** informing mental spheres three and four.

From the **seventh** mental sphere, mentally direct the **Sirius B52/Element 113** to the **heart** chakra and impress it above the **Silio** seal. Hold this with four alternate nostril breaths (four times in and out through each nostril), followed by one breath through both nostrils.

Descend down the central column (spine), secreting the **Sirius B52** hyperplasma into all 144,000 etheric fibers of the astral body. Practice the **breath of fire,** rapid shallow breathing through the nose, transmuting any blockages or obscurations into streams of crystal clear **hyperplasmic enlightenment** spreading throughout your entire nervous system.

Etheric blue Sirius B52/Element 113 vibrates subtle activating force into all etheric fibers. Descend back down central channel until you get to the root chakra where you discharge the mental electron-neutron to the center of the Earth. Ascend back up central channel and leave **Silio** at the **heart** chakra. Return your consciousness to the seventh mental sphere in the center of the crown chakra, then close and seal all seven Heptad Gates with the Sirius B52/Element 113. Relax and breathe slowly and deeply at least 13 times.

 Harmonic UR rune 113, Sirius-Beta 52/Element 113, hyperplasmic enlightenment: *Tonality of Sirius-Beta Encodes Seven Days of Creation as Interval of Lost Time Redeemed.*

For additional practice: Locate Heptad Gate 441 on the Hunab Ku 21. Note that it corresponds to the Magus of the Infinite, Lord of the Cube, Teacher of the Unity of Totality, Hunab Ku 21, the Source of All Movement and Measure. Study the connections (see graphic at the end of this chapter).

CHAKRAS 8 AND 9: ROOT OF ROOT AND CROWN OF CROWN

Root of Root chakra extends to and encompasses the Earth's octahedral core; it is the matrix for grounding cosmic mediumship. The Earth core chakra is what gives us the ability to communicate with elemental spirits.

Crown of Crown chakra extends to and encompasses the Earth's noosphere. The noospheric crown is the higher mind control that tunes us into the higher telepathic collective consciousness, the field of the planetary logos, and to supreme supermental superconscious states of cosmic consciousness.

The central activity of these two chakras is to coordinate evolutionary functions or processes within the celestial body (one planet) wherein they hold their energy field. The higher celestial logoi act on every aspect and facet of consciousness evolution through the mental spheres; this opens up a diverse range of possibilities of consciousness, perception, sensation, etc.

This extends to the upper realms into the laws of destiny, laws of creation and the absolute. This is the realm of cosmic design that defines the infrastructure of the universe we live in. It is the realm of the 5-D higher self, the body of radiance of the planetary logos as the transductive accumulator of all hierarchies, commands and ordinances. As the root of root is the reservoir of cosmic mediumship, so the crown of crown is fulfillment and realization of all cosmic consciousness possibilities.

SEVEN HEPTAD GATES OF THE HOLOMIND PERCEIVER

CIRCUIT 2

HEPTAD GATE 1: ALPHA-ALPHA/PROFOUND SAMADHI

First Time Dimension (Cosmic Creation)
First Mental Sphere (Preconscious)

Galactic Life Whole Becomes
Medium of Transmission

84

GATE 108
V11:H2

CIRCUIT 5

HEPTAD GATE 2: ALPHA-BETA/INFORMATIVE SAMADHI

Third Time Dimension (Cosmic Synchronization)
Second Mental Sphere (Subconscious)

Galactic Life Whole Realized
as Cosmic Consciousness

88

GATE 291
V11:H5

CIRCUIT 2

HEPTAD GATE 3: BETA-BETA/CONSCIOUS WAKING MEDIUMSHIP

Fourth Time Dimension (Cosmic Cube)
Third Mental Sphere (Waking Conscious)

Galactic Art Whole
Defines Space

91

GATE 144
V11:H20

CIRCUIT 5

HEPTAD GATE 4: BETA-ALPHA/HIGHER MIND CONTROL

Second Time Dimension (Cosmic Ascension)
Fourth Mental Sphere (Continuing Conscious)

Galactic Art Whole Becomes
Meditation of Reality

95

GATE 315
V11:H17

CIRCUIT 8

HEPTAD GATE 5: HYPERELECTRON/HYPERELECTRONIC SUPERCONSCIOUS (INFORMS 1ST & 2ND MENTAL SPHERES)

Fifth Time Dimension (Red Kuali Force Field, Right-hand Time)
Fifth Mental Sphere (Superconscious)

Galactic Art Whole
Defined by Time

90

GATE 414
V11:H14

CIRCUIT 8

HEPTAD GATE 6: HYPERNEUTRON/HYPERNEUTRONIC SUBLIMINAL CONSCIOUS (INFORMS 3RD & 4TH MENTAL SPHERES)

Sixth Time Dimension (Blue Duar Force Field, Left-hand Time)
Sixth Mental Sphere (Subliminal Conscious)

Radiogenesis Establishes
Galactic Life Whole

81

GATE 402
V11:H8

CIRCUIT 11

HEPTAD GATE 7: SIRIUS BETA 52 ELEMENT 113/HYPERPLASMIC ENLIGHTENMENT

Ninth Time Dimension (Inner Core Time)
Seventh Mental Sphere (Holomind Perceiver)

Tonality of Sirius Beta Encodes Seven Days
of Creation as Interval of Lost Time

441

GATE 441
V11:H11

THE 40 +1 [41] MYSTIC GATES AND THE FOUR QUADRANTS OF SPACE
SHOWING THE 7 HEPTAD GATES + THEIR CIRCUITS

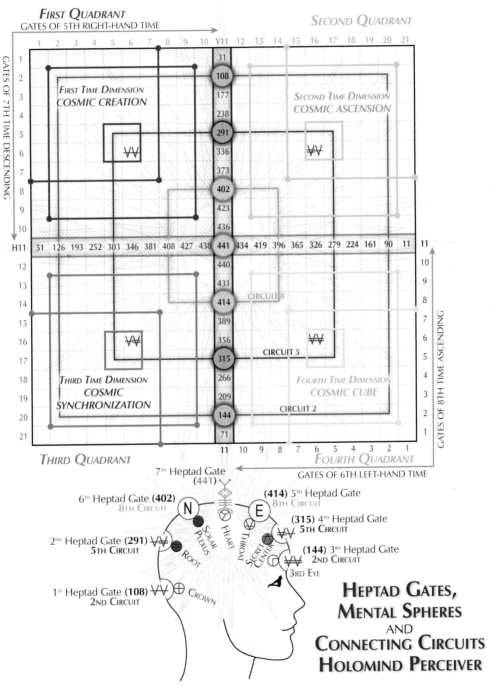

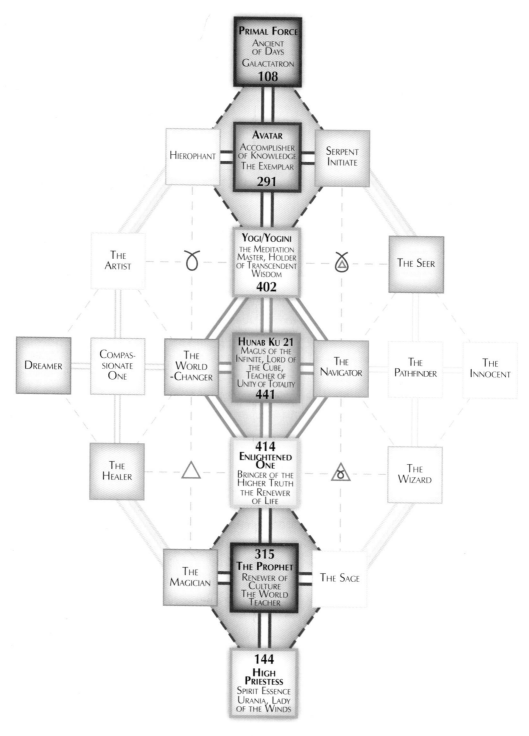

CHAPTER **6**

HOLOGRAPHIC YOGA

The mind should be kept independent of any thought that arises within it.
                                        —*Diamond Sutra*

1. As an application of Synchrogalactic Yoga, Holographic Yoga lifts us beyond dualism and is rooted in a veneration of the whole Earth as a hologram of total galactic consciousness. Planetary consciousness transcends history.

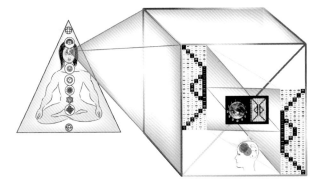

2. The planet is a member of the local star system and the star is a member of the galaxy. The human is a facet, texture or layer in the cosmos woven into the electronic structure of the universe. The cosmos is the sphere of consciousness. The Earth's biosphere is a microcosm of the cosmos; and we, humans are a microcosm of Earth's biosphere.

3. The purpose of Holographic Yoga is to liberate and expand the mind and spirit into greater levels of consciousness and knowledge of its electronic nature and how it is interwoven into the cosmos. By understanding cosmos as it is holographically imprinted within us, we become co-creators in the grand unfolding of consciousness.

4. According to the *Dynamics of Time,* the next geological era is brought about through the synchronization of the planetary noosphere with stellar evolutionary programming. The noosphere is an irreversible condition—there can be no turning back to the old time.

5. Holographic Yoga helps us discover ourselves as an integrated circuit reflecting the entirety of the noosphere. We are meant to become cosmically activated bioelectromagnetic plasma generators. Our function in the cosmic unfolding is to stabilize and dynamize, by turns, the planet's solar-cosmic interactions.

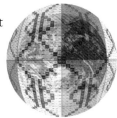

6. While the first phase of Synchrogalactic Yoga takes into account the activation of chakras, radial plasmas, mental spheres and holomind perceiver, Holographic Yoga takes it a step

further. Journeying into the cosmos, Holographic Yoga reveals a key that unlocks the psychic channels extending from the human chakra system through the various levels that encompass the galactic whole.

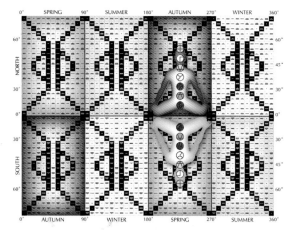

7. The psi bank is the working mechanism of the noosphere, Earth's mental sheathe. The psi bank also contains the timing codes for the release and establishment of different changes and mutations in the evolutionary process. Psi bank is to noosphere what brain is to mind. Noosphere, in this sense, can be thought of as the all-containing, all-embracing eighth—planetary—mental sphere.

THE GALACTIC BRAIN

Realizing ourselves as reflective circuits of the noosphere arouses the AC/CA current of the planet which opens us to the knowledge contained within the akashic register. How? Through perfect resonance, an electronic charge is deposited into the psi bank. This activates the AC and CA Manitou, the planetary guardians of the Galactic Brain on Earth. In this way, each of us becomes an embodiment of the AC/CA Planetary Manitou and thus we bring to life the seventh mental sphere, holomind perceiver.

8. The practice of Holographic Yoga helps us activate and merge our electromagnetic field with that of the Earth, creating an interactive force field. This force field establishes communication with both the core of the Earth and noosphere, while simultaneously reconnecting our biophysical apparatus with that of the Earth, stabilizing and lifting the collective frequency.

9. First we will give a cosmic overview, describing how this holographic system works and then offer 7 practices.

- *The purpose of higher intelligence is to see to it that the Velatropa system becomes stabilized at a higher frequency. The key to this is the relationship of Earth (V.24.3) with the other planets in the system and their various ratio relations to the Sun.*

- *The orbital frequencies of the planets in the system maintain the frequencies of different stages and levels of consciousness. The main focus of integrative consciousness is on V.24.3 and the relationship of the V.24.3 planet to the local star V.24. It is the star that is actually undergoing a massive inner transformational convulsion as it passes to a higher stage of galactic resolution—which has a lot to do with the present polarization and necessary stabilization of consciousness on V.24.3.*

7 Cosmological Components of Creation
1: V.24.333 (internal human/chakras)
2: V.24.33 (human)
3: V.24.3 (planet)
4: V.24 (star, Sun)
5: V. (Vela pulsar, where star V.24 is located)
6: V.0 (Orion Arm)
7: V.00 (Hunab Ku)

- *The human species is in the ultimate stage of a process where the experiment in the laws of karma and intentional thinking (as they have evolved on a number of different star systems in the Velatropa zone) have now all come to be focused on this particular planet. For this reason, at this time, specific beings have incarnated in order to serve as principle information probes for this cosmic intelligence plan. This is part of a larger planetary engineering project.*

- *The purpose of the project is a) to keep the planet from self-destructing and b) to stabilize the consciousness of the planet into cosmic resonance with the local galaxy, which directly affects the Sun.*

- *As the Sun goes through its internal convulsions, a stabilization of the solar frequency is created that directly affects, and elevates, the frequency of consciousness on this particular planet. This is a unique situation in the final stage of this experiment within the Vela sector, a zone 6,000-light years in diameter for which the Vela pulsar defines the circumference and the V.24 star and the V.24.3 planet define the central point.*

10. The most important point to grasp in practicing Holographic Yoga is that we are involved in large cycles of interlocking phases of the cosmos. The first phase begins with V.24.333, the internal generator chakra system. From this basic internal structure the chakras emanate an energy field through the human component, V.24.33, that includes the auric field.

11. The *quantinomio citiobarico* is the primary structure of the internal generator chakra system; it is the structure of the sole atom from which the chakras arise. All human and planetary chakras have the same structure. The human represents the intentional thinking element of the cosmos. Practice of Holographic Yoga as an application of Synchrogalactic Yoga helps make conscious the resonance between the sole atom and the human and planetary chakra systems.

HUMAN CHAKRA SYSTEM AND QUANTINOMIO CITIOBARICO

12. To practice Holographic Yoga it is important to have a firm understanding of the quantinomio citiobarico as the structure of the sole atom pulsing from the center of this (or any other) galaxy. This is the starting point from which to build.

NEUTRONIO
CHAKRA GENERATOR

SOLE ATOM
QUANTINOMIO
CITIOBARICO

13. The quantinomio citiobarico is characterized by holonomic consistency, meaning it contains everything and is contained by everything. As the structure of the sole atom, the quantinomio citiobarico can be understood as the *underlying master chakra*; the generating chakra from which all chakras arise.

14. As we have seen from previous volumes, *quanto* is number, *citio* is cell, and *barico* is pressure. Therefore, the quantinomio citiobarico is the *quantic number of cell pressure of the main energy circuits in the body, chakras, or force fields that hold the etheric body together within the aura.* So the uniform pressure on the cell from every direction creates the form of spherical consistency.

CROWN
1000 PETALS

THIRD EYE
2 PETALS

THROAT
16 PETALS

HEART
12 PETALS

15. The quantinomio citiobarico is also known as the sole atom in the sense that it is the primary atom which, experiencing its own cellular pressure, becomes the generator from which all energy and electricity in the cosmos is derived. The combination of two elements, *actinio* and *animio,* within the membrane of the cell, creates pressure that releases *quon* rays (see *CHC Vol. II*).

SOLAR PLEXUS
10 PETALS

SECRET CENTER
6 PETALS

ROOT
4 PETALS

NEUTRONIO
CHAKRA GENERATOR

16. These quon rays are condensed into 36 compressors, divided equally into three rings (like a holonomic topocosm). The release of the quon rays into space then form quantars and quasars from which galaxies are formed. This same quantinomio citiobarico also provides the essential structure to each of the chakras, but instead of 36 (4 × 9) compressors there are four neutrons that wrap around each chakra in radial form to create one *neutronio.* This is an example of holonomic consistency.

The internal generator of each chakra is composed of four neutrons arranged circularly in a radial form to create one neutronio. These neutronios generate fastenic or auric lines of force. When activated through yogic practices, these fastenic lines release radiance into the auric field to create healthy hyper-charged individuals.

QUANTINOMIO
CITIOBARICO
STRUCTURE OF
THE SOLE ATOM

36 COMPRESSORS

PERILIOS

ACTINIO
ANIMIO GAS

QUON RAYS

QUASARS

CICLOQUON
LUMINIC RAYS

MAURI TUBES

QUANTAR

ELECTROTHERMIC FIELD

IGNITION (IGNEO) FIRE

QUANTINOMIO CITIOBARICO AND HUNAB KU

17. All life is dependent on the Sun, the local stellar administrator. But the Sun itself receives its programs and energy from the Hunab Ku, the core or hub of the galaxy. It is here at the center of each galaxy that we find the sole atom or quantinomio citiobarico, from which the mass and energy of the galaxy originates, and continues to emanate.

18. As a galactic core, Hunab Ku, inclusive of the sole atom, is also an intelligence function or intergalactic thought core, which is like a super nanochip that contains the entire program of the galaxy.

19. The intelligence programs contained in the sole atom's three rings—known as gravitational, electromagnetic and biopsychic resonators—contain the information that spans the spectrum of galactic evolution. This is why it is called Hunab Ku—one giver of movement and measure—as it is also a reflex of a divine cosmological command of unity. Cosmic Science elucidates the unity of all creation and forms the basis for Holographic Yoga.

20. Cosmic Science demonstrates how everything is derived from interactions of certain fundamental levels of electricity and elemental structures that are common to, and can be found in a variety of ways in different stages and levels of existence and dimensions.

21. Just as the biosphere is the unity of life and the heliosphere is the unity of the Sun and all of the planet bodies, so also is the cosmos the unity of all of its constituent elements: galaxies, quasars, etc.

22. Cosmos is unified through common plasmatic electronic flows and interactions in a continuous genesis extending from the internal generators of the human body to the outer reaches of the most evolved supernova. Cosmos is telepathically webbed by mutually interpenetrating dimensions knowable to the intentional thinking element of the universe. Everything is always evolving toward communion with the One Creator.

23. The Law of Time, Cosmic History and Holographic Yoga all deal with the law of holonomic consistency, whether it is in the human aura of interactive generators or in the definition of the primary structures of a stellar or galactic phenomena, including the galaxy itself.

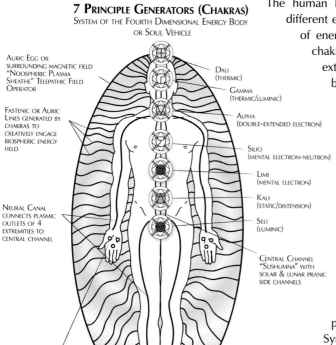

7 PRINCIPLE GENERATORS (CHAKRAS)
SYSTEM OF THE FOURTH DIMENSIONAL ENERGY BODY
OR SOUL VEHICLE

AURIC EGG OR SURROUNDING MAGNETIC FIELD "NOOSPHERIC PLASMA SHEATHE" TELEPATHIC FIELD OPERATOR

FASTENIC OR AURIC LINES GENERATED BY CHAKRAS TO CREATIVELY ENGAGE BIOSPHERIC ENERGY FIELD

NEURAL CANAL CONNECTS PLASMIC OUTLETS OF 4 EXTREMITIES TO CENTRAL CHANNEL

VRITIS OR NEUTRONIOS PALMS OF HANDS & SOLES OF FEET, PLASMIC FLOW (RECEIVER/TRANSMITTERS)

DALI (THERMIC)

GAMMA (THERMIC/LUMINIC)

ALPHA (DOUBLE-EXTENDED ELECTRON)

SILIO (MENTAL ELECTRON-NEUTRON)

LIMI (MENTAL ELECTRON)

KALI (STATIC/DISTENSION)

SELI (LUMINIC)

CENTRAL CHANNEL "SUSHUMNA" WITH SOLAR & LUNAR PRANIC SIDE CHANNELS

The human body is a system of generators producing different electrical streams of energy. Being a generator of energy, the quantinomio citiobarico (sole atom/chakra generator) works both internally and externally. Internally, each chakra is completed by four neutronios consisting of four neutrons. (By holonomic transposition the sole atom becomes the neutronio).

Through the neutronios, radioplasmic lines of force are generated by the chakra system to create the auric field. What you experience, not only through your five senses but coming in through your vritris (hands and feet), enters your system and is then transmitted through the neuronal canals, up to the brain, into the chakras, releasing *marsines*. Information is constantly streaming into us and out of us, but the process is largely unconscious. To bring this process to consciousness is the function of Synchrogalactic and Holographic Yoga.

Note: Marsines are the final stage in the process of the *quantified parton*, in which 8 *partons* incessantly occupy the same time space, establishing material for the radial plasmas.

PLANET COMPONENT OF HOLOGRAPHIC YOGA

"A planet is understood by analogy to be a macroatomic particle, functioning as a cosmic generator with its own magnetic field, motion and conductor (the plasma surrounding the Earth)"

—CHC Vol. II, p. 189

24. The human (V. 24.33) revolves around its own nucleus and has its own magnetic field, just as a planet does. Human consciousness is not apart from the evolution of planetary consciousness. As Chief Joseph put it, "the Earth and myself are one mind."

25. V.24.3 represents the planet component within planetary consciousness. The planet has an electronic shell and behaves much like an orbiting electron in an atom, with different electronic mantles and layers. V.24 is the star, the solar/stellar field, the nucleus of this particular thought atom.

 The Earth is a receptacle of plasmas; the thermic and luminic effect of the Sun. The outer part of the Earth has an electrical cover or atmospheric caps which include radiation belts, the ionosphere, the atmosphere and stratosphere. These mantles provide insulation to the Earth. Radial plasmas are stored in the core of the Earth. The North and South poles create the planetary axis that serves as the connecting point where the different plasmas, subatomic particles, protons, mesons and alpha mesons pass through.

26. The star provides the plasmas and the electronic energetics of the planet. The next level out from the star is V. (Vela)—this is the Velatropa sector. This is part of the next larger unit, or the Orion arm (V.0), of the galaxy. The galaxy (V.00) is the main supplier of the plasmic energetics to the star.

27. The galaxy contains different gases, spinning phenomena like quasars, quantars and pulsars which actually supply types of information and high frequency "radio waves." From the galaxy there is the galactic neighborhood which is a cluster of galaxies. The entire universe consists of countless galactic neighborhoods representing every phase and variety of evolutionary development.

28. All of the different galactic-cosmic levels and galaxy neighborhood types constituting the index of the myriad galaxies represent different kinds of electroplasmic interactions of the same

electronic fluids, plasmas, charges, discharges, and lines of force. These are capacitated, stepped up, stepped down and transduced.

29. Cosmic Science describes four interactive levels of cosmos: a) Biosphere at the planetary level; b) Heliosphere at the stellar level; c) Galactosphere at the galactic level; and d) Cosmosphere at the universal level. (Note the cosmosphere includes the whole of the cosmos as an equalizing set of interactive forces that unify different orders of quantifiable reality).

GRADATIONS OF CONSCIOUSNESS AND INTELLIGENCE CONSTITUTING THE UNIVERSAL MIND (ACCORDING TO COSMIC SCIENCE)

1. All phases of the cosmos in its cosmological sequencing are interlocked by a common set of electroplasmic interactions, ultimately generated from the sole atom.

2. These electroplasmic interactions reduce down to the simplest levels of the six types of cosmic electricity.

3. These six types of cosmic electricity are contained in the basic cubic parton structure.

4. From the combination of these six types of electricity come the twelve electronic lines of force.

5. These twelve electronic lines of force combine to create the seven primary radial plasmas.

6. Between the six types of cosmic electricity, the twelve types of cosmic force and the seven radial plasmas, virtually everything else is engendered.

7. These electroplasmic components are interactive throughout the different stages and levels of the cosmos.

"ACCORDING TO COSMIC SCIENCE, THE INFORMATION OF THE PARTON PLUS 6 TYPES OF ELECTRICITY IN THE COSMOS, IS HIDDEN IN THE 13TH SECRET CHAMBER OF THE GREAT PYRAMID OF RA IN EGYPT. RA REPRESENTS THE SUN GOD, THE SOURCE OF SOLAR ELECTRICITY."

SIX TYPES OF COSMIC ELECTRICITY
GENERATE
TWELVE LINES OF COSMIC FORCE
GENERATE
SEVEN RADIAL PLASMAS

LITMIO	L	ᐃ+ᐃ
DALMI	D	△+△
SIGMA	⋜	ᐃ+△
DALTON	ᓚ	ᐃ>△
NEMUR	ᘉᐃ	△>ᐃ
KAPPA	K	◓+◭
DUAL	≈	E+E
KUTMI	T	N+N
NAUR	∧	E+N
SELDI	S	E<N
DISLE	I	N>E
PUR	P	◭+ᐃ

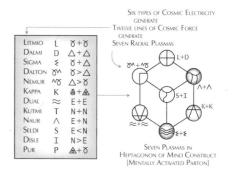

SEVEN PLASMAS IN
HEPTAGONON OF MIND CONSTRUCT
[MENTALLY ACTIVATED PARTON]

---

30. These interacting levels also unify the multi-leveled orders of the different dimensions from subquantifiable to super transcendent non-quantifiable realities of consciousness and meta- or supraconsciousness (the "invisible" realms, dimensions and universes).

31. The whole of this cosmic complex represents a composite or spectrum of different levels of interactions and dynamics of primary electronic forces and types of cosmic electricity. This is a vastly dynamic phenomenon that we can actively participate in.

THREE RINGS OF THE SOLE ATOM

As a generator of energy and information, the key to the sole atom/quantinomio citiobarico lies in its three rings. These define three grades or levels of information/energy:

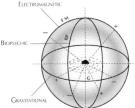

1) Gravitational (physical mass in all its forms and varieties, organic and inorganic).
2) Electromagnetic (all forms of electricity, energy, solar and cosmic radiation, plasmas, auroras, etc).
3) Biopsychic (intelligence programs activating the universal mental layers, creating planetary psi fields of which the noosphere/psi bank is an example).

PSYCHONE OR RESONANT FIELD MODEL "HOLONOMIC TOPOCOSM"

In its purest essence, the quantinomio citiobarico generates the biopsychic potential of the psi bank, the storage and retrieval system of the evolving planetary life programs. Knowledge of the sole atom/quantinomio citiobarico is programmed into the psi bank and was first channeled by Charles Henry in 1926 who referred to it as the "psychone". (Note that the term "noosphere" was also coined in 1926.)

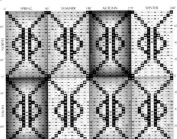

The psi bank is the telepathic switchboard of the noosphere, the future collective consciousness of the Earth. Different keys open different psycho mathematical levels helping the individual transform into the collective whole.

The comprehension of the psychone was further evolved into the resonant field model/holonomic topocosm and defined as the static equilibrium of the gravitational, electromagnetic and biopsychic fields (see *Earth Ascending: A Treatise Governing Whole Systems* (1984), J. Arguelles. This was affirmed by the extraterrestrial channeled text *Introduction to Cosmic Science* (1971), which contains the full description of the prototype of the psychone, the quantinomio citiobarico. At the same time, Arguelles, without knowledge of the text, first presented information about the psychone and its resonators in 1972 in his book, *Charles Henry and the Psychophysical Aesthetic.*

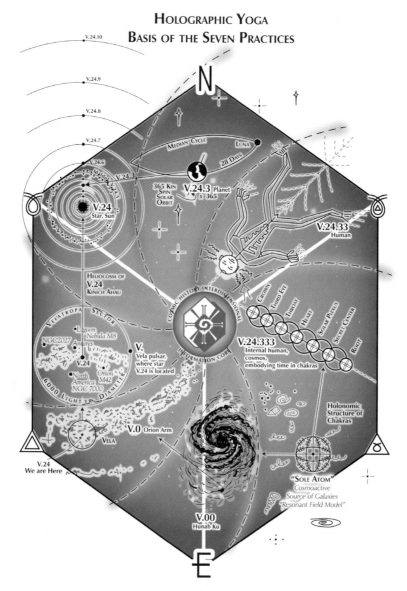

HOLOGRAPHIC YOGA
BASIS OF THE SEVEN PRACTICES

HOLOGRAPHIC YOGA: 7 PRACTICES

32. Holographic Yoga is based on the premise that we are all a living projection of a particular cosmic experiment. The projector is in another world, another dimension in another plane of reality. When we realize this, then we can return our attention back to the projector. By doing this, we create an increasing harmonic resonance in the field around us. This is also helpful in stabilizing our present planetary consciousness.

33. These exercises build on the practices from Synchrogalactic Yoga. The first practice focuses on integrating our chakras through time, and then building up from micro- to macrocosmic. By beginning with the underlying structure of the human chakra system, passing through the noosphere, we reach the galactic core.

34. A main purpose of Holographic Yoga is to activate the psi bank, realizing it as the mechanism of our own consciousness, and to activate our mental spheres as well, so our psychology becomes a cosmocentric cosmology. As described in previous volumes, any knowledge that we avail ourselves to regarding the noosphere and psi bank quickens and precipitates the mental/spiritual quantum shift in our conscious self-perception.

35. These seven practices of Holographic Yoga are based on the 7 cosmological components of creation as introduced above. The purpose of these practices is to attain holonomic understanding and resonant consistency within the cosmos.

36. Let us first look at the human chakra system and expand it out to show how the human embodies time.

Practice 1: V.24.333

365 +

364

312

260

208

156

104

52

Holographic Yoga
Synchrogalactic
Internal Activator
V.24.333
364 (7 x 52)
Plasmic Flows
+ 365th
Central Nadi (Channel)

In this visualization/practice we embody the time of the solar cycle by integrating the chakras to connect to the Earth at the deepest root level.

Each of the seven psychic generators (chakras) is potentiated by 52 flows—13 red, 13 white, 13 blue and 13 yellow—for a total of 364 flows. The 365th flow is the central channel connecting the seven plasmic generators.

Visualize the 52 four-colored flows from each generator, and feel them vibrating at a super cosmic frequency. This frequency corresponds to that of the Sirius B, which takes 52 years to revolve around Sirius A. The two new chakras—crown of crown and root of root—are activated by the spin generating the 364

115

flows in full movement through the 365th flow, or central channel. The two new chakras are actually extensions of the two poles of the 365th flow.

The seven chakra generators are also known as the seven days (castles) of Sirius. This connects primordially to the seven days of creation and the interval of lost time in eternity, the ratio of seven. Since 52 is 1/7th of the 364 + 1 orbital frequency code, 52 is the redemption of the interval of lost time in eternity, and the key to the generation of the seven days of the Second Creation.

Note that four Earth rings equal one "moon" of *Sirius Beta*, or "28 castles". (4 rings, seven castles per ring (7 × 4) = 28 52-day castles or five galactic spins plus three castles = one "moon" of Sirius B: 260 × 5 = 1300 + 156 (52 × 3) = 1456 = 52 × 28 = one "moon" of Sirius B).

PRACTICE 2: V.24.33 (HUMAN)

In this visualization practice, we enclose the seven generator system within the prototype of the human form: V.24.33. From the perspective of Cosmic Science, the human is the component element of intelligence on V.24.33—the cosmic vibratory root that inhabits the surface of the Earth.

It is a cosmic vibratory root because when the seven chakras are fully activated with their 364 flows, then the etheric body vibrates the physical body and the plasmas begin to secrete through the permeable membrane of the skin to create the electromagnetic aura. (Note: The flows are purely plasmatic and appear from the 144,000 etheric flows or nadis which are functions of the pranic activation of the soul body.)

What the mind of evolution seeks is for the human to be in high resonance, vibrating at a phenomenally higher frequency, emitting an auric field so intense that it glows visibly, altering the electromagnetism of everything in its immediate environment.

For this to occur, and for this practice to be effective, visualize the seven chakras each with their four sets of flows in the four colors and see the flows vibrating faster and faster until they begin to release from the pores of your skin as fastenic lines of force to create a brilliant spectral rainbow aura. Practice this repeatedly.

PRACTICE 3: V.24.3 (PLANET EARTH)

Once the plasma streaming spectral human aura has been established, the practice extends to the next component element, the planet: V.24.3. We are already aware of the three principle points of holonomic resonance: crown chakra (North Pole), root chakra (South Pole), and heart chakra, through the equator penetrating to the Earth's core, Earth's own holonomic resonator.

This practice connects the human auric field, plasmas and mental spheres with the Earth, while directing plasmas back to Earth's magnetic field. Our goal is to create a plasmic resonance with the Earth's poles.

Visualize the North Pole in your crown chakra and the South Pole in your root chakra. Connect the heart chakra to the equatorial zone penetrating to the Earth's core. In this way; transfer your psychoplasmic chakra energy to the Earth, focusing on these points.

Visualize streams of plasma vibrating from these points in your own aura extending outward to create the spectral auric field of Planet Earth, condensing into the two parts of the circumpolar rainbow bridge. Now the rainbow human and the Rainbow Earth are in the common resonance, you are in the Earth and the Earth is in you, two interchangeable holograms.

PRACTICE 4: V.24 (THE SUN AND ITS HELIOSPHERE)

Now that your aura and Earth's aura are in plasmic resonance, the Earth is seen spinning in its 365-day orbit, matching your 364 + 1 flows. Its orbit is in inseparable resonance from the other nine orbits creating the heliosphere.

At the center holding it all in place is V.24, the local star. It too has its aura, a fiery dynamic pulsed in 23-year cycles to create great phases of solar activation that continuously energize the electromagnetic fields of each of the planets, whose orbits, in turn, create ever more harmonic resonances for the entire heliosphere.

Feel this rich pulsing dynamic, listen with your inner ear to the symphonies of the music of the spheres. Visualize the 364 + 1 flows of your seven generators extending like 365 etheric fibers to each of the 365 positions of the Earth in its orbit around the Sun. Feel the excitation of knowing that your vitality is participating in the dynamic of Earth's daily rotation occurring repeatedly 365 times per orbit!

PRACTICE 5: V (VELA SECTOR, VELATROPA)

Now, expanding from the heliosphere of V.24, extend yourself 3,000 light years to the circumference of the 6,000-light year diameter Velatropa sector of the Orion Arm of our Galaxy. Our star V.24 is at the center of this galactic "suburb." It is defined by the pulsar "Vela", which pulses signals at ultra high frequencies that come in intelligently paced bursts that are, in essence, cosmic codes, with V.24 as their core target, though the codes are also transmitted to other principle stars in this sector including: Sirius, Arcturus, Antares, Alpha Centauri, the Pleiades and Aldebaran.

As a pulsar, Vela is the remnant of a star that exploded as a supernova some 6,000 years ago, so these higher frequency pulsations have been encoding the historical program of Earth. Now a shift is occurring.

Feel in your innermost mind the pulsations increasing their frequency. Tune into this process. Visualize the Vela pulsar directing its bursts of information to V.24 and its planetary system. Your mind is now changing.

PRACTICE 6: V.0 (THE ORION ARM)

The Orion Arm is one of the principle spiral arms of our Galaxy. The Vela sector is only a small zone towards the far edge of the Orion Arm. Consider that the galaxy is 100,000 light years in diameter and you can see that the Vela sector is but a small slice of the whole.

Visualize the galaxy like a large pinwheel. Now, visualize that one of these swirling arms is the Orion Arm. Then visualize that toward the tip of that arm is the Vela Sector, a small, minute little circle. In the center of that miniscule circle is the V.24 heliocosm. That's where you are, vibrating and resonating the whole structure. Now place the galaxy in your third eye and know that its wisdom has penetrated your palace of wisdom.

PRACTICE 7: V.00 (HUNAB KU)

Within your wisdom eye continue to visualize the galaxy spiraling at an enormous rate of speed, like a giant pinwheel whirling in the cosmic wind of creation. Now penetrate with your wisdom eye to the center of that pinwheel, the galactic core, the Hunab Ku—"one giver of moment and measure." As you approach, you pass through an incredible density of radio waves and a mass of hot gas swirling rapidly around on a small but super massive "object".

This is the interdimensional portal, mistakenly thought of as a black hole: The heart of the Hunab Ku.

Here is received the transmission of the sole atom, downloading higher-dimensional programs and broadcasting them out. Seen from its side, our galaxy has the shape of a galactic disc. Think of the Hunab Ku in the very center of your third eye sending out its broadcasts to the galaxy which is like a compact disc (CD) spinning as it plays its higher harmonics condensed into tens of billions of stars, each holding a note, a resonant frequency, in a galactic symphony that only God could possibly hear.

PART III
RECONSTRUCTING THE UNIVERSE

On the Planet Holon, straddling the line between the red galactic/karmic Neptune memory and red solar/prophetic Uranus navigation zones on the Arabian Peninsula, not far from the Red Sea, you will find the Earth's most singular power point and interplanetary memory node, the Ka'bah in Mecca. What is the source of this magnetic interplanetary memory attractor?

If we look up, past the red galactic/karmic Neptune zone, we come to the generator of the red chromatic sequence, galactic/karmic Maldek—the destroyed planet. Herein lies the root and cause of the Ka'bah's potent drawing power.

The memories of Maldek (now the Asteroid Belt) are transmitted in a downward flow to the galactic/karmic memory zone—the hub of the Old World to be condensed into a supremely concentrated point in Mecca. Just beyond Mecca is the Red Sea, and on the other side of the Red Sea is the next sequence of the chromatic red zone, the solar/prophetic Uranus navigation zone.

From the interplanetary vantage point, Uranus is Earth's biotelepathic twin and the object of the evolutionary advancement of the

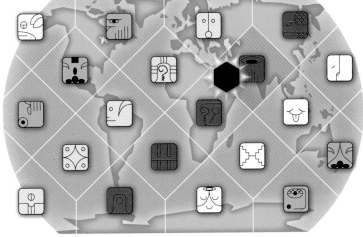

human once the time tunnels are opened. The migrations of spirit, generated in Maldek, its memory stored in Neptune to be focalized in the Ka'bah, are finally released as time travel navigation to Uranus. In this interplanetary saga, the terrestrial focus is the Ka'bah. Let us examine the story behind this singular geomantic site.

CHAPTER 7

KA'BAH AND THE CUBE

1. Every day more than one billion humans bow five times in prayer to one single point on the surface of the Earth, the Ka'bah in Mecca.

2. Every year more than 1 million Muslims make a pilgrimage (al-hajj) en masse to this point in Saudi Arabia, a shrine called the Ka'bah where there is a black stone (some say dark red)—the magnetic object with 5 billion prayers a day literally directed to it. There is no other phenomenon that compares with this on Earth. Why is this so and what does it mean for the destiny of our Planet?

3. The Ka'bah functions as the *Kiblah* (or *Qibla*), the direction a Muslim faces while praying. Muslims consciously orient themselves, at five specified times per day, to the Ka'bah, a 35 × 40 × 50 feet cube-shaped structure, with a 12-inch diameter black oval stone set within its northeastern corner. It is amazing to consider the number of people directing their energy and prayers to that particular point.

4. Those millions who make the pilgrimage at hajj or on their own to Mecca circumambulate seven times around the shrine. Why is it that in this remote place in the desert of Saudi Arabia, the Ka'bah is the basis or object of the most synchronized form of spiritual practice on the planet?

5. Think about the numbers: Each pilgrim that visits the Ka'bah circumambulates the stone seven times. Five times a day, approximately 1.3 billion Muslims make Salat prayers in the conscious orientation toward the Ka'bah; that is more than 6 billion prayers a day directed to one specific place. It is thus distinguished from any other place on Earth. This is often spoken of, but rarely explained.

6. Ka'bah is derived from the Arabic word *kab* which means cube. The Ka'bah is literally the "house of the cube" and the main shrine for all of Islam. The heart and purpose of the Ka'bah lies in its eastern corner that contains a small black stone. This mysterious black stone is the reason for the shrine of the Ka'bah, or cube. Why is it that a cube that enshrines the stone? What is this stone?

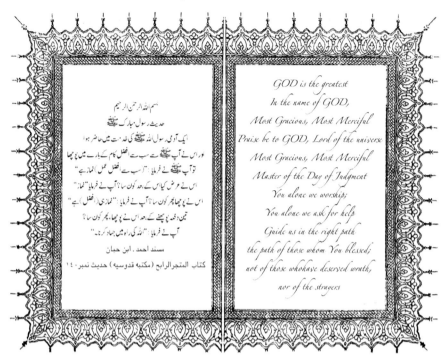

بِسْمِ اللهِ الرَّحْمٰنِ الرَّحِيمِ

حدیث رسول مبارک ﷺ

ایک آدمی رسول اللہ ﷺ کی خدمت میں حاضر ہوا
اور اس نے آپ ﷺ سے سب سے افضل کام کے بارے میں پوچھا
تو آپ ﷺ نے فرمایا : "سب سے افضل عمل نمازہے "
اس نے عرض کیاس کے بعد کون سا ؟ آپ نے فرمایا "نماز"
اس نے پوچھا پھر کون سا ؟ آپ نے فرمایا : "نماز ہی (افضل) ہے "
تین دفعہ پوچھنے کے بعد اس نے پوچھا پھر کون سا ؟
آپ نے فرمایا : "اللہ کی راہ میں جہاد کرنا"۔

مسند احمد ، ابن حبان

کتاب المتجرالرابع (مکتبہ قدوسیہ) حدیث نمبر ۱٤۰

GOD is the greatest

In the name of GOD,

Most Gracious, Most Merciful

Praise be to GOD, Lord of the universe

Most Gracious, Most Merciful

Master of the Day of Judgment

You alone we worship;

You alone we ask for help

Guide us in the right path

the path of those whom You blessed;

not of those who have deserved wrath,

nor of the strayers

7. Some scholars have suggested that the stone is a meteorite fallen to Earth. One Islamic tradition suggests that the black stone fell from heaven to a place near the Red Sea during the time of Adam and Eve. This stone traces back to Abraham who was sent by God on a journey through Arabia with Hagar, the mother of his second son, Ishmael. Abraham had originally set off from Ur near present day Baghdad. He made the journey south into the Arabian Peninsula where he found the black stone.

8. The rare stone is said to have a celestial origin: It was originally an angel, as the story goes. God appointed a guardian angel to Adam, an angel of knowledge. At the beginning of creation, God asked all beings in the universe to take a vow before incarnation that they would remember Him after their incarnation to this planet.

9. This vow of remembrance was placed in the heart of every being. God then asked the angel to swallow the declaration so that this knowledge would be inside of him. This was to ensure that no being could say that they had no knowledge of God. This was the angel of Adam's knowledge.

10. When Adam and Eve were tempted by Satan to eat from the forbidden tree, he promised them that they would possess all knowledge of the entire universe. The tree of knowledge was meant for Adam and Eve, but only at the right time. Satan tempted them to eat of this tree prematurely

and at that moment, when Adam forgot, the angel was turned to a precious white stone. Adam and Eve were then sent to Earth.

11. When Adam fell to Earth, he awoke, so it is said, in Ceylon. Nearby, he saw a stone and heard it speak: "Don't you remember who I am before Satan made you forget?" Then the angel Gabriel appeared to Adam with the message to carry that stone until he found the place that is the replica of the house above the seventh heaven or the house of universal intelligence, called *Al-Bait ul-Ma'mur*. Adam finally carried that stone to where Mecca is today and he built the house with that stone in place.

12. Several cycles later, Abraham was guided to find that stone. When he found it, it was now black, covered with the accumulated sins and corruption of humanity. Abraham and his son, Ishmael, retrieved the stone and placed it in the house that they had built for it. This was the second Ka'bah; the first was built by Adam.

13. The pillar of that stone connects to the place of universal intelligence. This is the place where Muhammad went on his Night Journey, "the ascent to the seventh heaven", where he saw 70 thousand angels who, every seven days, make a complete circumambulation around this house: the Al-Bait ul-Ma'mur, Allah's house. This is the model or template of the earthly Ka'bah. This is where Muhammad received the instructions for the five daily (Salat) prayers.

MUHAMMAD AND ISLAM

Muhammad established historical Islam and was the last of the three messengers of the awakening preceded by Buddha and Jesus. He completed his mission on Earth in the second year of Pacal Votan's cycle of power. When Muhammad's soul ascended (June 8, 632), Islam split into two schools: Shi'ite and Sunnah.

Shi'ite refers to the belief in the succession of the imams, beginning with Muhammad's nephew, Ali. Sunnah refers to the tradition of following the teachings and sayings of the life of Muhammad. The whole of Islamic law, called the Shari'ah, was derived primarily from the Qu'ran and Sunnah texts.

Toward the end of the eighth century (but still during the classic period of the Mayan civilization in the New World) the Shi'ites split into two schools: the Ishmaelite tradition with seven Imams and the 12 Imam school.

---

14. By the time of Muhammad, the Ka'bah, built by Abraham and Ishmael, was filled with 360 idols (some say 365). One story tells that when Muhammad first saw the Ka'bah stone, tears fell from his eyes and he touched and kissed its surface. Muhammad was directed to purify the Ka'bah, making him the third, following Adam and Abraham, to purify and rebuild the Ka'bah in its present form. Muhammad himself placed the stone in the place where it is now enshrined.

15. This telling of the story of the stone points to a direct line of prophetic transmission from Adam to Abraham to Muhammad, a lineage that runs from the first man (and prophet), Adam, to the "seal of the prophets", Muhammad.

Adam Kadmon
In the Kabalistic tradition, the original Adam was Adam Kadmon, the "red Adam". In the interplanetary cosmology, this red Adam originated on Maldek, place of the original Garden of Eden. The sacred stone was a remnant from Maldek that fell to Earth after the planet was destroyed. In this regard, the stone signifies a memorial fragment of the catastrophe of Maldek, the karma of which everyone on Earth is now living out.

16. Since that stone was originally the angel of knowledge, when Muslim pilgrims visit that stone they are going to the point that holds the original vow of remembrance that God placed in their heart before their incarnation. When they make a pilgrimage to the stone they are redeeming what Adam forgot when he was cast out from paradise. So the rite of touching the stone becomes a recapitulative and redemptive cosmology.

17. This particular telling of the story of the Ka'bah comes from the Persian mystic, Qadi Sa'id Qummi, who lived a 52-year cycle (1639-1691), and wrote about the history of the black stone along with numerous chronologies and histories of the Ka'bah. Qummi was a Shi'ite Muslim and a believer in the 12th Imam in the lineage of Muhammad. The symbology of the 12th Imam is woven into the cosmology of the black stone. But it is not just the stone that is significant but also the Ka'bah itself, the "cube" in which it is enshrined. What is the origin of the cube?

18. The 8th Imam said that divine religion will never perish as long as the Ka'bah endures. This is because the Ka'bah contains the stone that extends back to the original creation; and that stone is believed to have originally been an angel.

19. The cube has 6 sides, 8 corners and 12 edges. According to Shi'ite cosmology, the 12 edges represent the twelve Imams; the 8 corners are the eight supports of the throne; and the 6 sides are the six days of creation. Quranic cosmology says that on the day of resurrection eight angels will support the throne; an angel at each of the eight corners. On the day of resurrection the 12th Imam will reveal himself—and the cube will be manifest spiritually.

Many Shi'ite Muslims are awaiting the return of the 12th and final Imam, or the *Mahdi*, who is believed to be in occultation until the "end of time." The Imams trace their descent from Ali, the nephew of Muhammad who was the first Imam.

20. The 12th Imam remains hidden or occulted until the day of resurrection. His occultation occurred in AD 873/AH 260 (AH refers to After Hejira). There is some echo of the occulted element

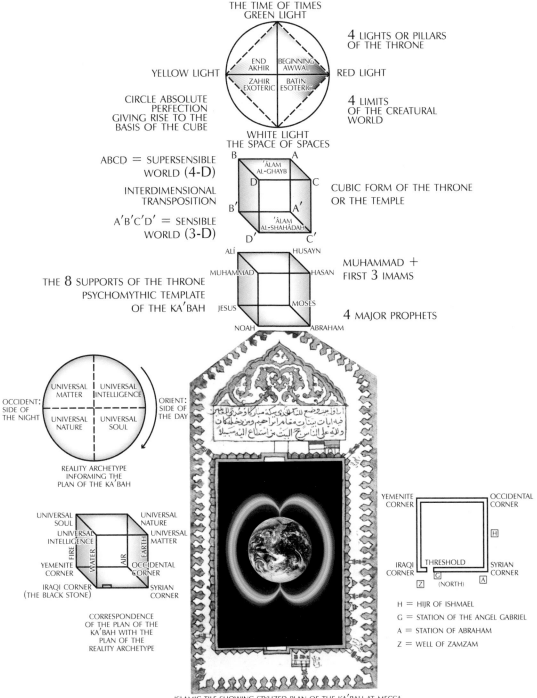

ISLAMIC TILE SHOWING STYLIZED PLAN OF THE KA'BAH AT MECCA
WITH RAINBOW BRIDGE AS SIGN OF THE RETURN OF THE 12TH IMAM, THE MAHDI

in the story of Joseph in the Qu'ran. Joseph is the 12th son with 11 brothers. In the most significant part of his story, Joseph remains occulted from his brothers and family until the predestined moment when he reveals himself. Also, *Joseph* is the title of Sura 12 of the Qu'ran.

21. Twelve is the number of the temple, the highest complex number (of 13) that consists of multiples: 2, 3, 4, 6. It is a complex harmonic that creates a stasis. This is why plus one is thirteen, the frequency of the circulation of cosmic time.

22. In the tradition of the 12 Imams, the plus one, 13 is Fatima—the female principle, while the fourteen is Muhammad. In that tradition they say that each Imam comes to the world bearing four different kinds of light and each light has seven degrees; equaling 28.

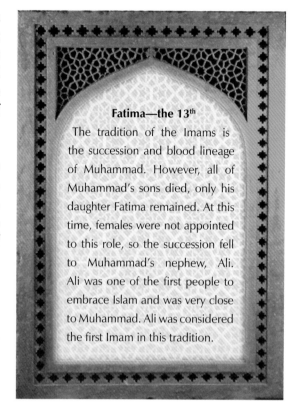

Fatima—the 13th

The tradition of the Imams is the succession and blood lineage of Muhammad. However, all of Muhammad's sons died, only his daughter Fatima remained. At this time, females were not appointed to this role, so the succession fell to Muhammad's nephew, Ali. Ali was one of the first people to embrace Islam and was very close to Muhammad. Ali was considered the first Imam in this tradition.

23. According to the Shi'ite tradition, if it were not for the occulted 12th Imam, the world would fall apart. This is due to the belief that the 12th Imam holds the axis of the world. (This is an interesting point to consider in light of the circumpolar rainbow bridge). Seen symbolically, it is this occult spiritual knowledge that maintains the world order. Without the role of the imams in maintaining the spiritual axis of our world, there would be absolute chaos and the world would have been destroyed a long time ago. This information is also interesting in light of a potential pole shift.

OCCULTATION OF THE 12TH IMAM

In the tradition of the 12 Imams, 11 are known and one is in occultation. No name is given to this one, though he is believed to have been born in 869 (Christian calendar) on the day 15 Shaban, the eighth moon of the lunar calendar. (Note that in the Sunnah tradition the date 15 Shaban marks the day when Muhammad supposedly presents the record of all births and deaths that were to occur in the next year).

The 12th Imam appeared early during the 11th baktun of the Holy Wars, AD 830-1224. For this reason, the 12th Imam went into occultation and supposedly remains alive (at least in the fourth dimension) until the end of time. It is believed that he will appear as the *Mahdi*, or the manifestation of the 12th Imam, to close the aeon.

SYMBOLISM OF THE KA'BAH AND THE CUBE (OF THE LAW)

24. The cube is derived from the foundation of the plan of the Throne of God as a two-dimensional square made three-dimensional into a cube. The cube represents the form of self-perfection, making the Qiblah of the Ka'bah, the "center of the cosmos." The cube maintains symmetrical perfection and remains constant throughout all scales; it always has six sides that are equidistant from an invisible center point.

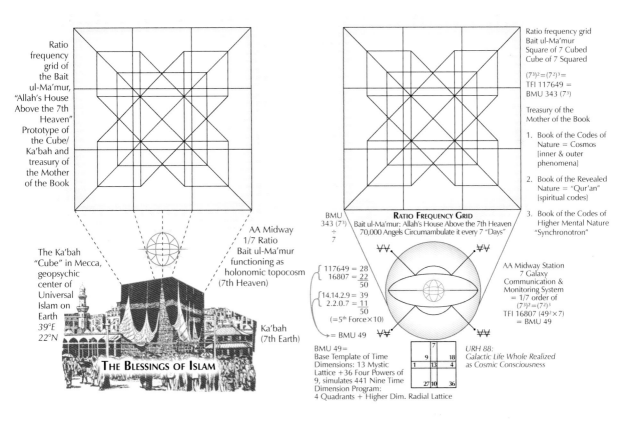

Ratio frequency grid of the Bait ul-Ma'mur, "Allah's House Above the 7th Heaven" Prototype of the Cube/Ka'bah and treasury of the Mother of the Book

The Ka'bah "Cube" in Mecca, geopsychic center of Universal Islam on Earth 39°E 22°N

THE BLESSINGS OF ISLAM

AA Midway 1/7 Ratio Bait ul-Ma'mur functioning as holonomic topocosm (7th Heaven)

Ka'bah (7th Earth)

Ratio frequency grid Bait ul-Ma'mur Square of 7 Cubed Cube of 7 Squared

$(7^3)^2 = (7^2)^3 =$
TFI 117649 =
BMU 343 (7^3)

Treasury of the Mother of the Book

1. Book of the Codes of Nature = Cosmos [inner & outer phenomena]

2. Book of the Revealed Nature = "Qur'an" [spiritual codes]

3. Book of the Codes of Higher Mental Nature "Synchronotron"

BMU 343 (7^3) ÷ 7

RATIO FREQUENCY GRID
Bait ul-Ma'mur: Allah's House Above the 7th Heaven 70,000 Angels Circumambulate it every 7 "Days"

$\begin{cases} 117649 = 28 \\ 16807 = \underline{22} \\ 50 \end{cases}$

$\begin{cases} 14.14.2.9 = 39 \\ 2.2.0.7 = \underline{11} \\ 50 \end{cases}$
(=5th Force×10)

= BMU 49

AA Midway Station 7 Galaxy Communication & Monitoring System = 1/7 order of $(7^3)^2 = (7^2)^3$ TFI 16807 $(49^2 \times 7)$ = BMU 49

BMU 49=
Base Template of Time Dimensions: 13 Mystic Lattice +36 Four Powers of 9, simulates 441 Nine Time Dimension Program: 4 Quadrants + Higher Dim. Radial Lattice

		7	
	9		18
1		13	4
27	10		36

URH 88:
Galactic Life Whole Realized as Cosmic Consciousness

25. The Ka'bah is a perfect geomantic anchor that encompasses a complete cosmology. It is also a template or model of the potential of the universal cube as a holder or carrier of different systems of knowledge. The four corners of the Ka'bah represent the four prophets: Moses, Abraham, Jesus and Noah.

26. In the Shi'ite tradition on the four upper corners, there is Muhammad followed by the first three Imams. There are stones placed at each corner, representing physical places on Earth, with the most significant one being the black stone.

27. Above the black stone is the place of universal intelligence and above the other three corners are the universal soul, nature, and matter. There is a whole cosmology of the universal cube—and the cube of the universe. The symbolism of the cube relates to the human going toward the self-perfection of his/her own divine nature, the yoga of self-perfection. In this sense the cube is eternal, it has no history.

28. The eternal cube represents the divine religion that will never perish as long as the temple of the Ka'bah endures—as prophesied by the 8th Imam. In this sense, the cube signifies a structure of fourth-dimensional intelligence that is projected into our mind that symbolically epitomizes our journey to self-perfection. Its prototype is the *Al-Bait ul-Ma'mur*, the House of Allah, above the seventh heaven.

29. As the form of the Al-Bait ul-Ma'mur, the cube correlates to systems of divine knowledge. For example, the cube with its eight opposite corners can represent the eight triplets of the I Ching. The time triplet is at the upper left with the moon triplet, and the space triplet is at the upper right with the sun triplet. The other four corners represent the sensible world: Thunder, mountain (stillness), lake and wind. These eight triplets, in all of their permutations, create the 64 (8×8) codons. The six lines of the codon also fit the six sides of the cube in a process called "cubing the codon."

FROM THE THRONE TO THE CUBE

The origin of the cube (Ka'bah) goes back to the template of the original Throne of God. This throne is seen in a form like a diamond or a square, much like the *Hunab Ku 21* and the four gates of light: red, green, yellow and white (see graphic at the end of Chapter 5). These are the colors of the four gates of light of the throne of God. It is divided into two parts: beginning and esoteric; and ending (of things) and exoteric.

The Throne of God manifests at the beginning and end. Exoteric is revealed knowledge and esoteric is hidden knowledge. These four gates of light form a square. When this square is projected it forms a foundation of the cube—the four pillars of the cube create an upper part that signifies the fourth-dimensional world—the supersensible—while the lower part of the cube is the sensible realm signifying the third-dimensional world. There are 8 supports to the throne. The cube has 8 corners which signify these supports.

30. As the visual form of the Law of Time, the cube first appeared to Valum Votan as a galactic time atom cube composed of four nested tetrahedra: red, white, blue, yellow. Within this tetrahedra there is a perfectly blue corner where the three blues meet,

In the higher-dimensional reality, the cube represents complete integration of the timespace. From the point of view of the fourth and fifth dimensions, timespace is a cube.

and a perfect red corner where the three reds meet, and likewise for the white and yellow—these are similar to the light gates of the throne.

31. Not long after the time atom cube revealed itself, came the perception of the imploded cube containing three internal planes: plane of mind, plane of will and plane of spirit. The time atom cube was perceived as an explosion of these planes (this occurred on Resonant 15, 1/24/91). The cube has six sides: top and bottom; left and right; and front and back.

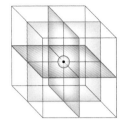

32. The top and bottom planes are created by the horizontal plane that cuts across the center. The two sides (left and right) are created from a plane at the center that is perpendicular to the horizontal plane. The front and back sides are created by another plane perpendicular to the plane that creates the left and right sides. The locus of consciousness, or the center of creation, is at the center where these three planes meet: plane of mind (top and bottom); plane of will (left and right), and plane of spirit (front and back).

DIMENSION OF NUMBER

Number is a dimension unto itself. Six is actually the value of the cube. The plane of mind is space; the plane of spirit is time; the plane of will is number; and the point at the center is the plane of transcendence which is the Throne of God. Each of the planes has two sides, for a total of six sides of the cube.

Number + Space = Matter.
Number + Time = Energy.
Space + Time + Number = Quantity.
Space × Time × Number = Cube.

Space represents matter; time represents energy; number represents measure; cube represents consciousness. Space becomes quantity/measure; time becomes telepathy.

Each plane is one dimension, corresponding to the six dimensions of consciousness and the six days of creation, so the cube is the perfect form of creation and is the manifestation of the base triplet which is the same as the binary triplet.

The cube has six sides and eight vertices—which is the galactic harmonic or the octave. Six plus the center point is zero or seven, the Throne of God. If you add the eight vertices plus the one in the center you get nine. Each plane or face has four edges, for a total of 12. So there are 12 edges, 6 faces and 1 center point, which totals 19. The 12 edges plus 1 center point = 13.

CUBE OF KNOWLEDGE

The Black Stone of Adam is enshrined in the Ka'bah (Ka'b = Cube in Arabic) because the Cube is the self-perfect form. Kab'ah = Qiblah.

CUBE FUNCTION 6:

6 = Perfect number $(1+2+3=1\times2\times3 = 6)$
$6^3 = 216$ = Perfect Cube Frequency $[108\times2]$
= Arcturus $(121=11^2)$ + Sirius $(95=19\times5) = 216$

$$1^3$$
$$+2^3$$
$$+3^3$$
$$+4^3$$
$$+5^3$$
$$+6^3$$
$$+7^3 = 28^2$$
$$[784]$$

$28^2+13^3 =$
2981 (7.9.1)
$= 11\times271$ [271 = KIN 11]
= BMU 335 = URH 107
= KIN EQ 121 [11^2]
4 DRAGON, KEY CODE TO DISCOVERY OF LAW OF TIME

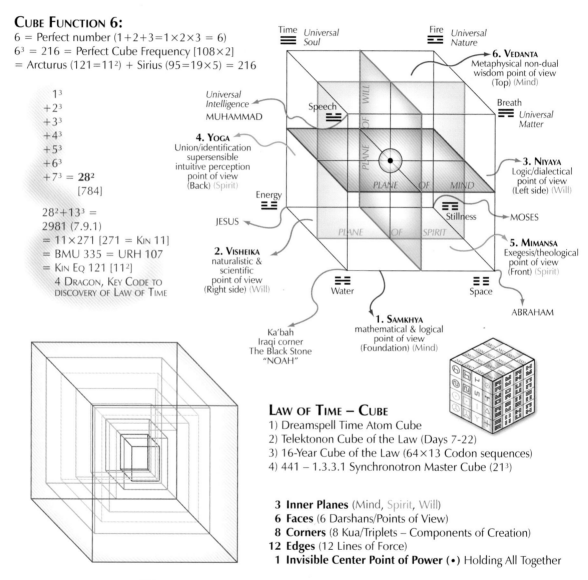

Time — Universal Soul
Fire — Universal Nature

6. VEDANTA Metaphysical non-dual wisdom point of view (Top) (Mind)

Universal Intelligence MUHAMMAD
Speech
Breath — Universal Matter

PLANE OF WILL

4. YOGA Union/identification supersensible intuitive perception point of view (Back) (Spirit)

3. NIYAYA Logic/dialectical point of view (Left side) (Will)

PLANE OF MIND

Energy
JESUS
Stillness → MOSES

PLANE OF SPIRIT

2. VISHEIKA naturalistic & scientific point of view (Right side) (Will)

5. MIMANSA Exegesis/theological point of view (Front) (Spirit)

Water
Space
ABRAHAM

1. SAMKHYA mathematical & logical point of view (Foundation) (Mind)

Ka'bah Iraqi corner The Black Stone "NOAH"

LAW OF TIME – CUBE

1) Dreamspell Time Atom Cube
2) Telektonon Cube of the Law (Days 7-22)
3) 16-Year Cube of the Law (64×13 Codon sequences)
4) 441 – 1.3.3.1 Synchronotron Master Cube (21^3)

3 Inner Planes (Mind, Spirit, Will)
6 Faces (6 Darshans/Points of View)
8 Corners (8 Kua/Triplets – Components of Creation)
12 Edges (12 Lines of Force)
1 Invisible Center Point of Power (•) Holding All Together

The Cube is the primal knowledge. It is the epitome of self-perfection. It is the goal and limit of knowledge. It is the Alpha & Omega of the projection of the supramental into the domain of discriminating awareness or higher mental understanding.

CUBE OF KNOWLEDGE

33. The cube is fundamentally a foundation of knowledge. The psychomythic drama of Adam is the drama of knowledge. Adam desired knowledge. Satan said: "You can have it all now." Then came the Fall and the saga of history. A process has unfolded throughout history of determining and defining what knowledge is and what is valid knowledge.

34. Today, information is mistaken for knowledge; there is so much information that we do not know what to do with it; as a result there is little understanding as to what genuine knowledge is.

35. As a system of knowledge, the six sides of the cube correspond to the six darshans, or points of view, of the Vedic system, where the foundation (bottom) darshan is called *Samkhya*, the mathematical, logical or cosmological point of view. The top corresponds to Vedanta, the metaphysical non-dual point of view.

36. The plane of mind consists of *Vedanta* (above) and *Samkhya* (below). The plane of will corresponds to *Visheika*, the scientific naturalistic point of view (right side) and *Niyaya*, logic or dialectical point of view (left side). In the plane of spirit, the back side is *Yoga* or supersensible point of view, and the front side is *Mimansa*, the theological point of view. This is how the Vedic system corresponds to the three planes and six faces of the cube.

37. We can define a whole system of knowledge, whether it is the Vedic system or I Ching system through the intrinsic metaphysics or logics of the cube. Meditation on the cube reveals its structure as a manifestation of primal knowledge; it is what is before and after the realm of conceptualization. It is the primal self-perfection and yet it is the self-perfection that we all aspire to. It is the Alpha and Omega of the projection of the supermental into the domain of the

We have created the heavens

and the earth, and everything

between them in six days, and

no fatigue touched us.

—Qu'ran, 50:38

discriminating mind. This is the final metaphor of the goal of our self-perfection where the final goal has been equalized.

38. The cube is a metaphor of our own perfection and transcendence. It is the projection of a supermental structure of knowledge into the realm of our discriminating mind and awareness. Through illuminating projections into our mental layers, the angel of knowledge implants structures of intelligence into our mind and intellect. When we come to know something we recognize, or re-cog-nize, a structure that conforms to what has already been planted in the mind.

Through illuminating projections into our mental layers, the angel of knowledge implants structures of intelligence into our mind and intellect.

39. The cube defines the perfection of the Law of Time. The 16-year Cube of the Law, derived from the 16 cube positions of days 7-22 in the Telektonon define the matrix cube of time. Within the matrix cube of time are the 64 codons in each of their 13 permutations to create an 832-week ($64 \times 13 = 52 \times 13$) cycle, summarized as a higher-dimensional time cube constructed over a 16-year cycle of time.

CUBE AND 441 MATRIX

40. The final supermental projection of the cube is the 441 matrix—Hunab Ku 21—which creates the cube of 21 cubed, or 9261, written as 1.3.3.1 in vigesimal code.

41. This 441 cube matrix contains a basic grammar of telepathy condensed into a set of 441 numbers—the constituent syllables or mathematical mantras. These 441 frequencies constitute the resonant building blocks of the Second Creation. All of the previous accumulations of knowledge, whether Islamic, Vedic, Taoist, etc. are contained within this matrix and cube structure of the 441, 1.3.3.1.

42. Because it is literally a supermental projection, the 441 cube matrix structure is the basis of a purely mathematical form of knowledge. In order to attain perfection, we have

to enlarge our consciousness to encompass a larger domain of meaning—one that transcends verbal language.

43. According to the effort we make to expand our consciousness, the divine force will respond, making us superconscious, supermental, superhuman entities. This is the actual means of transformation.

44. One way to expand our consciousness is to understand the way different number matrices operate and inform us. To realize this we follow a disciplined process, such as yoga, in order to transcend or transform the lower self into the higher self. Keeping our mind focused on the highest outcome we displace our ego with higher thoughtforms, by shedding the doubts and anxieties of the lower mind which is beset with questions and worries.

45. The 441 cube is the final manifestation of this supermental cube projection. The structure of the meaning of the cube, from the point of view of Adam and the angel of knowledge, is a universal experience where we enter the vortex that unifies with universal intelligence.

46. This structure of meaning is similar to the system of the holomind perceiver with its four intergalactic channels. These are precisely like the four pillars of the cube: cosmic creation, cosmic ascension, cosmic synchronization and cosmic cube—universal matter, universal soul, universal nature and universal intelligence.

Each moment is an opportunity to transcend ourselves by remembering God. In communion with the angels of knowledge we become the cube enshrining the mystery of the stone.

47. Everything is brought into the present so that we are now being given a structure for organizing and giving a new meaning to our knowledge. This structure helps us organize the different aspects or facets of knowledge: scientific, yogic, theosophical, mathematical, aesthetic, philosophical, etc. The different levels of knowledge converge to create a cubic structure. Everything is inclusive.

48. A cube has six sides (the point in the center is the 7th); eight corners (the point in the center is the 9th); and twelve edges (the point in the center is the 13th). The fundamental number cosmologies of the even numbers of 6, 8 and 12 create the 26 (13 × 2). The dimension of time is contained in the numbers: 7, 9 and 13. They create the cosmology of the cosmic constant: 7 + 9 + 13 = 29. Even numbers represent space; odd numbers represent time. All possibilities of thought and knowledge are condensed into this cosmology and reformulated as fundamental numerical frequencies existing in a cosmology of mathematical meaning.

ISHMAELITES AND 7 IMAMS

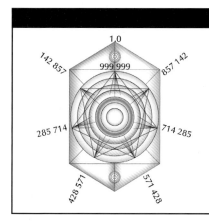

Seven is the key number of the interval of lost time in eternity. In the tradition of the Ishmaelites, there were no more than seven Imams. The mystical numerology accords with the Law of Time and the key numbers of the synchronic order. Similarly, the Sakyamuni Buddha, who was born at the midpoint of the seventh baktun of the 13 baktun cycle, was supposedly the seventh of the Buddhas born in this world system during this great superkalpa of time. After him there were 28 enlightened masters in succession from Mahakasyapa to Bodhidharma.

49. This supermental projection into our consciousness and our discriminating awareness is meant to be meditated on and studied in order to discover its hidden matrices. This is the governing structure of the multidimensional universe. The opposite of the cube is the sphere. The sphere has no corners or edges, it is absolute. It is the light universe.

50. From the light universe is projected the existential universe. The perfection of the existential universe is synthesized by the cube; this is why Adam, who fell from the heavenly sphere, built the first shrine to God in the form of a cube—the existential universe.

51. Pacal Votan in his tomb held a jade sphere in his right hand and a jade cube in his left hand. This represented the absolute light universe and the absolute of the relative. Within the sphere, the cube is inscribed. There is a hypothetical sphere around the cube as well as a hypothetical sphere at the center of the cube. One is implicit in the other and the two go together to define each other.

52. In the cube and Ka'bah are the keys to the temple of universal religion/remembrance (UR). The stone symbolizes remembrance of our cosmic origins and holds the memory of our capacity for self-perfection; this is also the purpose of all yogic systems.

CHAPTER 8

RETHINKING THE SOLAR SYSTEM

1. The universe we see through a telescope and experience via the Internet is the secondary universe. The universe within is the primary universe.

2. Human consciousness is actually a participation in the greater Earth consciousness. It is not we who possess consciousness, but it is the planet that allows us to participate in its consciousness. Likewise, each planet in our solar system contains its unique consciousness and frequency, all contributing to a larger multi-leveled heliospheric consciousness.

3. How can we perceive a new level and way of thinking about the universe or even the solar system? By withdrawing our attention from the outer realm and placing it on the inner realm. Once we are established within the center of our own being we can ask again: What are planets? How can I experience them? What relation do they have to me? To the Earth? To the Sun? To evolution?

4. The galaxy is the fundamental building block of the universe. The Galactic Being is the whole galaxy itself, awakened as a super being. We are each cells that make up one Galactic Being.

5. The solar system is a galactic thought molecule and the planets are its electronic thought units. This is one whole system, a whole entity with multi-leveled facets, each with its own set of frequencies.

6. Earth, or planetary consciousness is merely an attribute of solar consciousness, the consciousness of the local star and its planetary system. The human brain, in relation, is merely a processing system. The human is literally a walking biopsychic antenna. The transistor circuit of our antenna connects with the planetary orbits and the resonances held by each planet.

Earth's orbital circumference = 585,000,000 miles @ 365 days = approximately 1,600,000 miles per day = approximately 45,000,000 miles per 28-day Moon = 66,666 miles per hour = 1111 miles per minute = 19 miles per second! Where are we going so fast?

7. The interplanetary field is the largest area in our solar system held together by the local star (the Sun), but this is still only a micro part of the total area of the solar system. The Milky Way is part of a cluster of about 3 dozen galaxies called the Local Group, and only constitutes a small volume of the total area of the Local Group, its neighborhood. The largest member of the Local Group is the Andromeda Galaxy, a spiral galaxy visible to the eye.

8. The billions of solar systems in our galaxy rotate around the center of the Milky Way at a speed of approximately 300 km per second. It takes more than 200 million years to finish a complete cycle around the center of the Milky Way. In 4 billion years, Earth has traveled 20 times around the center of the galaxy. Alpha Centauri is the solar system nearest to us. But what does this mean? What does it mean in relation to the Law of Time and the evolution of consciousness?

Our solar system is not what it appears. It is not what the scientists would have us believe. How can we derive fresh perspectives and come to a new level of thinking about the solar system, galaxy and universe?

The Planets

9. The word "planet" means "wandering star", for the planets seem to move faster and more erratically than "fixed" stars. To the galaxy, the planets are infinitely small electron-like objects orbiting a central star. Each planet has a specific function in the solar system, just as each solar system has a specific function within a whole galaxy. The purpose of a planet is to hold different levels or stages of consciousness in orbital order.

10. In prehistory, planets are recognized by people of different cultures to play different mythological roles. Some of this has been passed down to us in the Western astrology system. Hindu astrology has its own system, as do Taoist and Chinese astrology.

11. In most traditions, the planets are viewed as symbols of the personality and emotional/social human behaviors. These traditions view the planetary world as the world of the soul, with the Sun as the middle point, or core field of consciousness. These meanings are derived from mythic or preliterate levels of consciousness.

12. In the historic consciousness or scientific consciousness of the last five or six hundred years, planets are no longer understood from a prehistoric or prematerialistic view. Modern day scientists focus mainly on the physical traits of the planets, such as atmosphere, density, weight, etc. Little, if any, credence is given to the psychological or consciousness aspects. Scientists are genuinely looking for life, but life as defined on Earth. Information feedback varies according to the quality of input.

13. Consider the influence of the planets on our psyche according to their harmonic periodicity. The Saturn synodic cycle is 378 days (18 × 21). There is great resonance in these numbers indicating a larger harmonic orchestration to the solar system—and the universe. The planet Mars has a 780-day (13 × 60) synodic cycle, and Venus has a 584-day (73 × 8) synodic cycle as the evening and morning star. The 378-day Saturn loops coincide with Earth's annual orbit to create a return cycle every 29 years. These harmonic periodicities resonate with various flows of consciousness within our biological order that affect us in ways of which we are mostly unconscious. This is a main focus of astrology.

14. Cosmic History places special interest on the orbital positions of the different planets to each other. The influence of the other planets to Earth is actually the influence of the frequency of the other planets in their orbits, and in their synodic and cyclical occurrence in relationship to the noosphere. They have certain patterns, for example, the moon sets up a pattern of 27, 28 and 29 days.

PLANETS, HELIOSPHERE AND THE LAW OF TIME

15. From the heliospheric perspective, planets are arranged and interpreted according to their orbital position in relation to the Sun. In the heliospheric planetary arrangement there are 10 primary planets, each with two flows: a Galactic Karmic flow (G/K) and a Solar Prophetic flow (S/P).

The Earth, the stars, the Sun and all the planets are ultimately divine creation thought-forms emanated from a Central Source.

16. G/K represents the heliospheric inhalation, when the Sun inhales galactic/karmic energy into itself, and S/P represents the heliospheric exhalation when the Sun exhales solar/prophetic energy. G/K represents the preconscious field of influence and the primal powers of *becoming*. S/P represents the subliminal field of influence and the resonant powers of *return*.

17. These two flows represent the circulation of time within the solar system or heliosphere. The two flows are like a heliospheric Ida and Pingala. The right side of the body (hand and foot) is galactic/karmic and the left side (hand and foot) is solar/prophetic.

PLANETS AND HUMAN BODY

The entirety of the solar interplanetary thoughtform is contained within the human body. The planets can be found within the digits of the four extremities, which hook up the body in a binary crossover pattern: right hand (five outer planet frequencies) and left hand (five inner planet frequencies); right foot (five inner planet frequencies) and left foot (five outer planet frequencies). This is the fundamental structure of cosmic essence within the body.

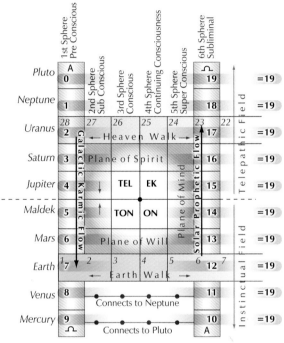

TELEKTONON
4-D INTERPLANETARY CIRCUIT BOARD

18. From this perspective, there are 20 attributes of planetary relationships. Each planet has a galactic/karmic aspect and also a solar/prophetic aspect. These correspond with 20 solar seals, each being in either the G/K or S/P heliospheric flow. Incidentally, the sum of the two solar seals of each pair of adjacent planets in the flows adds up to 19.

19. The ten planetary orbits are paired with each other to form five circuits that carry different qualities of heliospheric consciousness: Pluto/Mercury (circuit 1); Neptune/Venus (circuit 2); Uranus/Earth (circuit 3); Saturn/Mars (circuit 4); Jupiter/Maldek (circuit 5).

20. These ten planetary orbits and five-circuits are contained within the 140-unit Telektonon interplanetary master grid that serves as a fourth-dimensional map of the solar system. $140 = 5 \times 28$ or 7×20. These 140 units serve as the telepathic coordinates of all five circuits.

21. Orbits three and eight—Earth and Uranus—located on the third circuit, hold great significance as they are connected by the 28-day solar/lunar orbital cycle which holds both the atomic and

PLANETS

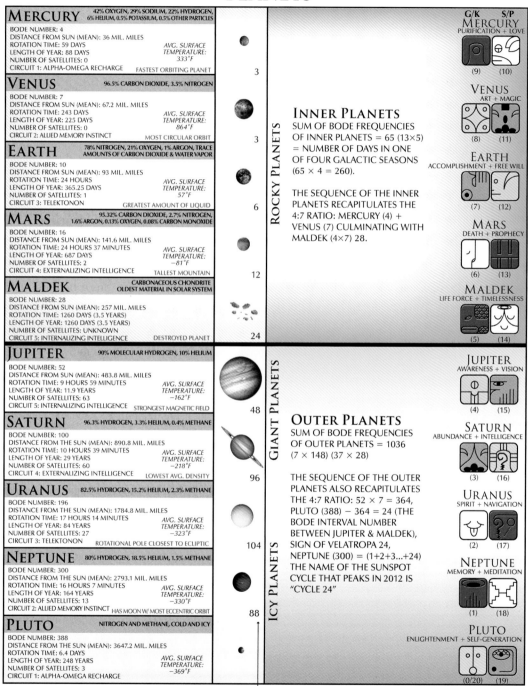

MERCURY
42% OXYGEN, 29% SODIUM, 22% HYDROGEN, 6% HELIUM, 0.5% POTASSIUM, 0.5% OTHER PARTICLES

BODE NUMBER: 4
DISTANCE FROM SUN (MEAN): 36 MIL. MILES
ROTATION TIME: 59 DAYS
LENGTH OF YEAR: 88 DAYS
NUMBER OF SATELLITES: 0
CIRCUIT 1: ALPHA-OMEGA RECHARGE
AVG. SURFACE TEMPERATURE: 333°F
FASTEST ORBITING PLANET

3

VENUS
96.5% CARBON DIOXIDE, 3.5% NITROGEN

BODE NUMBER: 7
DISTANCE FROM SUN (MEAN): 67.2 MIL. MILES
ROTATION TIME: 243 DAYS
LENGTH OF YEAR: 225 DAYS
NUMBER OF SATELLITES: 0
CIRCUIT 2: ALLIED MEMORY INSTINCT
AVG. SURFACE TEMPERATURE: 864°F
MOST CIRCULAR ORBIT

3

EARTH
78% NITROGEN, 21% OXYGEN, 1% ARGON, TRACE AMOUNTS OF CARBON DIOXIDE & WATER VAPOR

BODE NUMBER: 10
DISTANCE FROM SUN (MEAN): 93 MIL. MILES
ROTATION TIME: 24 HOURS
LENGTH OF YEAR: 365.25 DAYS
NUMBER OF SATELLITES: 1
CIRCUIT 3: TELEKTONON
AVG. SURFACE TEMPERATURE: 57°F
GREATEST AMOUNT OF LIQUID

6

MARS
95.32% CARBON DIOXIDE, 2.7% NITROGEN, 1.6% ARGON, 0.13% OXYGEN, 0.08% CARBON MONOXIDE

BODE NUMBER: 16
DISTANCE FROM SUN (MEAN): 141.6 MIL. MILES
ROTATION TIME: 24 HOURS 37 MINUTES
LENGTH OF YEAR: 687 DAYS
NUMBER OF SATELLITES: 2
CIRCUIT 4: EXTERNALIZING INTELLIGENCE
AVG. SURFACE TEMPERATURE: −81°F
TALLEST MOUNTAIN

12

MALDEK
CARBONACEOUS CHONDRITE OLDEST MATERIAL IN SOLAR SYSTEM

BODE NUMBER: 28
DISTANCE FROM SUN (MEAN): 257 MIL. MILES
ROTATION TIME: 1260 DAYS (3.5 YEARS)
LENGTH OF YEAR: 1260 DAYS (3.5 YEARS)
NUMBER OF SATELLITES: UNKNOWN
CIRCUIT 5: INTERNALIZING INTELLIGENCE
DESTROYED PLANET

24

ROCKY PLANETS

JUPITER
90% MOLECULAR HYDROGEN, 10% HELIUM

BODE NUMBER: 52
DISTANCE FROM SUN (MEAN): 483.8 MIL. MILES
ROTATION TIME: 9 HOURS 59 MINUTES
LENGTH OF YEAR: 11.9 YEARS
NUMBER OF SATELLITES: 63
CIRCUIT 5: INTERNALIZING INTELLIGENCE
AVG. SURFACE TEMPERATURE: −162°F
STRONGEST MAGNETIC FIELD

48

SATURN
96.3% HYDROGEN, 3.3% HELIUM, 0.4% METHANE

BODE NUMBER: 100
DISTANCE FROM THE SUN (MEAN): 890.8 MIL. MILES
ROTATION TIME: 10 HOURS 39 MINUTES
LENGTH OF YEAR: 29 YEARS
NUMBER OF SATELLITES: 60
CIRCUIT 4: EXTERNALIZING INTELLIGENCE
AVG. SURFACE TEMPERATURE: −218°F
LOWEST AVG. DENSITY

96

URANUS
82.5% HYDROGEN, 15.2% HELIUM, 2.3% METHANE

BODE NUMBER: 196
DISTANCE FROM THE SUN (MEAN): 1784.8 MIL. MILES
ROTATION TIME: 17 HOURS 14 MINUTES
LENGTH OF YEAR: 84 YEARS
NUMBER OF SATELLITES: 27
CIRCUIT 3: TELEKTONON
AVG. SURFACE TEMPERATURE: −323°F
ROTATIONAL POLE CLOSEST TO ECLIPTIC

104

NEPTUNE
80% HYDROGEN, 18.5% HELIUM, 1.5% METHANE

BODE NUMBER: 300
DISTANCE FROM THE SUN (MEAN): 2793.1 MIL. MILES
ROTATION TIME: 16 HOURS 7 MINUTES
LENGTH OF YEAR: 164 YEARS
NUMBER OF SATELLITES: 13
CIRCUIT 2: ALLIED MEMORY INSTINCT
AVG. SURFACE TEMPERATURE: −330°F
HAS MOON W/ MOST ECCENTRIC ORBIT

88

PLUTO
NITROGEN AND METHANE, COLD AND ICY

BODE NUMBER: 388
DISTANCE FROM THE SUN (MEAN): 3647.2 MIL. MILES
ROTATION TIME: 6.4 DAYS
LENGTH OF YEAR: 248 YEARS
NUMBER OF SATELLITES: 3
CIRCUIT 1: ALPHA-OMEGA RECHARGE
AVG. SURFACE TEMPERATURE: −369°F

GIANT PLANETS

ICY PLANETS

BODE INTERVAL NUMBERS

INNER PLANETS
SUM OF BODE FREQUENCIES OF INNER PLANETS = 65 (13×5) = NUMBER OF DAYS IN ONE OF FOUR GALACTIC SEASONS (65 × 4 = 260).

THE SEQUENCE OF THE INNER PLANETS RECAPITULATES THE 4:7 RATIO: MERCURY (4) + VENUS (7) CULMINATING WITH MALDEK (4×7) 28.

OUTER PLANETS
SUM OF BODE FREQUENCIES OF OUTER PLANETS = 1036 (7 × 148) (37 × 28)

THE SEQUENCE OF THE OUTER PLANETS ALSO RECAPITULATES THE 4:7 RATIO: 52 × 7 = 364, PLUTO (388) − 364 = 24 (THE BODE INTERVAL NUMBER BETWEEN JUPITER & MALDEK), SIGN OF VELATROPA 24, NEPTUNE (300) = (1+2+3...+24) THE NAME OF THE SUNSPOT CYCLE THAT PEAKS IN 2012 IS "CYCLE 24"

G/K   S/P

MERCURY
PURIFICATION + LOVE
(9)   (10)

VENUS
ART + MAGIC
(8)   (11)

EARTH
ACCOMPLISHMENT + FREE WILL
(7)   (12)

MARS
DEATH + PROPHECY
(6)   (13)

MALDEK
LIFE FORCE + TIMELESSNESS
(5)   (14)

JUPITER
AWARENESS + VISION
(4)   (15)

SATURN
ABUNDANCE + INTELLIGENCE
(3)   (16)

URANUS
SPIRIT + NAVIGATION
(2)   (17)

NEPTUNE
MEMORY + MEDITATION
(1)   (18)

PLUTO
ENLIGHTENMENT + SELF-GENERATION
(0/20)   (19)

telepathic fields. This circuit is located entirely within the heart chakra, signifying that only unconditional love can activate the biotelepathic earth spirit speaking tube.

22. In Cosmic Science, Earth is viewed as a particular genre among many types of planets, within a highly fluid, electronically interactive plasma universe. Within the plasma universe different levels and stages are divided up for transducing (stepping up and stepping down) electrical charges. Flux tubes, at one time, connected the consciousness circuits of the 10 planets at their magnetic poles—etheric spiraling electronic force fields meant to pulse with the binary sunspot cycles.

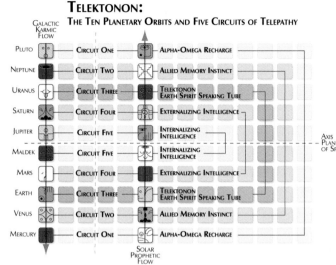

TELEKTONON:
THE TEN PLANETARY ORBITS AND FIVE CIRCUITS OF TELEPATHY

GALACTIC KARMIC FLOW

PLUTO	CIRCUIT ONE	ALPHA-OMEGA RECHARGE
NEPTUNE	CIRCUIT TWO	ALLIED MEMORY INSTINCT
URANUS	CIRCUIT THREE	TELEKTONON EARTH SPIRIT SPEAKING TUBE
SATURN	CIRCUIT FOUR	EXTERNALIZING INTELLIGENCE
JUPITER	CIRCUIT FIVE	INTERNALIZING INTELLIGENCE
MALDEK	CIRCUIT FIVE	INTERNALIZING INTELLIGENCE
MARS	CIRCUIT FOUR	EXTERNALIZING INTELLIGENCE
EARTH	CIRCUIT THREE	TELEKTONON EARTH SPIRIT SPEAKING TUBE
VENUS	CIRCUIT TWO	ALLIED MEMORY INSTINCT
MERCURY	CIRCUIT ONE	ALPHA-OMEGA RECHARGE

AXIS PLANE OF SPIN

SOLAR PROPHETIC FLOW

HORIZONTAL LINES OF FORCE
(DETERMINED BY THE PAIRED PLANETARY ORBITS WHICH CREATE 5 CIRCUITS)

SUN SPOTS AND POLES

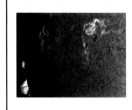

Solar flares can be linked to a solar thoughtform moderated by the Sun as a binary sunspot cycle. The solar flares directly affect Earth's electromagnetic field, increasing its plasmas and electromagnetism. The excess plasmas flow into the magnetic poles and create what are known as the auroras—australis (south) and borealis (north). According to Cosmic Science, information regarding the poles is stored in the fifth secret chamber of the Great Pyramid of RA.

23. These flux tubes were disturbed by the destruction and disruption of planetary orbits 4 and 5 (Mars and Maldek), and further disturbed by the artificial time frequency of planetary orbit 3 (Earth). When the fifth planet, Maldek (now the Asteroid Belt), was destroyed and Mars rendered inoperable, these interplanetary flux tubes were shut down, as explained in previous volumes.

24. Now, during this present time of (inter)planetary electromagnetic disorder, oceanic life, namely whales and dolphins, have been assisting in holding the Earth's frequencies in balance. When the cycle commences and begins again, the Sun will gain a new level of evolutionary balance.

PLANETARY ORBITS, CONSCIOUSNESS AND BODE'S LAW

From a fourth-dimensional viewpoint, a planet is an atomic electron that holds a particular frequency in place. The frequency pattern is the orbit. Frequency is the rate of vibratory oscillation of particular levels, or kinds, of analphs or thoughtforms.

—CHC, *Volume IV*

25. The planetary orbits are the resonant frequency constants of the noosphere. Resonance refers to any harmonic interaction between two or more bodies. The noosphere is directly related to the planetary orbital frequency system. We cannot isolate one planet and say it does not have a relation to the others. Each planet is essential in creating an integrated orbital circuit.

26. All planets are interconnected and form one cosmic body. The sum of the resonant frequencies of all the planets in relation to each other impacts the quality of resonance of the noosphere.

27. The noosphere is the sum of the complex of interactions of the orbital frequencies of the various planets in relationship to each other; and, in particular, as they relate to the Earth. How can we tune into the frequencies of these planetary orbits?

28. According to the Law of Time, the frequencies of the planetary orbits are determined primarily by the Bode numbers as first proposed by Johann Daniel Titius of Wittenberg and then evolved and popularized in 1768 by German astronomer Johann Elert Bode.

29. Bode, who lived at the end of the eighteenth and early nineteenth century, determined that the planetary orbits could be assigned sets of whole numbers which define the orbital ratios of the planets in relation to each other and their distance from the Sun. According to the Law of Time, those frequencies coordinate different levels, or stages, of consciousness. Included in the planetary Bode numbers is Maldek, now known as the Asteroid Belt.

30. Bode discovered the orbit of the lost planet between Mars and Jupiter on September 11, 1801. On that date, 9-11, he discovered a band of asteroids orbiting the Sun. He had been following (Johann) Kepler's law of the progression of planets and was certain there should have been a planet between Mars and Jupiter. Note the number assigned to the missing planet is 28, the harmonic standard.

BODE NUMBERS AND PLANET FREQUENCIES

Bode numbers take the planet as a whole reduced to a set of intervals that have relation in proportion to each other and their distance from the Sun. The Bode numbers sequence breaks down into two sets: the five inner planets and the five outer planets. The five *inner planets* are: Mercury (4); Venus (7); Earth (10); Mars (16); and Maldek (28). The five *outer planets* are: Jupiter (52); Saturn (100); Uranus (196); Neptune (300); and Pluto (388).

INNER PLANETS	OUTER PLANETS

Mercury (4). Frequency of self-existing form power.

Venus (7). Frequency of resonant creation.

Earth (10). Frequency power of the 10 orbits, half of 20. Earth is the place of the transmigration of memories and programs from Maldek and Mars. Karma of previous world systems was transferred to Earth to see if it could be resolved or redeemed.

Note the frequency of Earth is 7.8 hertz, fractal of 78 and also a fractal of 780, the number of days in the Martian synodic cycle as viewed from Earth. Seventy-eight is also the key in the decipherment of the tomb of Pacal Votan; 78 is the sum tonal frequency of the 13 seals carved on the sarcophagus lid.

Also note the relationship of Earth to Mercury is a 10 to 4 relationship. This is a close relation. 10 is the triangular of 4 (1 + 2 + 3 + 4 = 10). Venus (7) to Earth (10) is an even tighter relation. The relation of Earth to Mars is 16 to 10. Look at the ratio intervals and see what kind of whole number differences these create.

Mars (16). Frequency of the Cube of the Law. 4 squared. There are 16 positions between days 7 and 22. Through the system of whole number ratios, Titius and Bode both determined there was a missing planet between Mars (16) and Jupiter (52).

Maldek (28). Frequency of the harmonic constant, 4 × 7 (Mercury × Venus). This harmonic standard represents the mental organization of time. Note: the perfect harmonic ratio of Maldek is attained by doubling the distance between Maldek (28) and Mars (16). By observing the 28-day harmonic cycle, Earth can redeem the karma of the lost planet Maldek. 28 is the triangular of 7.

Jupiter (52). Frequency of time. 52 weeks = 1 year (solar orbit). The ratio of Sirius B is converted to 52 weeks in the Babylonian system of 7-day weeks. Saturn is associated with third-dimensional circuits and the creation of structures supporting time is money. Also to be noted, 52 is 4 × 13, 13 × 28 (Maldek) = 364 = 52 (Jupiter) × Venus (7).

Saturn (100). Frequency of currency. 100 is 10 × 10 (Earth). Basis of the monetary system which is the 3-D material application of T(E) = Money or Time is Money, where money equals the value 100.

Uranus (196). Frequency of multidimensionality (28 × 7). Uranus represents the connection to Earth that has to be made; this connection is being short-circuited by Saturn (100) and Jupiter (52), which destroyed Maldek (28) and made civilization on Mars (16) extinct. Uranus (196) is 28 × 7. Note: Uranus (196) = Saturn (100) + Jupiter (52) + Maldek (28) + Mars (16). Uranus (196) is occulted by the Tower of Babel (represented by the sequence Mars, Maldek, Jupiter, Saturn).

Neptune (300). Frequency of oceanic memory. 300 is the triangular of 24 (1 + 2 + 3 + ... + 24 = 300), Kinich Ahau is designated Velatropa 24. This signifies that the power of the cumulative memory of Velatropa 24 is kept in Neptune, planet of oceanic consciousness.

Pluto (388). Frequency of 4 × 97 (96 + 1); 96 is 24 × 4, so 97 is (24 × 4) +1.

Inner and Outer Planets

31. The Bode number sequence breaks down into two sets: the five inner planets and the five outer planets. The sequence of the five inner planets is 4, 7, 10, 16 and 28. The sequence of the five outer planets is 52, 100, 196, 300 and 388. The sequence of the inner planets recapitulates the 4:7 ratio; Mercury (4) and Venus (7), culminating with Maldek (28) 4 × 7.

32. The interval between Maldek (28) and Jupiter (52) is 24; Velatropa 24, place of the human free will experiment, and indicator of the AA Midway station. This is the galactic surveillance unit locked in interdimensional "air space" between Maldek and Jupiter (see Chapter 13).

33. The sequence of 52-388 of the outer planets also recapitulates a ratio of 4:7 that is 52 × 7 = 364. Pluto (388) less 364 is 24, the interval between Maldek and Jupiter and the sign of Velatropa 24. Neptune (300) = 1 + 2 + 3…+ 24. The solar sunspot cycle that peaks in 2012 is known as Cycle 24. Also note 388 − 52 = 336 = 28 × 12 = 28 (Maldek) less than 364, one moon less than 13 Moons.

34. The sum of the Bode frequencies of the inner planets (4 + 7 + 10 +16 + 28) is 65 (13 × 5), the number of days in one of four galactic spectra, or seasons. The sum of the Bode frequencies of the outer planets (52 + 100 + 196 + 300 + 388) is 1036 (7 × 148).

35. The key number of the inner planets is 13 and the key number of the outer planets is 7. The 148 is equivalent to kin 148, 5 Star, representing the Arcturus command. Also, 148 × 7 = 37 × 28 (=1036). Note: 13 and 28 factors of the inner and outer planet frequency sums.

36. Therefore, the 28 factor appears in both the inner and outer planets in multiple combinations. This further demonstrates that 28 is the cosmic harmonic standard, the solar/biotelepathic frequency and the rhythm of a single interplanetary thoughtform. This thoughtform is available as the noospheric mental frequency index to humans who have established themselves in the 13 Moon 28-day cycle.

Outer Planets: Expand and Release Consciousness

37. The function of the five outer planets is to expand and release consciousness. The function of the five inner planets is to focalize and concentrate consciousness.

Pluto (388): Power of Enlightenment and Self-generation. Enlightenment and self-generation are intrinsic to our being. The self-generation of enlightenment is the gateway to and from interstellar and intergalactic space.

Neptune (300): Power of Birth/Memory and Meditation. Birth is a function of memory. At the time of birth all cosmic memory is within us. Meditation functions as a conscious remembering by which we are able to see clearly and maintain ourselves in the higher course of cosmic enlightenment.

Uranus (196): Power of Spirit and Navigation. Navigation is the intrinsic power of knowing where to go and how to get there in both the spiritual and physical dimensions. Spirit is the basis of any navigation beyond the physical dimension. Spirit endows birth with purpose. Navigation is Spirit's means of returning to source. The Earth/Spirit holds the 28-unit harmonic frequency, the biotelepathic "time tunnel."

Saturn (100): Power of Abundance and Intelligence. Abundance refers to the spiritual power of consciousness, rather than accumulation of material possessions. Spiritual abundance of consciousness is the capacity to establish any number of levels of intuitive orientation. Intelligence is the power of multi-leveled discrimination and discernment of any potential path to attain a specific mission or goal. As the seventh planet, Saturn is the focalizer of consciousness in the interplanetary system.

Jupiter (52): Power of Flowering and Vision. Flowering is a function of consciousness. A flower exemplifies solar consciousness as it opens to the Sun. Vision is a function of the same solar power—if there is no light then you cannot see. Flowering of vision represents the visionary capacity of forever expanding in consciousness.

Inner Planets: Focalize and Concentrate Consciousness

Maldek (28): Power of Life-force and Timelessness. The function and purpose of life-force is to attain timelessness or self-realization. This was the pattern of the original Adam—Adam Kadmon—the first human "manufactured" in the solar system. Life-force is always flowing, remaining in the flow of moment-to-moment timelessness.

Mars (16): Power of Death and Prophecy. Where there is life-force there is death (transcendent door to the beyond). Everything in the biosphere is a continuous recirculation, or migration, of atoms—the recirculation of life within death and death within life. Prophecy is the gift of seeing the true meaning of life and death and receiving from akashic space the message to be spoken.

Earth (10): Power of Accomplishment and Free will. Relates to the two poles of consciousness. The power of accomplishment relates to the power of memory at birth. How? By remembering purpose and bringing to completion the order of the universe through the correct use of free will. Free will is the choice to align with the Divine Plan: this is true accomplishment.

Venus (7): Power of Art and Magic. Art is a natural function of the power of accomplishment. Magic is what arises from the correct alignment of free will with the Divine Plan. To align with the Divine Plan is to put the mind in its correct place. Mind and time precede space and physical order—realizing this, magic becomes possible and art becomes supernatural.

Mercury (4): Power of Purification and Love. Purification is a natural function; we are in a continuous process of purification. When we have purified, then we can truly love. This is all a process of the solar/prophetic generation of love. We purify ourselves to heal ourselves. When we heal ourselves, then we naturally generate love for ourselves and for all beings. Only when we truly love and accept ourselves can we love others. Love is the greatest natural healing.

Five Circuits of Consciousness

38. The five circuits of Earth's consciousness reflect how the noosphere functions through the planetary orbits. The orbital frequencies of the planets create one large field of resonance. Within this large field, every planet has some unique function and vibrational frequency. Each planet has a double charge, a flow coming in from the galaxy (G/K) and a flow going out from the Sun (S/P).

39. These five circuits are the consciousness "grooves" where the field of intelligence interacts with the phenomenal world. The circuits go from the outermost to the innermost. Each circuit has

a frequency and the sum of these frequencies is 140 ($28 \times 5 = 20 \times 7$). This is the Telektonon sacred ratio.

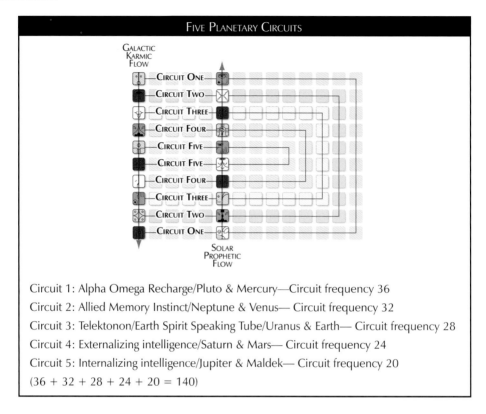

FIVE PLANETARY CIRCUITS

GALACTIC KARMIC FLOW

CIRCUIT ONE
CIRCUIT TWO
CIRCUIT THREE
CIRCUIT FOUR
CIRCUIT FIVE
CIRCUIT FIVE
CIRCUIT FOUR
CIRCUIT THREE
CIRCUIT TWO
CIRCUIT ONE

SOLAR PROPHETIC FLOW

Circuit 1: Alpha Omega Recharge/Pluto & Mercury—Circuit frequency 36
Circuit 2: Allied Memory Instinct/Neptune & Venus— Circuit frequency 32
Circuit 3: Telektonon/Earth Spirit Speaking Tube/Uranus & Earth— Circuit frequency 28
Circuit 4: Externalizing intelligence/Saturn & Mars— Circuit frequency 24
Circuit 5: Internalizing intelligence/Jupiter & Maldek— Circuit frequency 20
($36 + 32 + 28 + 24 + 20 = 140$)

40. The five circuits are the defining orders of Earth's consciousness within the resonant field. The circuits give a sequence of formal order to the whole field of resonance in a descending order of 4 ($36\text{-}32 = 4$, etc.). This formal order is fractally, microscopically transmitted into the noosphere as a four-fold organizing factor which also recapitulates a set of fundamental power from 20 to 36.

41. Each circuit has two basic fields of consciousness: Telepathic (five outer planetary orbits) and instinctual (five inner planetary orbits). There are six different telepathic and instinctual alignments that correspond with the six mental spheres. The seventh mental sphere, the holomind perceiver, is the auric egg that encloses the other six.

42. Consciousness is a function of the star (Kinich Ahau), which functions like a gyroscope to hold the orbits of its electrons called planets. The sequence of the planets is embedded in an interplanetary cosmogenesis and each interplanetary circuit represents a different quality of consciousness and intelligence.

FIVE INTERPLANETARY CIRCUITS

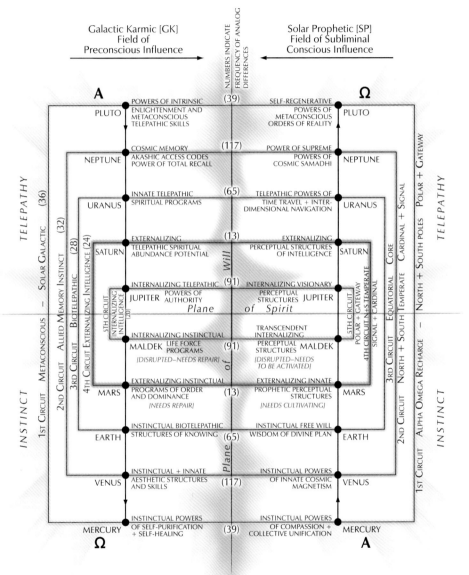

NOOSPHERE ORGANIZATION
INTERPLANETARY CIRCUITS OF CONSCIOUSNESS
BASIC PROGRAMS

Pluto & Mercury: Metaconsciousness/Alpha-Omega Recharge circuit. Frequency 36 (9 × 4): regenerative power of mind (fourth power of nine). This is the highest heliospheric plane of consciousness that connects with the whole galactic order. It is akin to the supramental order—beyond mind. It is purely solar-galactic force.

Neptune & Venus: Allied Memory-Instinct circuit. Frequency 32: Crystalline order of consciousness. This circuit connects telepathic memory with instinctual organic preconscious and subconscious analphs.

Uranus & Earth: Biotelepathic circuit. Frequency 28: Key circuit for the activation and transformation of the biospheric field into the telepathic order of the noosphere.

Saturn & Mars: Externalizing intelligence circuit. Frequency 24: The Velatropa factor. This circuit externalizes inner perceptions as well as receives external perceptions that are transferred to the internalizing intelligence circuit.

Maldek & Jupiter: Internalizing intelligence circuit. Frequency 20: Totality of being and consciousness. This circuit internalizes outer perceptions as well as transferring perceptions that flower from inner experience to the externalizing intelligence circuit.

The Law of Time places great significance on the relations of the planets to the Sun. Star histories are loaded into planetary positions.

PLANETS AND MYTHS

43. Do planetary myths hold validity now? Is Mercury really the messenger? For the most part this may be the case. Mercury's orbital position is closest to the Sun, and, with its 88-day orbital cycle, it moves the fastest of all the planets. Because of this speed, Mercury is associated with the messenger bringing communication. Mercury was depicted with wings on his feet. We see those associations have some type of scientific validity. Beyond this it is questionable.

44. Do the physical characteristics of planets have anything to do with the quality of consciousness of that planet? For example, Jupiter is the biggest planet; Saturn is the lightest, etc. Is this fact not important for the determination of consciousness and psychological aspects?

45. In this solar system there are five inner planets. These are all relatively small in size, and there is a very distinct dividing line made by the Asteroid Belt between the inner planets and the outer ones. With the exception of Pluto, the outer planets are giant compared with the inner ones, which are small Earth-sized planets. If the Creator has created everything for a purpose, then all design has purpose, and there is nothing in the universe that is not designed according to a law or principle.

46. It appears that this system is designed so that the inner five original planets were all roughly the same size and mostly rocky; then there were at least four if not more gaseous and fiery outer planets which were very large, with, again, the exception of Pluto.

47. In 2006, Pluto was downgraded by the scientific community to a planetoid. This is psychologically interesting given the aspects of the psyche that are associated with Pluto. If it is not really a planet, then what is it and how does it affect the field? Does this mean that its astrological and psychological attributes are invalid? Nonetheless, it maintains an orbital frequency that harmonizes with the other planetary orbits. But there is a clear distinction between the Asteroid Belt and then the very large size of Jupiter—what is the meaning of this?

The five circuits are functions of the Planet Holon and signify Earth's consciousness reflecting the noosphere. Study the location of the circuits on the Planet Holon. We participate in consciousness but we don't own or possess it. Spiritual practices make our biopsychic organism a receptor of consciousness.

48. The planets are children of the Sun. It seems like the planets have everything to do with the star system that they are arranged around; just like the electrons going around a particular nucleus. The significance of the division into outer and inner planets, so physically obvious, has everything to do with the thought construct that the Sun is evolving and maintaining.

PLANETARY ARCHETYPES

OUTER PLANETS

G/K ⊖
Enlightened One
PLUTO
S/P
World-Changer
WE HOLD THE POWERS OF ENLIGHTENMENT & SELF-GENERATION, YOU WILL FIND US IN CIRCUIT 1: ALPHA-OMEGA RECHARGE
388

G/K •
Primal Force
NEPTUNE
S/P
Yogi/Yogini
WE HOLD THE POWERS OF MEMORY AND MEDITATION, YOU WILL FIND US ON CIRCUIT 2: ALLIED MEMORY INSTINCT
300

G/K ••
High Priestess
URANUS
S/P
Navigator
WE HOLD THE POWERS OF SPIRIT AND NAVIGATION, YOU WILL FIND US ON CIRCUIT 3: TELEKTONON EARTH SPIRIT SPEAKING TUBE
196

G/K •••
Dreamer
SATURN
S/P
Pathfinder
WE HOLD THE POWERS OF ABUNDANCE AND INTELLIGENCE, YOU WILL FIND US ON CIRCUIT 4: EXTERNALIZING INTELLIGENCE
100

G/K ••••
The Innocent
JUPITER
S/P
Seer
WE HOLD THE POWERS OF FLOWERING AND VISION, YOU WILL FIND US ON CIRCUIT 5: INTERNALIZING INTELLIGENCE
52

INNER PLANETS

G/K —
Serpent Initiate
MALDEK
S/P
Wizard
WE HOLD THE POWERS OF SEX AND TIMELESSNESS, YOU WILL FIND US ON CIRCUIT 5: INTERNALIZING INTELLIGENCE
28

G/K •
Hierophant
MARS
S/P
Prophet
WE HOLD THE POWERS OF DEATH AND PROPHECY, YOU WILL FIND US ON CIRCUIT 4: EXTERNALIZING INTELLIGENCE
16

G/K ••
Avatar
EARTH
S/P
Sage
WE HOLD THE POWERS OF ACCOMPLISHMENT AND FREE WILL, YOU WILL FIND US ON CIRCUIT 3: TELEKTONON EARTH SPIRIT SPEAKING TUBE
10

G/K •••
Artist
VENUS
S/P
Magician
WE HOLD THE POWERS OF ART AND MAGIC, YOU WILL FIND US ON CIRCUIT 2: ALLIED MEMORY INSTINCT
7

G/K ••••
Healer
MERCURY
S/P
Compassionate One
WE HOLD THE POWERS OF PURIFICATION AND LOVE, YOU WILL FIND US IN CIRCUIT 1: ALPHA-OMEGA RECHARGE
4

49. What happens if an atom is stripped of its electrons? It ceases to be an element. By analogy, if you take the planets and their orbits away from the Sun, that would have a very destabilizing effect, and the thought structure that the Sun/heliosphere is meant to evolve would cease altogether.

50. The Law of Time places great significance in the relations of the planets to the Sun and their roles as defined by this solar relationship. Many planets have moons or satellites; *pay attention to these.* Mercury and Venus are the only two planets with no moons. Earth and Pluto have only one moon; Mars is the only planet with two moons and Neptune is the only planet with 13 known moons.

Earth contains the greatest amount of liquid of any planet and Mars has the tallest mountain. Jupiter has the strongest magnetic field and Maldek's electromagnetic field is now only a memory

51. What is the relation of the moons to the planets and the planets to the Sun? Moons are objects that go around planets, like planets are objects that go around the Sun. According to Anthroposophy (Rudolf Steiner), the Earth is the physical place where the human soul connects with the body. Earth, Sun and Moon provide the basic energies for the development of humanity. According to Cosmic Science, moons are planetoids that have no electrical fields and thus function solely as gravitational stabilizers.

52. The solar system, with its star at the center, has ripples of planets going around it. In this way, the Sun is seen as having an etheric body and the planets actually mark certain points of density within the etheric body of the Sun. What part of this galactic being are we? What is the nature of solar being? Solar consciousness? What thoughtform is the solar system configuring? Is this thought Cosmic History?

PREAMBLE TO CHAPTER 9

The New Earth Geomancy was inspired by and is in some ways an update of Alice Bailey's work in The Destiny of the Nations *written after the Second World War (1949). At that time, both pessimism and optimism were in the air. The United Nations (UN) had recently been founded and Alice Bailey put much trust in the possibility of the UN being the vehicle for the unification and positive fulfillment of the destiny of the nations.*

Particularly significant in The Destiny of the Nations *is the idea of the influence of different astrological signs or planetary bodies—and even the seven rays—upon specific cities or nations. This notion is among the most fertile presented in the book, illustrating that the destinies of the nations are bound with the particular astrological sign that govern them. For example, Bailey says Australia is governed by Virgo, etc. Though this idea may seem outdated, it remains highly provocative.*

Bailey peers through a cosmic lens at the influence of the planets on Earth and at Earth as being a repository of different planetary programs, which is similar to the ideas of traditional astrology. Rather than the astrological perspective, Cosmic History takes the heliospheric perspective of the planets. In the astrological perspective, planets have meaning according to what particular constellation they happen to be moving through and what particular house they happen to be in.

As we enter the time of the noosphere our consciousness becomes the mind of the Earth. This is a different mental geography than we are familiar with. This is the psychogeography of the Earth—our new mental foundation. Read on about the New Earth Geomancy...

157

CHAPTER 9

NEW EARTH GEOMANCY

The world is one world and its sufferings are one and humanity is in truth a unity; but many are still unaware of this.

—Alice Bailey, *Glamour, A World Problem*

1. Geomancy—literally divination by signs or by means of the Earth itself— is an ancient art and science. In China it is known as Feng Shui—winds and water—and has much to do with finding auspicious sites and/or orientations in nature. However, the New Earth Geomancy is not just what is happening on the surface of the planet, but consciously engages the internal workings of interplanetary forces.

2. From the heliospheric perspective, planets are arranged and interpreted according to their orbital position in relation to the Sun. As we have seen from the previous chapter, there are different Bode numbers that indicate the various types of frequency ratios that the planetary orbits hold in relation to each other, to the Sun, and to the whole.

3. The notion of a planetary grid traces back to Plato who conceived of Earth as being shaped like a dodecahedron ball. R. Buckminster Fuller further developed this idea and laid out a dodecahedron on the world map, and even made dodecahedron globes.

4. In the 1970s Russian scientist, Kiril Lachugin, conceived of the Earth as a giant crystal structure. This crystal structure creates a grid that is constructed of an icosahedron integrated with a dodecahedron. This model was adopted by American Researchers, Bill Becker and Bethe Hagens, and developed as the Planetary Grid System (1983).

5. The specific New Earth Geomancy grid system (Planet Holon) was discovered by Valum Votan in 1986. Inspired by Buckminster Fuller's dymaxion dodecahedron world map, the Planet Holon is a 20-unit geometrical design overlaid on a Becker-Hagens planetary grid. This was first known as the Arcturus Protectorate Zone and later as the Planet Holon.

6. As a harmonic frequency grid to stabilize the dissonance of the Earth's biopsychic field, the Arcturus Protectorate Zone is divided into 20 zones that correspond with the seals of the Mayan calendar. Each of the 20 zones contains a solar seal that belongs to either a galactic/karmic or solar/prophetic interplanetary flow. Each seal corresponds to a planet, either in its position in the galactic/karmic flow or in its position in the solar/prophetic flow. Each planet has two

seals. Each flow is divided into two chromatic runs of five seals (planets) each which diagonally span the planet from North Pole to South Pole.

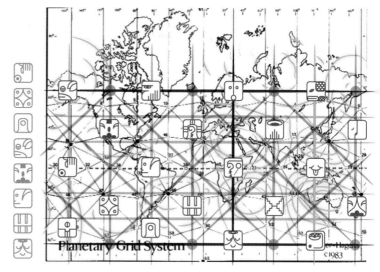

Planetary Grid System c1983

7. The Planet Holon is a pure projection from the AA Midway Station and serves as a fourth-dimensional etheric protective grid around planet Earth. The AA Midway Station serves as an intergalactic telepathic supervisor that focalizes this particular grid onto planet Earth. This grid can be followed daily in 20-day sequences: Sun to Storm. The holon grid is also divided into five horizontal zones—Earth Families—which have particular functions with corresponding attributes.

8. The grid creates five horizontal zones. Each of the zones are activated with equal frequency in the 20-day runs. When consciously directed by human thought-force, higher interplanetary frequencies can penetrate the chaotic frenzy of happenings on Earth. This structure makes up the skeleton of the fourth-dimensional body of the planet. By continuously activating this grid, slowly but surely, the higher fourth-dimensional frequency will moderate and help lay a foundation for the emergence of a new order or state of being: The noosphere.

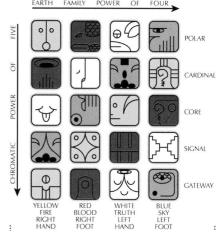

EARTH FAMILY POWER OF FOUR

FIVE / OF / POWER / CHROMATIC POWER OF

POLAR
CARDINAL
CORE
SIGNAL
GATEWAY

| YELLOW FIRE RIGHT HAND | RED BLOOD RIGHT FOOT | WHITE TRUTH LEFT HAND | BLUE SKY LEFT FOOT |

9. Through contemplation of this planetary grid we can better grasp, as galactic citizens, the various levels and methods of the New Earth Geomancy. In time we may even be chosen to become the new planetary shamans—the diviners of the Earth, whose science and knowledge is based on a telepathic engagement of the Planet Holon/Arcturus Protectorate Grid.

The Earth families are five sets of four seals each. Any day of the solar year is coded by one of these sets, such that every four years, the same four seals code that day in a succession of red, white, blue, yellow seals). One sequence of Earth families creates a chromatic of time: 73 chromatics, 5 days each = 365 (days in a solar year).

160

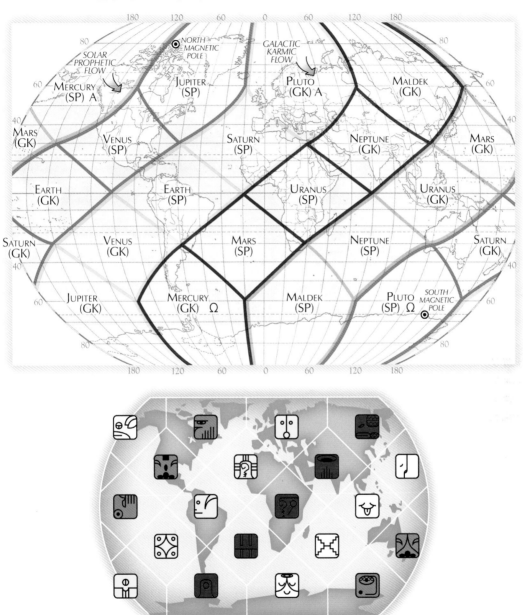

PLANET HOLON — PLANET DESIGNATIONS

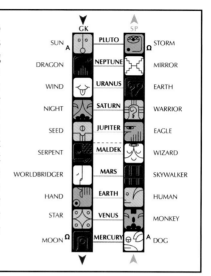

The galactic/karmic flow runs from Pluto to Mercury and the solar/prophetic flow runs from Mercury to Pluto accommodating the ten planetary orbits. The Yellow Sun seal corresponds to G/K Pluto at the North Pole, the Red Moon seal to G/K Mercury at the South Pole. The White Dog seal corresponds with S/P Mercury at the North Pole and the Blue Storm with S/P Pluto at the South Pole. There are four runs that go diagonally from the upper left to the lower right. Each flow has two parts. One part takes us to the midpoint of the solar system (Jupiter and Maldek) and the other takes us to the end of either the solar or galactic spectrum (Mercury and Pluto).

New Earth Geomancy: Three Levels

There are three levels to consider when working with the New Earth Geomancy: 1) Outermost; 2) Plate Tectonics; 3) The Core. These three components define a whole system for the reactivation of Earth as a living, evolving being.

Level 1: Outermost Level

This is the level of the electromagnetic field, the Van Allen radiation belts, in particular the psi bank/noosphere with its division into four plates or eight seasonal divisions (four in the North and four in the South). The eight seasonal plates are further subdivided into 24 psi nimboid membranes, six per seasonal plate.

Each of the psi nimboid membranes is coded by one of the 24 Elder Futhark runes. By studying the color patterns of the different seals we can see how each of these psi nimboid plates is affected by the Planet Holon in its color formation. The psi plates belong to the outer most aspect; the etheric form of the psi bank located in between the outer and inner Van Allen radiation belts. It is here that the programs from the solar binary sunspot cycle first affect the electromagnetic field, and are dispersed to the 24 membranes.

Consciously directed collective thought-force will increase the receptive interaction at this noospheric psi bank level as the information coming in from the binary sunspots hits the electromagnetic field. The noosphere's electromagnetic programs are activated through the psi field—four plates and 24 membranes—and channeled through the poles into the Earth as well as being radiated onto the surface level of the Earth. This is the first stage of receiving the information/energy from the binary sunspot cycles, the activation of the noosphere's psi information flows.

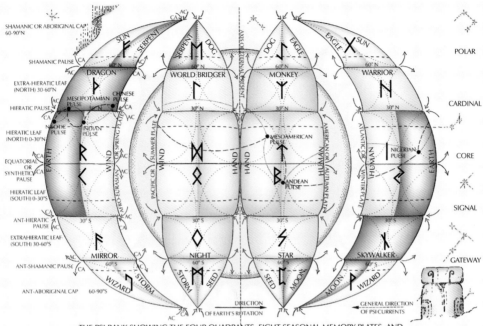

THE PSI BANK SHOWING THE FOUR QUADRANTS, EIGHT SEASONAL MEMORY PLATES, AND
24 PSIONIC NIMBOID MEMBRANES – ALSO SHOWING ZONES OF INFLUENCE WITH 24 ELDER FUTHARK RUNES

Level 2: Plate Tectonics

Geomagnetically, the second level is governed by the tectonic plates that create the surface tension of the planet. There are three types of tectonic plate boundaries: 1) Divergent boundaries, where the plates are pulling apart, (this creates a "positive" energy while the next two boundary types set off "destructive" forces); 2) Convergent boundaries, when plates come into collision with each other (like the Chilean fault line and the fault line causing the Boxing Day tsunami in Indonesia); 3) Transform boundaries, when plates slide or grind past each other, such as the San Andreas Fault, in California.

These are the three types of boundaries that connect the different tectonic plates. There are about 20 main tectonic plates that are always in motion with a fluid foundation. This creates the surface tension that also contributes to the dynamic of life on Earth. Different types of Earth energies emerge through different plates. The Arcturus Protectorate Grid, indicating the planetary zones of influence, is overlaid on Earth to help stabilize the plates by creatively reconfiguring the biopsychic influence and the psychic field as we know it.

Level 3: The Core

The third level refers to the Earth core. At the center of the Earth there is an outer and inner core. The inner core has a radius of 1216 km (19 × 64, DNA code). The octahedral crystal core is inside of this. The eight facets of the octahedron correspond to the eightfold division of the 4 psi plates. There is a correspondence and dynamic connection between the octahedral core and the four psi plates of the seasons with which they are in resonance.

The dynamic inner core, like a gyroscope, is intended to stabilize the planet. It has an electrodynamic connection to the poles which receive solar cosmic transmissions that are then stored within the core. There are intermittent points and radial diffusions from the core to the surface where codes are received and transmitted as information to the different plasmas, and that subliminally affect the consciousness of receptive human beings. The practice of Synchrogalactic Yoga helps to tune us in to these frequencies.

BIOPSYCHIC SURFACE TENSION AND THE SEVEN RAYS

As a collective species, we are transitioning from what Alice Bailey calls the sixth ray of idealism into the seventh ray of ceremonial magic. This transition contributes to the biopsychic tension and dynamic on the surface of the planet.

The sixth ray of devotion/idealism results in ideological fanaticism at its most negative. This influence is waning. As it wanes the fanaticism or conservatism intensifies. The seventh ray influence of the Aquarian age of the future is getting stronger. As it becomes stronger through biopsychic unification, the sixth ray recedes. The seventh ray represents the passage from conscious to continuing conscious and the passage from instinct to telepathy. It leads to synthesis and fusion that blends spirit and matter.

The interaction of the fourth, sixth and seventh rays also account for chaos, turbulence and confusion on the planet. As the strong-willed sixth ray begins to fade and the seventh ray increases, a psychic vacuum is created so that the majority of people feel more confused—they cannot make sense of what is going on. The masses are unequipped to resolve within themselves the idealism of the new and the idealism of the old; they are too extreme. This larger group, countless millions or billions, feel that there is no hope, no future—though through the cybersphere they have created outlets for their egos, such as social networking sites like Facebook and Twitter.

"A large number of seventh ray egos or souls and men and women in the seventh ray personality are coming into incarnation. To them is committed the task of organizing the activities of the new era and of ending the old methods of life and the old crystallized attitudes of life, of leisure and of the population."

—Alice Bailey

This advanced new age thinking is increasingly widespread and sees no way but for the old to end. This contributes to the surface tension and makes the interplanetary Arcturus Protectorate Zone all the more significant.

THREE LEVELS OF NEW EARTH GEOMANCY

A) Outermost: Electromagnetic Field
Van Allen Radiation Belts, Cosmic-Solar radiation receiver-transformers, Earth broadcast studio: "Noosphere Live"

Binary Sunspot Cycle, information keys via 260/441 programs

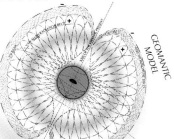

PSI BANK = RINGS = CUMULATIVE PSION DEPOSIT + SYNTHESIS OF STAGES OF PSYCHOCULTURAL DEVELOPMENT

Plate Boundaries

B) Surface Tension: Geomagnetic Field
Tectonic plates, underlying zones of cosmic interplanetary influence.

Planet Holon/Arcturus Protectorate superimposed on the geomagnetic field

C) Dynamic Inner Core
Iron Crystal Octahedron provides gyroscopic dynamic stabilizer, radial diffuser of solar galactic plasma information codes received and transmitted as information waves to surface and electromagnetic field.

Three Types of Plate Boundaries
Constructive boundary – Plates pulling away
Destructive boundary – Pushing against
Transform boundary – Sliding over each other

NEPTUNE-URANUS CELL GOVERNS RED + WHITE CHROMATICS

INNER CORE

OCTAHEDRON CRYSTAL HUNAB KU 21

RADIUS = 19×64 (1216 KM)

VENUS-EARTH CELL GOVERNS BLUE + YELLOW CHROMATICS

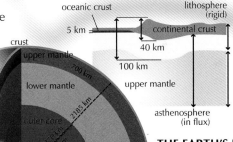

oceanic crust

lithosphere (rigid)

5 km

continental crust

40 km

100 km

crust
upper mantle
lower mantle

outer core

inner core

upper mantle

asthenosphere (in flux)

THE EARTH'S INTERIOR
The Earth's interior is divided as follows:

1. **Crust** (5-40 km thick): The thin outer skin of the planet.
2. **Mantle** (2,885 km thick): The origin of most magma.
3. **Core** (3,486 km thick): A dense metal-rich ball inside the Earth. The core is composed of liquid **outer core** and solid **inner core.**

20 INTERPLANETARY ZONES OF INFLUENCE

10. A main point of study in New Earth Geomancy is the 20 interplanetary zones of influence. The Polar Earth Family holds the frequency of the North Pole and the Gateway Earth Family holds the frequency of the South Pole. Here, there is a complete correspondence with the planets Jupiter, Mercury, Maldek and Pluto, which hold the four positions around each of the two poles.

11. The two outermost planets of the interplanetary circuit, Mercury and Pluto, hold the poles and mediate information coming in from and going out to the galaxy; and the two innermost planets of the circuit, Maldek and Jupiter, mediate the information going to and coming from the Sun.

12. In the Planet Holon, all four of these planets—two outermost and two innermost of the interplanetary circuit—are at the Polar Regions. Pluto (Sun) is the transmitter of galactic information. Mercury (Dog) is the transmitter of solar information. The Dog zone occupies a position that straddles the Asian and American landmass. Here is found the shamanic bridge that spans from the Serpent to the Dog zone.

13. Maldek and Jupiter are the innermost planets of the interplanetary circuit. Jupiter is the sixth orbit and Maldek the fifth. These two planets also hold Earth's poles. Jupiter, the largest planet, signifies the potentiality of expansive spiritual vision. It is also the storehouse of spiritual texts and scripture. Songs, tunes and melodies of the lost chord reside in Maldek's orbit. As the midpoints of the two flows (S/P and G/K), these two planetary orbits represent a density of information that is gathered and distributed.

14. Constituted and governed by the influences of Maldek and Jupiter, the circumpolar rainbow bridge serves as the spiritual rejuvenation center that contains all harmonies of the universe. Note that the magnetic poles are located at the beginning and end of the Sky Clan, North Magnetic Pole (Eagle/Jupiter); South Magnetic Pole (Storm/Pluto). (When studying the Planet Holon graphics, note that the four chromatic runs are designated as four clans: Yellow Fire; Red Blood; White Truth; and Blue Sky. Also note the different crossover polarities and relations between planets).

15. Maldek is represented by the Serpent in the North and the Wizard in the South. The songs and melodies of the lost chord are always drifting into our space through the influence of the auroras and the continuous emission of electromagnetic energy and information from the poles. (see *CHC Vol. III*).

16. Many poets, musicians and rocks stars say their songs were just floating in the air, they just hear them; this is because Maldek is one of the planets that govern the poles, emitting the songs and

GEOLOGIC TIME

Geologists consider time from the formation of the Earth to today, following a **geologic timescale** that breaks Earth history into manageable pieces. Geologic time is divided and subdivided into **aeons, eras, periods, epochs** and **ages.**

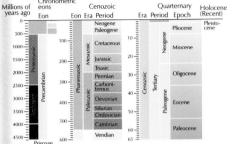

The boundaries on the geologic timescale are set by major events that have been preserved in the rock record. For example, the mass extinction of dinosaurs and some marine invertebrate species 65 million years ago forms the **Cretaceous/Tertiary boundary, or K/T boundary.**

AEONS, ERAS, EPOCHS AND AGES

are all functions of fluctuations of the solar frequencies due to shifts in the sun's electromagnetic field and evolutionary adjustments of the solar logos in response to signals from the galactic/cosmic hierarchy.

It is this same hierarchy in coordination with the solar logos sunspot cycle mechanism that imprinted the Arcturus Protectorate on the Earth.

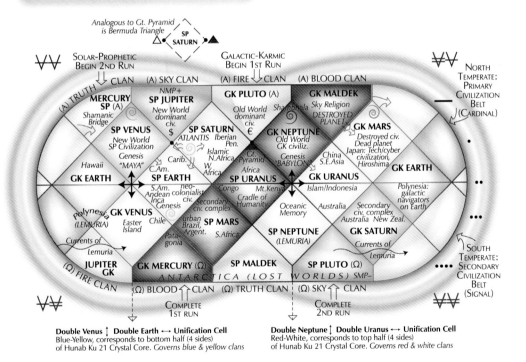

Study the graphic showing the 20 fields, or zones, of interplanetary influence, subdivided into four, 5-part chromatic runs. At top the G/K run begins with Pluto. The S/P run begins with Mercury. The G/K run is completed with Mercury and the S/P run with Pluto. These can be followed on a daily basis. Note the names of planets and the two flows transposed to the Planet Holon: Mercury (A), North Pole; Mercury (Ω), South Pole; Pluto (A) North Pole; Pluto (Ω), South Pole.

sounds into the collective psychic atmosphere between the poles. Note also how Maldek is paired with Pluto.

17. The next horizontal band after the Polar is the Cardinal Family, who establish the genesis. Located in the North temperate civilization belt, the Cardinal family guards the space where the major civilizations of the world are located. There are two geneses of civilizations: Old World and New World.

18. The Old World genesis is located in the red Neptune (Dragon) zone and holds the key to the Babylonian genesis. This is also the place that is the genesis of virtually all major world religions: Buddhism, Hinduism, Zoroastrianism, Taoism, etc., as well as the monotheistic religions: Judaism, Christianity and Islam. These are the galactic/karmic civilizations in the Neptune zone of the Dragon, indicating cosmic memory and primal being.

The memory of the "lost chord" or "lost planet" is deeply embedded in the unconscious human psyche. What is this memory? What happened?

19. The New World genesis is located in the blue Venus (Monkey) zone that contains the solar/prophetic genesis in the Mayan-Toltec Mexican vision of civilization. This is where the prophecy of time originates. The blue Venus (Monkey) and red Neptune (Dragon) zones are an antipode pair, signifying that the karmically denser Old World civilization is to be challenged by, or challenges, the New World civilization. Venus and Neptune also hold the second telepathic circuit of consciousness, the *Allied Memory Instinct circuit*. This is the circuit that activates the generation of all civilizations.

20. The yellow Saturn Cardinal Family (Warrior zone) represents the psycho-mythic genesis of old Atlantis. Presently, it includes the North Atlantic, Iberian Peninsula (Spain and Portugal), as well as Islamic North Africa and the great Sahara Desert. The white Mars (Worldbridger) zone represents the destroyed civilization of Mars, the red planet. Note that Atlantis is paired with the ill-fated Mars. The Martian karma is now reincarnate in present-day Japan.

The genesis of the post WWII New Atlantean technosphere established Japan as the front runner of technological civilization.

21. The challenge for Japan is to overcome its isolated ethnocentrism, as it is susceptible to suffer the same fate as Mars or Atlantis. This could indicate why Japan, so far, has been the only nation bombed with nuclear weapons. As a counterpoint these same people continue the mass slaughter of whales and dolphins that is disrupting the balance of nature. Japan is also just below the Maldekian (Serpent) zone of influence, which circulates the destroyed planet memories into that zone, reflected in the thriving manga and pop subculture of Japan.

22. Most of North American civilization lies in the blue Venus zone: Mexico, Central America, Florida up to the state of Washington, including California, where we find the New World civilization. However, the northeastern part of the United States, which includes the power centers that dominate the world, is in the blue Jupiter (Eagle) zone. This is the Jupiter effect, seat of the New World dominance of Washington DC and New York City. This is where the dollar comes from. In Europe, as well, the main dominant financial centers lie in the yellow G/K Pluto (Sun) zone.

23. These two polar signs, Eagle and Sun, are where the world financial markets are generated. The power center of Europe is in the Sun zone, which includes London, Rome, Paris, Moscow, and the general area of Western and Eastern Europe and parts of Russia as well.

24. The concentration of power in civilization, as it developed toward the end of the cycle, gravitated toward the S/P Jupiter New World of the dollar, and the G/K Pluto Old World of the euro. These Polar family power zones concentrate the two main planetary centers of monetary influence. However, the later technological dominance emanates from Japan (in

Was there a world we destroyed before? Where did this happen? Are we doing this again? How can we break out of this cycle?

the G/K Mars Worldbridger zone), the only Asian nation in the G-7. This completes the North temperate civilization belt.

25. Across the equatorial center is the Core Family—Earth and Uranus—which together form the biotelepathic circuit. China, the ultimate world power, is divided into three zones: Serpent, Dragon and Wind (Maldek, Neptune and Uranus)—all galactic/karmic—creating a complex of overwhelming force and karmic liability.

26. Note that the two Uranus flows (G/K and S/P) are adjacent to each other, as are the two (G/K and S/P) Earth flows. Joining the double Earth West/East axis are the two flows (G/K and S/P) of Venus in a North/South axis, and joining the double Uranus West/East axis is the North/South axis of Neptune.

27. Saturn and Mars have a reverse crossover relationship that creates a dynamic polarity—Mars (G/K) and Saturn (G/K) (West Pacific) and Saturn (S/P) and Mars (S/P) (Atlantic). Between the Mars/Saturn zones are the two sets of joined planets, Neptune-Uranus and Venus-Earth; these eight zones comprise the two unified protectorate cells of primary Arcturian control. Venus and Neptune have a parallel vertical relationship and Earth and Uranus have a continuous horizontal relationship.

28. The core influence that holds the planet together—two unified cells at the center of Earth (Neptune and Uranus; and Venus and Earth) establishes the inner core of Earth with a radius 1216 km. Earth's outer core is held together by a super hyperparton: Dum Kuali, Dum

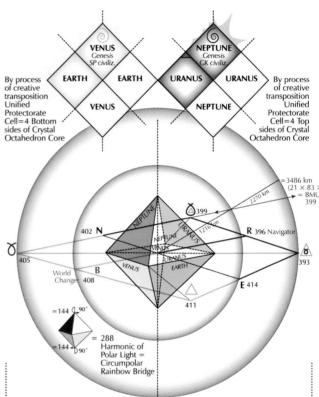

The two Venus and two Earth seals are blue and yellow, while the two Neptune and two Uranus seals are red and white. The Uranus/Neptune cell transposes to become the red and white upper half of the octahedral center of the Earth, and the Venus/Earth cell transposes to become the lower half of the octahedron. These two unified cells are governed by the iron octahedral core. This creates the stabilization at the center of the Earth and at the equatorial zone that also resonates the four psi plates in their eight-fold seasonal divisions. These transpositions are manifestations of a higher-dimensional energy principle used in planet engineering design science.

Duar, Kum, Kemio, the hyperelectron and hyperneutron along with the red and blue transformers, "Navigator" and "World Changer." This forms a hyperparton grid around the octahedron.

PLANET HOLON – TWO PRIMARY CELLS

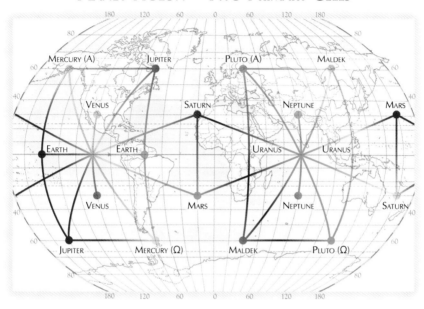

29. The octahedron then transposes itself into the unification cells on the surface as the Earth-Venus and Uranus-Neptune zones. This creates the dynamism on Earth and is how the Earth core affects the surface level. The surface level then mutually transposes down to the octahedron crystal core.

30. Unlike astrology, which excludes Earth as a planetary influence, in the New Geomancy, Earth is considered as an influence upon itself—in conjunction with its twin, or ally, Uranus.

The next three pages consist of index zones coded according to the psi bank plates and Earth Families and their positions on the planet taking into account the principle geographical-historical-biophysical aspects of each of these areas of influence. This becomes the content basis of the New Earth Geomancy.

THE NEW PLANETARY GEOMANCY

PLANET HOLON PSI BANK–PSI NIMBOID MEMBRANE + 4 QUADRANTS + 8 SEASONAL MEMORY PLATES
ZONES OF INFLUENCE OR STRATEGIC PSYCHOGEOGRAPHIC LOCATIONS
PSI BANK PLATES + PLANET HOLON ZONES ESTABLISH BIOPSYCHIC FIELD COORDINATED BY NOOSPHERE

PLANET HOLON

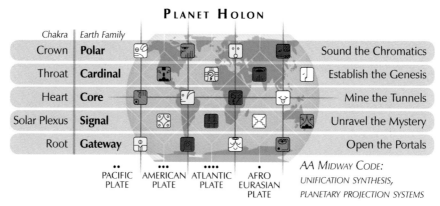

Chakra	Earth Family					
Crown	**Polar**					Sound the Chromatics
Throat	**Cardinal**					Establish the Genesis
Heart	**Core**					Mine the Tunnels
Solar Plexus	**Signal**					Unravel the Mystery
Root	**Gateway**					Open the Portals

PACIFIC PLATE   AMERICAN PLATE   ATLANTIC PLATE   AFRO EURASIAN PLATE

AA MIDWAY CODE: UNIFICATION SYNTHESIS, PLANETARY PROJECTION SYSTEMS

$0 = \dot{\ominus}$

SUN ZONE
NORTH POLAR

Psi Plate I   ⼽
Psi Plate IV   X

Begin
Yellow Chromatic/Fire Clan

Polar Family Yellow (Sound the Chromatics)
Zone of the Enlightened One, (A) GK Pluto, Inflow of Galactic Influences
Zone of psychogeographic influence: European subcontinent, from western Siberia, Slavic land, across all of Europe, but not including Iberian Peninsula [Spain & Portugal], projecting upward from Great Pyramid of Egypt, Syria, Turkey, the Caucasus, much of the Mediterranean and Black & Caspian Seas, Stonehenge, heartland of Western Civilization, Christianity, ancient Rome, Greece, Egypt, Russia, Byzantum, Ottoman Empire.

DRAGON ZONE
NORTH TEMPERATE

Psi Plate I   ⼂

The Vedas, I Ching, Qur'an

Cardinal Family Red (Establish the Genesis)
Zone of the Ancient of Days, GK Neptune, Activation of Galactic Memory
Zone of psychogeographic influence: projecting east from Great Pyramid and north from mid-Indian Ocean, Arabian Peninsula, Middle-East, including Israel, Mecca, Jerusalem, Baghdad, "Cradle of Civilization", Iraq, Indian subcontinent, Vedic root, Himalayas, Afghanistan, Tibet, much of China, into southern Siberia, root of monotheistic religions, as well as Hindu, Jain, Buddhist, Sikh, Yoga, Taoism, Hunza, Shambhala, the mother of human civilization.

WIND ZONE
EQUATORIAL

     N   S
Psi Plate I   ⼓   ⼃
Psi Plate II   ⼗   ⼇

Straddles Equator (North/South)

Core Family White (Mine the Tunnels)
Zone of the High Priestess, GK Uranus, Galactic Spiritual Communication
Zone of psychogeographic influence: projecting south from south China & China Sea, and north from Arabian land, Aboriginal North and Western Australia, includes all of New Guinea, Indonesia, Java, Bali, Borabadur, Southeast Asia, Buddhist, Hindu, Islam overlays, the Philippines and into the West Pacific Ocean, Aboriginal, Oriental and Polynesian mix.

NIGHT ZONE
SOUTH TEMPERATE

Psi Plate II   ◇

Aboriginal/Tribal
overlays of Christian Colonialism

Signal Family Blue (Unravel the Mystery)
Zone of the Dreamer, GK Saturn, Distillation of Galactic Power of 7
Zone of psychogeographic influence: projecting from southwestern-most point of Australia, includes most of Aboriginal Australia [Oceania], Uluru, Tasman Sea, Melanesia, Polynesia, Aotearoa and Southeastern South Pacific, land of great Polynesian navigators, followed by Captain Cook & British imperialism, making present Australia & New Zealand part of the British Commonwealth.

SEED ZONE
SOUTH POLAR

Psi Plate II   ⼳
Psi Plate III   ⼓

Gateway Family Yellow (Open the Portals)
Zone of the Innocent, GK Jupiter, Magnification of the Flowering of Galactic Power
Zone of psychogeographic influence: Antarctica, Transantarctic Mountains, Ross Sea and Ross Ice Shelf, West Antarctica, Amundsen Sea, Southern Sea, southernmost South Pacific Ocean, treasure vaults of the secrets of Lemuria & Atlantis. Completes Yellow Chromatic/Fire Clan.

SERPENT ZONE
NORTH POLAR

Psi Plate I ᚠ
Psi Plate II ᛘ

Begin Red Chromatic/Blood Clan

Polar Family Red (Sound the Chromatics), Zone of the Serpent Initiate, GK Maldek
The Lost Planet Primal Initiations of Power & Knowledge
Zone of psychogeographic influence: Northeast Asia, the Great Tundra, Siberian plains & plateaus, Arctic Ocean, Mongolia, the Gobi Desert, northeastern China, Beijing, the Forbidden City, Eastern Kazakhstan, Altai, the Korean Peninsula, Hokkaido, Sea of Japan, Sea of Okhotsk, northwest North Pacific, ancient shamanic magic zone, Genghis & Kublai Khan, home of Sky Religion, Magic, Taoism, Buddhism.

WORLDBRIDGER ZONE
NORTH TEMPERATE

Psi Plate II ᚱ

Cardinal Family White (Establish the Genesis), Zone of the Hierophant, GK Mars
The Lost Civilization of Galactic Mars, Seat of the Hierarchical Knowledge
Zone of psychogeographic influence: North Pacific Ocean, Japan, Land of the Rising Sun, ancient mysteries of the Takenouchi, 7 Generations, Shinto and flowering of Zen Buddhism, leader of the later industrial civilization, Mt. Fuji, North Mariana Islands, Hiroshima, Nagasaki, atomic bomb/memory of Mars.

HAND ZONE
EQUATORIAL

N   S
Psi Plate II ᛘ ᛉ
Psi Plate III ᛏ ᛒ

Straddles Equator (North/South)

Core Family Blue (Mine the Tunnels), Zone of the Avatar, GK Earth
Focalization Point of the Influx of the Lost Knowledge of the Otherworlds
Zone of psychogeographic influence: Central, North & South Pacific, northern & eastern Polynesia, farthest reaches of the ancient Polynesian navigators, principle zone of influence, Hawaiian Islands, Hawaiian volcanos, last Polynesian kingdom contested by Japan, USA, WWII.

STAR ZONE
SOUTH TEMPERATE

Psi Plate III ᚴ

Signal Family Yellow (Unravel the Mystery)
Zone of the Artist, GK Venus, Focalization of Influx of Galactic Artistic Knowledge
Zone of psychogeographic influence: South Pacific Ocean, easternmost Polynesia, Easter island, Kontiki Aku Aku Ancient Star Mysteries, central Chile, and west Argentina, heart of Cordillera of the Southern Andes Mountain chain, southernmost reaches of Inca Empire, Mount Aconcagua seismic zone, Rim of Fire, Spanish Colonial Empire, liberator O'Higgens.

MOON ZONE
SOUTH POLAR

Psi Plate III ᚲ
Psi Plate IV ᚦ

Conclude
Red Chromatic/Blood Clan

Gateway Family Red (Open the Portals)
Zone of the Healer, (Ω) GK Mercury, Point of Influx of Galactic Healing Knowledge
Zone of psychogeographic influence: Western Antarctica, Antarctic Peninsula, southern South America, Patagonia, the Healing Heartland, southern Chile, southern Argentina, Falkland Islands, southernmost Atlantic Ocean, Tierra del Fuego, South Georgia, Sandwich Islands.

DOG ZONE
NORTH POLAR

Psi Plate II ᛗ
Psi Plate III ᚴ

Begin White Chromatic/Truth Clan

Polar Family White (Sound the Chromatics), Zone of the Compassionate One, (A) SP Mercury
Point of Influx of Solar Logos Love Frequencies
Zone of psychogeographic influence: North Pacific Ocean, easternmost Siberia, ancient land bridge to North America, shamanic migration of ancient Amerindians, Alaska, Mount McKinley, Eskimo culture, north-northwest Pacific coast cultures, now Alaska, 49th U.S. State and northwestern-most Canada/Yukon.

MONKEY ZONE
NORTH TEMPERATE

Psi Plate II ᚤ

Northwest Caribbean,
Mt. Shasta, Rocky Mountains

Cardinal Family Blue (Establish the Genesis)
Zone of the Magician, SP Venus, Point of Influx of Magical Powers of the Solar Logos
Zone of psychogeographic influence: Most of Temperate & Tropical North America, Mexico and Central America, Seat of great civilizations, Olmec, Maya, Toltec, Zapotec, Aztec as well as sedentary & nomadic North Amerindian cultures, Hopi, Navajo, Ute, Lakota, Cherokee, etc., seat of Mayan Calendar & Galactic Maya Home Base, prophecies of time (Sunstone), Quetzalcoatl, U.S.A. (except eastern seaboard), Mexico and Canada.

HUMAN ZONE
EQUATORIAL

N   S
Psi Plate III ᛏ ᛒ
Psi Plate IV ᛁ ᛇ

Straddles Equator (North/South)

Core Family Yellow (Mine the Tunnels)
Zone of the Sage, SP Earth, Point of Influx of Wisdom of Solar Logos
Zone of psychogeographic influence: South Central America, Central Caribbean, major part of South America, Amazon, Andes, Andean civilization, Chavin, Nazca, Tiahuanaco, Inca Empire, Macchu Picchu, Kontiki Viracocha, Keepers of the Wisdom of the Atlantean Star Elders, colonialist Catholic Empire, modern-day Brazil, Venezuela, Colombia, Ecuador, Peru.

SKYWALKER ZONE
SOUTH TEMPERATE

Psi Plate IV

Signal Family Red (Unravel the Mystery), Zone of the Prophet, SP Mars
Point of Influx of the Space of Prophecy of the Redemption of the Lost Planets
Zone of psychogeographic influence: South Atlantic (southern reaches of ancient Atlantean Empire), southwestern-most African continent, present-day Namibia & Republic of South Africa, Cape Town, Namib & Kalahari Deserts, mid-Atlantic coast of South America, urban Brazil (Rio, Sao Paolo), Uruguay and urban Argentina (Buenos Aires).

WIZARD ZONE
SOUTH POLAR

Psi Plate IV
Psi Plate I
Conclude
White Chromatic/Truth Clan

Gateway Family White (Open the Portals)
Zone of the Wizard, SP Maldek, Storehouse of the Lost Wisdom of the Otherworlds
Zone of psychogeographic influence: Antarctica, Queen Maud Land, east Antarctica, Valkyrie Dome, Atlantic Indian Antarctic Basin, point of generation: southeast African coast.

EAGLE ZONE
NORTH POLAR

Psi Plate III
Psi Plate IV
Begin Blue Chromatic/Sky Clan

Polar Family Blue (Sound the Chromatics)
Zone of the Seer, SP Jupiter, Planetary Fountainhead of Visionary Power
Zone of psychogeographic influence: North Magnetic Pole, Arctic Ocean, Greenland, Iceland, north Canada, Baffin Island, Queen Elizabeth Islands, Hudson Bay, Great Lakes, eastern Canada, eastern Seaboard, U.S.A. urban zone, global industrial world center, former Iroquois Nation, Eskimo shamans.

WARRIOR ZONE
NORTH TEMPERATE

Psi Plate IV

Cardinal Family Yellow (Establish the Genesis)
Zone of the Pathfinder, SP Saturn, Atlantean Pathways of Cosmic Consciousness
Zone of psychogeographic influence: projecting west from Giza Pyramid, northwest Africa, Sahara Desert, ancient Benin Empire, Ghana, Senegal, Algeria, Morocco, Libya, north Atlantic Ocean, ancient Atlantis "Beneath the sea she may be", pathways of the great sea-farers, Iberian Peninsula, Spain & Portugal.

EARTH ZONE
EQUATORIAL

Psi Plate IV
Psi Plate I
Straddles Equator (North/South)
Overlays of Hindu, Tribal with
Christian, Muslim

Core Family Red (Mine the Tunnels), Zone of the Navigator, SP Uranus
Synchrotronic Evolutionary Space of the Birth and Rebirth of the Human Race
Zone of psychogeographic influence: projecting south from Giza Pyramid, major portion of African continent, Egypt, Sudan, Ethiopia, Kenya, Mt. Kenya, Mt. Kilimanjaro, Nigeria, Congo River, Angola, Zimbabwe, Tanzania, Mozambique, the Heartland of the Human Race, zone of the rebirth from global industrial colonialist oppression, the original tribes of man.

MIRROR ZONE
SOUTH TEMPERATE

Psi Plate I

Signal Family White (Unravel the Mystery)
Zone of the Yogi(ni), SP Neptune, Oceanic Consciousness of Cosmic Memory
Zone of psychogeographic influence: Indian Ocean, Madagascar, Seychelles Islands, Mauritius, Chagos Archipelago, southwestern-most point of Australia, along with Hand zone as most oceanic of all the zones, Treasure Trove of the Lost Mysteries of the Cosmic Unconscious.

STORM ZONE
SOUTH POLAR

Psi Plate I
Psi Plate II
Conclude
Blue Chromatic/Sky Clan

Gateway Family Blue (Open the Portals), Zone of the World-Changer, (Ω) SP Pluto,
Magnetic/Transformative Field of Planetary Regeneration
Zone of psychogeographic influence: South Magnetic Pole, South Indian & Southern Oceans, Antarctica, Transantarctic Mountains, George V Land, Wilkes Land, Ross Sea & Ross Shelf, plasma generator of the Rainbow Bridge.

HUNAB KU 21
EARTH CORE
Psi Plate I
Psi Plate II
Psi Plate III
Psi Plate IV
Coordinates
Planetary Unification Cells

Generator of Solar-Galactic Electrodynamic Transmissions through Radio Polar Diffusion
Zone of the Magus of the Infinite, Solar-Galactic Root of Planetary Kuxan Suum
Seat of Noosphere Consciousness and Psi Bank Programs, Receptor of Solar Sunspot Cycle Transmissions

Crystal Iron Octahedral Inner Core: Radius 1216 km =64 (DNA) × 19 (command)
Outer Core Radius 2270 km. (1216+2270 = 3486 = BMU 399 ⊛) Lower Mantle Radius: 2185 km.
Upper Mantle to Crust: 700 km. Total Kilometers, Center to Crust Radius: 6371 km.

Planetary Zones of Influence

31. Contemplate the different positions and zones of influence—for example, from Atlantis into the Earth zone. The Yellow Human seal represents S/P Earth and is the genesis of the Inca civilization, south of the equator; this is the sole major exception to the Cardinal Family civilization genesis in the North. On the far right side/easternmost point of the yellow Saturn (Warrior) zone is the Great Pyramid. This is where Pluto, Neptune, Uranus and Saturn all meet. The westernmost point of this zone is where blue Jupiter, blue Venus, and yellow Earth meet with Saturn. This is the area of the Bermuda Triangle.

32. The civilization belt of the Cardinal Family comes into the Earth core—the red Uranus zone at the Great Pyramid—and then goes into Africa, the cradle of humanity. Note the location of the Congo River, Mt. Kenya on the Equator and the Great Pyramid at the northernmost point.

33. In the G/K Uranus Core Family zone is the ancient Hindu-Buddhist civilization centers as well as present day Southeast Asia and Indonesia. The island nation of Indonesia represents the easternmost point of Islamic civilization and is Islam's most populous nation.

34. The fourth horizontal band below the core is the secondary or subsidiary civilization belt of the Signal Family. This belt bears the imprint of the originating civilization that came from the north. Note that urban Brazil and Argentina, from Sao Paolo to Buenos Aires, are in the red Martian zone. These are all neo-European/neo-colonialist civilization centers. On the other side of the red Mars (Skywalker) zone is present-day South Africa which is also spawned by European civilization.

35. On the far right of the blue Saturn (Night) zone is Australia and New Zealand, which are also neo-colonialist civilizations, specifically British Commonwealth nations. Brazil, Argentina and Chile are all secondary civilizations. So, South America, subequatorial Africa, Australia and New Zealand with their major cities Santiago, Capetown, Buenos Aires, Sao Paolo, Rio de Janeiro, Sydney, Melbourne, and Auckland are civilization centers that originated in Europe.

36. The Signal Family complements the Cardinal Family and has similar effects or influence. These are the two hemispheric civilizational belts of the planet, and the principle zones of the consumer culture of globalization.

37. Just as the Polar and Gateway families share the same four planets (Pluto, Mercury, Maldek, and Jupiter), so do the Signal and Cardinal families (Mars, Saturn, Venus and Neptune). The equatorial core center holds the two biotelepathic circuit planets: Earth and Uranus. These two planets also control Earth's core, from which emanate the interdimensional time tunnels.

ACTIVATING EARTH'S MEMORY

38. Sixty years have now passed since Alice Bailey wrote *The Destiny of the Nations*, and the world has gone upside-down several times over. It is now clear that for the destiny of the Earth, the nation states need to be dissolved. This dissolution should be combined with a constructive changeover to bioregionalism and an organization of the human race into gatherings or groupings working with the five zones of interplanetary influence. These zones can be activated in several ways. The simplest way to begin is by locating the daily kin in the Planet Holon according to the 13 Moon, 28-day cycle.

---

13 MOON CALENDAR AND PLANET HOLON

The 13 Moon calendar is a daily program for identifying the human with the Planet Holon. The 20 solar seals combine with the 13 galactic tones to create the 260-unit synchronization sequence. This 260-day cycle is synchronized with the 365-day cycle to create the 13 Moon count. Note the prominent planet of each day. For example, if today we are in red Uranus, tomorrow will be in white Neptune, etc. This activation equalizes all zones.

---

39. From a higher-dimensional viewpoint, all zones share equal importance. For instance, the Mirror and Hand zones are mostly oceanic. The Mirror zone's main population center is Madagascar and the Hand zone's main feature is the Hawaiian Islands. The oceanic zones represent the aggregates of cosmic consciousness. The ocean represents the collective (un)consciousness of the planet. There is really only one ocean. The ocean is equalized; all zones include part of the ocean.

40. All continents and islands float in the one Earth Sea, as Ursula LeGuin called it. The Mirror zone, for instance, is the storehouse of Lemurian or "lost world" memories, "Neptune's bottom": the treasure house stored at the bottom of the ocean. The memories that are stored in the depths of the ocean in the Mirror zone set up different Lemurian currents that sweep through the bottom of Australia and enter the South Pacific where they seed Polynesia, Earth's present-day Lemurian culture.

41. Polynesia is in the Hand, Star, Night and Wind zones. Those Lemurian currents seed the Polynesian civilizations scattered across those islands, just like Atlantean currents go out from the North Atlantic swirling out into North and South America, Europe and Africa across the Sahara into Egypt and south into the heartland of the African continent.

42. The currents of consciousness of the previous races of humanity are oceanic. These oceanic currents are then picked up and recirculated as currents of consciousness by the wind and by the sea. That is why a visit to an ocean beach is so mystically all-absorbing.

43. Some currents on the surface of the ocean are activated through the wind, sending their influence into different parts of the world. For instance, Southern Australia continuously receives winds either from Antarctica (cold) across the Great Southern Ocean or from the northern desert regions (hot). The northern desert region is one of the largest desert areas on the planet.

44. Southern Australia is also one of the oldest continuously humanly inhabited places on the Earth tracing back 50,000 years or more with the Aboriginal civilization. These winds pick up the psychic currents of the Dreamtime (Night zone), and carry them to the rest of the world. However, with the disruption of the aboriginal people these are not always pleasant dreams.

45. Antarctica is the frozen continent of the "lost worlds." So when the winds blow up from Antarctica, the psychic charges stir and begin to circulate deep and ancient memories. All wind contains a psychic charge. Sometimes you can feel the "winds of change" or "ill wind blows no good"—these sayings indicate types of psychic currents carried in the winds. From the point of view of the interdimensional viewing screens in the AA Midway Station, every zone is of equal psychic importance.

PLANET HOLON – FIVE CIRCUITS

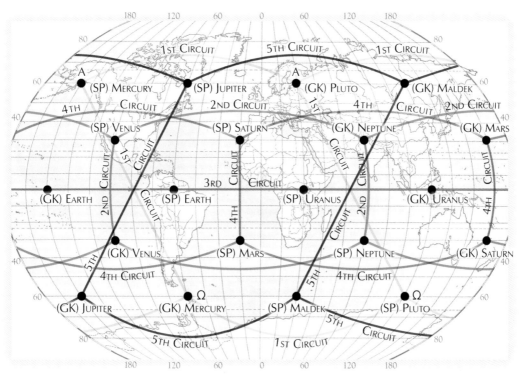

46. Every zone is a carrier of one of five circuits of planetary consciousness. On a daily basis, we can practice sending pulsations of conscious light into these zones by mentally activating the corresponding zone on the Planet Holon. We can also activate the zones through group meditations within our Earth families.

47. The Earth families create the structure of a new social organization. When a group of people consciously function within an Earth family then they can focalize their energies to charge one of the five horizontal bands of the planet. The group practice consciously engages the telepathic activation of a particular protectorate zone and thus, awakens the interplanetary force field. The more people practicing the greater the activation. This is a telepathic art that will increase as we move into the Aquarian Age, or age of the noosphere.

48. There are different psychic vortices of energy that ascend from each of the five zones, each containing its own particular quality of energy or interplanetary attributes. This energy is then absorbed through the electromagnetic field of the noosphere. This creates a cycle of reciprocal energy flows within the flux tubes at the poles.

49. Different vortices of energy open and send an impulse to those planets that represent the different zones. Once received, they come back as subliminal feedback from other worlds. It is the responsibility of the planetary geomants—the diviners of the Earth—to identify these vortices, cross-index them and keep them activated. Sometimes these are known as sacred centers.

50. We are at this very particular consciousness horizon at the brink of a new cycle. We can now develop our own biotelepathic feedback mechanism to raise and sustain higher levels of consciousness in different regions of the planet, and then stabilize at these higher levels.

51. When we reach the noospheric level, we will have raised the bar to fourth-dimensional continuing consciousness where we are susceptible to higher mind control. At this stage, our interdimensional selves are able to penetrate our waking consciousness, directing us on how to interpret or proceed with particular data, information and experiences, according to the zone that we might find ourselves in.

52. No metaphor in present-day consciousness can describe what will occur once we stabilize at this higher level. Subliminal and superconscious levels will open up and we will find ourselves engaged in unprecedented mental psychic activity. We will be a new evolved superhuman consciousness telepathically processing supermental orders of information and experiencing the cosmic evolution that characterizes Cosmic History.

PART IV
STAR MIND DESCENDING

Chapter 10

Pulsar Cosmology

"The wavespell is the primary template for evolutionary advancement provided by the codes of fourth-dimensional time. To understand the wavespell in its entirety is to reconstitute the epistemological bases and categorizations of human knowing."

—J. Arguelles, Call of Pacal Votan

1. Pulsar cosmology is a new methodology for modes of thinking that are capable of altering conditions in the material and immaterial worlds. Pulsar cosmology is the method. The wavespell is the form for practicing the method. With this method we enter Cosmic Creation.

2. Pulsar cosmology is a fourth-dimensional mental cosmology that is activated through practices of yoga and meditation. We are now well aware of the capabilities of the machine to recall vast amounts of information and connect us instantaneously with anyone anywhere on the planet. But what about exploring the vastly untapped potential of the mind?

3. We now have the telepathic/mathematical cosmological tools to penetrate into the higher dimensions. Pulsar cosmology is a key tool for learning to apply fourth-dimensional time science, which is essentially a science of the higher-dimensional mind.

4. Pulsar cosmology is a telepathic technology in its infancy on our planet, though it is similar to technologies used in previous world systems such as Atlantis. Telepathic technologies are utilized throughout the cosmos as civilizations advance and as human intelligence progresses from third- to fourth-dimensional operations.

5. Mind is the underlying power of machine technology. Soon, everyone will come to realize this. Pulsar cosmology is a mental technology that

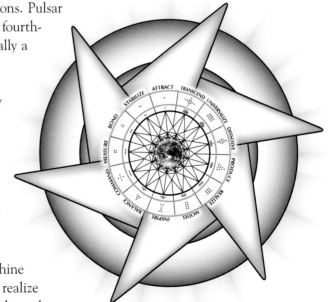

Radial Wavespell

relies solely on the development of mind power free from instrumentation and technological devices.

6. As we enter into cultivating mind more and more, we will realize that it is a tremendous vehicle and storehouse of methods and techniques that can replace altogether the material technology that is strangling the life of the planet.

7. Discovered in 1992 by Valum Votan, while working with and contemplating the pulsar geometries of the wavespell as first presented in the Dreamspell, pulsar cosmology is a largely unexplored telepathic technology with numerous implications. Pulsar cosmology is a dynamic creative capacity of telepathic mental visualization and projection that has been randomly utilized by people who can pick up certain paranormal techniques, i.e. clairvoyance, spoon bending, "mind over matter", etc.

8. As we develop these telepathic pulsar technologies we will see the potential of our mind as a powerful cosmic force. We will also realize other qualities of our mind that we may not have known existed. This knowledge of the true capacity and nature of mind will cause us to become morally enlightened as we see the actual nature of the universe.

9. While pulsar cosmology is a multi-leveled telepathic technology, is merely one aspect of the vast programs of time science revealed by the Law of Time. According to the Law of Time, the pulsar is a relational constant in time that can be plotted geometrically on the wavespell form. All numbers form a relationship with each other. Pythagoreans believed that humans could rise above their third-dimensional programs by meditating and telepathically communing with number "beings." This is also an aspect of the philosophy of the Law of Time.

10. In the cosmology of the Law of Time, several methods/tools are used to explore fourth-dimensional time, including: the wavespell and pulsars, the galactic compass (Sirian Wheel),

Maintaining a projective geometry form without mental thought formations cultivates continuing consciousness.

the Telektonon interplanetary circuit, and the 441 (21 × 21) number matrices (*see CHC Vol. V & VII*). For now we will explore more in depth the wavespell or pulsar cosmology.

11. Pulsar cosmology is based on the geometry of the fourth dimension. Geometry is a higher form of knowledge. Geometry is the study of spatial order through the measure and relationship of forms. Pulsar cosmology is the application of the spatial order in combination with the cyclic movement of time. This is a fractal order that has the power to increase or decrease in scale without losing its ratio and to move across time in fractal measures. We are talking about projecting a geometric structure in time.

GEOMETRY OF THE WAVESPELL

In the wavespell geometry of time, pulsars occur as a tetrahedron, the actual geometry of time that connects the first, fifth, ninth and thirteenth tones of the wavespell. This cosmic fractal of time, the most primary geometrical structure, also contains three triangulations.

Two of these triangles are isosceles. The second-dimensional sense pulsar, however, is an equilateral triangle connecting the third, seventh and eleventh tones. So we are dealing with three triangles and a tetrahedron. It is important to grasp the simplicity of the foundation of pulsar technology. The triangle is the most primary 2-D form. The tetrahedron is four triangles joined (when 3 triangles join to make a form, the 4th is naturally created). The tetrahedron is the primary geometry of 3-D form.

---

12. To begin to apply this cosmology it is important to first familiarize ourselves with the wavespell. Each wavespell can be thought of as a stairway, spiraling ever upward and onward. We are always evolving to a higher level, whether we perceive it in the moment or not. The idea is to work with the program and create increasingly conscious pulsars in time. (*Note: A supplemental pulsar cosmology leaflet is forthcoming for those who wish to study pulsar cosmology more in depth. Information about pulsars can also be found in the following works of Jose Arguelles/Valum Votan:* Dreamspell, The Arcturus Probe, Call of Pacal Votan *and* Time and the Technosphere).

A wavespell can be defined in the following ways:

1. A wavespell is a 13-unit geometry in time.
2. A wavespell is a cosmic, self-circulating fractal unit of measure.
3. A wavespell is a holonomic construct of multidimensional time.
4. A wavespell is a 13-unit form constant of fourth-dimensional time.
5. A wavespell is a lattice within which pulsars are structured.
6. A wavespell is a recapitulative and recombinant cosmology.
7. A wavespell is the primary template for evolutionary advancement profiled by the codes of fourth-dimensional time.

13. Plotting different durations of time onto a wavespell template allows us to see vast amounts of information as a single thoughtform. A wavespell can represent any proportion of time or it can be a means of encoding instructions, precepts, etc. Each unit can represent a day, a moon, a year or a billion years. *Cosmic History Vol. II* demonstrated the Wavespell of Cosmic Creation where the entire wavespell was equivalent to the 13.7 billion years of creation with each of the 13 units approximately equivalent to 1.054 billion years.

14. In the 13-unit wavespell there are two gates, two towers and nine chambers. Each of these 13 units has its own relation to each other.

1: **Magnetic Gate** (entry point)
2: Lunar chamber
3: Electric chamber
4: Self-existing chamber
5: **Overtone Tower**
6: Rhythmic chamber
7: Resonant chamber
8: Galactic chamber
9: **Solar Tower**
10: Planetary chamber
11: Spectral chamber
12: Crystal chamber
13: **Cosmic Gate** (exit point)

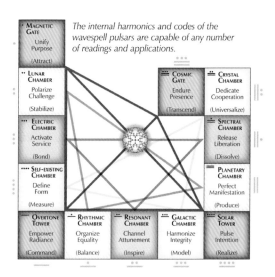

The internal harmonics and codes of the wavespell pulsars are capable of any number of readings and applications.

15. While the dimensional geometries of the wavespell are called *pulsars*, the definition of pulsar here differs from modern science's definition of the word. According to the Law of Time, a pulsar is an interdimensional intersection that penetrates the third-dimensional mind. A pulsar pulses at regular intervals within a 13-tone measure of time.

16. There are two types of pulsars: dimensional pulsars and overtone pulsars. The dimensional pulsars define the synchronically interconnected realms of the fourth dimension as functions of a four-color code. The overtone pulsars provide cross-dimensional time structures that reveal more

complex connections based on the fifth force power of 5. There are four types of dimensional pulsars and five types of overtone pulsars. The pulsar code allows us to track different patterns in space forward and backward through time.

17. By working with the pulsars we can: 1) Increase continuing conscious, whole systems and holographic thinking; 2) Move forward and backward in time—fractal time compression; 3) Encompass large spans of time in a single thoughtform; 4) Move from linear to radial/cyclical thinking/contemplation; 5) Organize and compile multi-leveled data and make connections that lead us to further distinctions of knowledge; 6) Perform many types of meditations and visualizations; 7) Plan our days, weeks and years in a simple, programmable, usable form; and 8) Increase our power of memorization and recall.

18. Working with pulsar cosmology brings the unification of universal telepathy into the present moment and provides the basis for multidimensional meditation. We use our focused mind to become the laser beams of these pulsars; this reorients and rearranges the synchronic order into a harmonic system, so that application of the pulsar cosmology augments telepathy.

PULSAR COSMOLOGY

185

DIMENSIONAL PULSARS (4 TYPES) AND THEIR FUNCTIONS

1. **Fourth-dimensional Time Pulsar**
    Tones 1 (Magnetic), 5 (Overtone), 9 (Solar) and 13 (Cosmic).
    Sum of tones = 28, the harmonic standard.

    Encompasses the realm of time and mind which enfolds all other realms. Unifies purpose through command, formalized action and magic flight.

2. **First-dimensional Atomic-Molecular Lunar Life Pulsar**
    Tones 2 (Lunar), 6 (Rhythmic) and 10 (Planetary).
    Sum of tones = 18, frequency of 18-dimensional universe.

    Encompasses the realm of biogeochemical changes (geobiology).

3. **Second-dimensional Sense Pulsar**
    Tones 3 (Electric), 7 (Resonant) and 11 (Spectral).
    Sum of tones = 21, frequency of unity of totality.

    Encompasses entire psychophysical realm of electrosensory thresholds (art and physics).

4. **Third-dimensional Mind-Form Pulsar**
    Tones 4 (Self-existing), 8 (Galactic) and 12 (Crystal).
    Sum of tones = 24, frequency of complex psychosocial mental reality.

    Encompasses the realm of mental and social development (cooperative cosmic order).

Note that the sum of all tones: $91 = 13 \times 7$, triangular of 13, mathematical basis of 13:20 frequency $(13 + 7 = 20)$

The two gates and two towers create the tetrahedron in time, or the fourth-dimensional time pulsar that informs, regulates and enfolds the other three pulsar movements. The tetrahedron is the minimal geometric form with maximum information-bearing capacity.

Each of the other three pulsars (life, sense and mind) form a triangle. So there is one master tetrahedron with three triangles inscribed within it. The tetrahedron represents the fourth dimension, while the three interlocking triangles represent the third dimension, or physical plane. However, the whole structure functions as one interlocking interdimensional whole.

OVERTONE PULSARS

Five Types of (Interdimensionally Integrating) Overtone Pulsars based on Vigesimal dot-bar Code

1. **One-dot (1, 6, 11):** Unify in the 1st tone, organize in the 6th tone, liberate in the 11th tone.

2. **Two-dot (2, 7, 12):** Polarize in the 2nd tone, resonate in the 7th tone, cooperate in the 12th tone.

3. **Three-dot (3, 8, 13):** Activate in the 3rd tone, harmonize in the 8th tone, transcend in the 13th tone.

4. **Four-dot (4, 9):** Measure form in the 4th tone, pulse intention in 9th tone = 1 line of force.

5. **Five-dot (5, 10):** Command in the 5th tone, manifest in 10th tone = 1 line of force.

The overtone pulsars are moved by the power of the overtone fifth as the units are all five tones apart.

Between the points creating the tetrahedron time atom there are a sum total of 26 vertices or axes. The differences and sums between the vertices create frequency intervals. The sum of the sums of the 26 vertices of pulsars and overtone pulsars is 364, the number of days in a solar year, $364 = 91 \times 4$. 91 is the sum of the tones of the wavespell (13:7) code. (See *The Arcturus Probe*, p. 191).

PULSAR MAGIC

Within a circle, inscribe the tetrahedron of the fourth-dimensional time pulsar; this represents the timeship. At the magnetic, overtone, solar and cosmic points, place one crystal each. The magnetic-point crystal represents the Earth and Moon; the overtone-point crystal represents the fifth force beam; the solar-point crystal represents the Sun; the cosmic-point crystal represents the Excalibur at the core.

At the central fifth point, the intersection of the two axes, is the human battery. Above is the sky, below is the Earth. According to your intention, chose one or more of the 26 vertices appropriate to whatever action you intend and practice your powers of mental projection.

—*The Arcturus Probe, Appendix*

---

26 Pulsar Vertices

4-D Time Pulsar
(6 vertices)

1-D Life Pulsar
(3 vertices)

2-D Sense Pulsar
(3 vertices)

3-D Mind Pulsar
(3 vertices)

One-dot Magnetic Overtone Pulsar
(3 vertices)

Two-dot Lunar Overtone Pulsar
(3 vertices)

Three-dot Electric Overtone Pulsar
(3 vertices)

Four-dot Self-existing Overtone Pulsar
(1 vertice)

Bar Overtone Pulsar
(1 vertice)

CELESTIAL HARMONICS

"Celestial harmonics, the dynamics of time, are to the fourth dimension what space dynamics or celestial mechanics are to the third dimension ..."

—*Dynamics of Time, 0.11*

19. The Dynamics of Time introduces us to *celestial harmonics*: the intelligent, purposive connections we make between different points in time or time vector points. A physical quantity has magnitude and direction. A time vector point has a frequency, magnitude and a direction (past, present, future); ascending, descending, radial, etc.

20. The main application of pulsar cosmology is to plot various cycles of time that represent specific time vector points. The connections that we unveil within the patterning illustrate different types of celestial harmonics. The 13 Moon calendar, along with other fourth-dimensional tools, such as the Dreamspell and Telektonon, familiarizes us with these basic patterns of celestial harmonics.

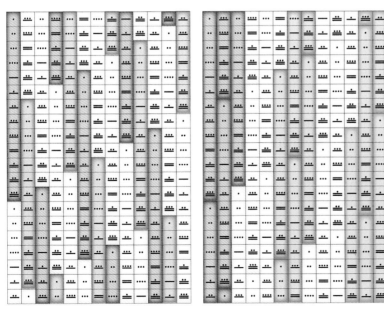

20 WAVESPELLS   **5 CASTLES**

In a 260-day Tzolkin cycle, there are 80 dimensional pulsars and 100 overtone pulsars. This creates numerous possibilities of celestial harmonics. Note that there are also more than 80 octaves of sound frequency, each governing a specific manifestation in the universe. Each 260-day cycle can be broken up into 20 wavespells. These 20 wavespells are arranged in five castles with four wavespells per castle.

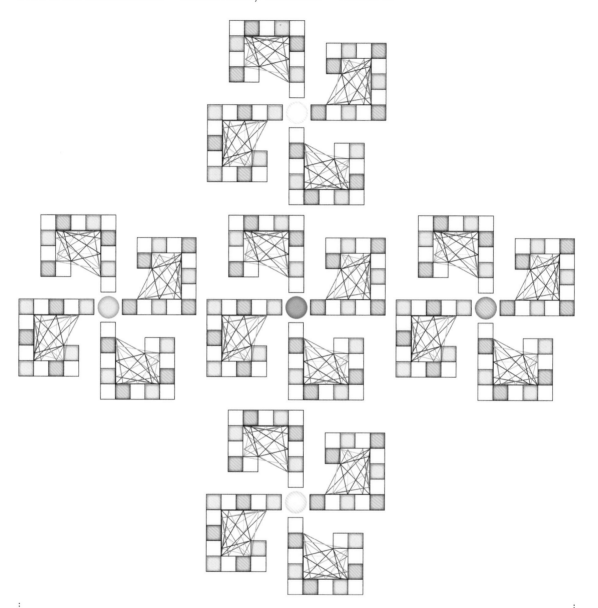

20 WAVESPELLS = 5 CASTLES

A castle of four wavespells (52 days = 13 × 4) consists of four tetrahedrons. Within each tetrahedron of time are the three other pulsars and five overtone pulsars. 52 (days) × 5 (castles) = 260. These are the internal structures.

a)   There are four dimensional pulsars per wavespell and 16 per castle (16 × 5 = 80 pulsars).
b)   There are five overtone pulsars per wavespell and 20 per castle (20 × 5 = 100 overtone pulsars).

WORKING WITH WAVESPELL/PULSAR COSMOLOGY

21. There are many applications of the wavespell and pulsar code that can be used in various meditation practices. These also can be seen as a means of planetary yoga. The wavespell can be applied in several ways in order to read information. It allows us to enter a particular cosmology that reformulates the history of the phenomenal world and the physical plane cosmos.

22. As we enter more fully into the noospheric phase of evolution on this planet, these types of mind technologies will be further developed. Following are a few examples of the many ways you can begin to work with pulsar cosmology. The more you work with them, the more they reveal to you.

23. Pulsar cosmology, like the time transport vehicles described in the *Dynamics of Time*, can be used/constructed for different actions in the following sequence:

   1. **Personal:** For restoration of personal magnetism and vitality.
   2. **Historic:** For correction of imbalanced collective social patterns including the elimination of toxic waste.
   3. **Interplanetary:** For the creation of the circumpolar rings for peaceful interplanetary relations; and for the restoration of the planetary flux tube system—or reconnecting and repairing the ruptured heliospheric program.
   4. **Galactic:** For exploration of higher-dimensional spiritual functions of the super- and subliminal consciousness.

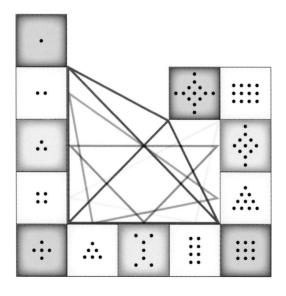

GALACTIC WAVESPELL

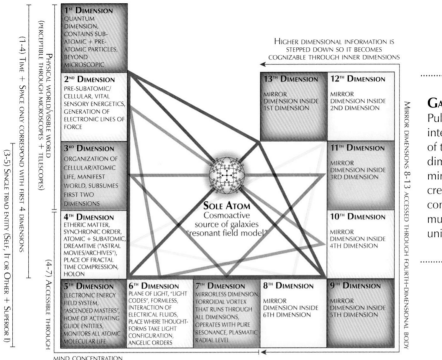

GALACTIC WAVESPELL: Pulsar demonstrates interactive relationships of the different dimensions and their mirror counterparts creating the rich complexity of the multidimensional universe.

HISTORIC WAVESPELL
THE HISTORICAL CYCLE AT A GLANCE
3113 BC – 2012 AD

HISTORIC WAVESPELL: Pulsar demonstrates the different karmic interactions between the various historical periods represented by the 13 baktuns. Each baktun is 144,000 days or a little less than 400 years. This wavespell example can be used to plot fractal time compressions.

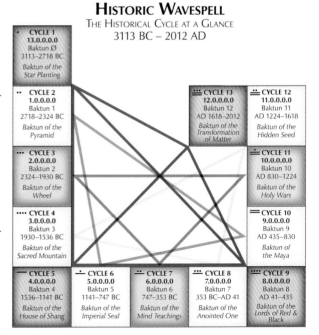

ADVANCED WAVESPELL/PULSAR COSMOLOGY PRACTICE

24. The galactic aspect is based on understanding biogeochemical transductions. It is also helpful to have some working knowledge of atoms, molecules and the periodic table of elements, as well as astrophysics especially as presented in Cosmic Science. This level has yet to be fully explored and activated.

    a) Reverse atomic/molecular spin through sensory teleportation exercises based on the wavespell geometry of time;

    b) Harmonic rearrangement of the synchronic order through biogeochemical transductions utilizing proton crystal geometries of different elements;

    c) Whole body sensory teleportation.

METHODOLOGY OF REVERSING ATOMIC-MOLECULAR SPIN

25. The key points to reflect upon and study are the wavespell geometry of the time pulsar consciously utilized to reverse atomic molecular spin.

26. To practice reversing atomic and molecular spin requires a corresponding system of knowledge. The first step is to understand what elements we are dealing with that constitute that particular atom or molecule. This can be found in the Periodic Table of Elements in which all of the elements are arranged in a particular order that corresponds to a type of binary arrangement.

27. It is important to understand that the elementary composite elements all have protons or nuclear structures that are constituted in crystalline geometric forms. These structures take the form of variations of tetrahedrons, octahedrons, hexagons and cubes. Octahedral is two tetrahedrons joined. The transposition of the cubic form and variations of the octahedron make it possible to formulate the pulsar geometries with proton crystal structures. Here is the step-by-step methodology:

    a. Determine the form structure of the particular proton molecule that the particular element you are working with takes. For example, we may choose to work with dissolving a particular uranium isotope so that it ceases to release radioactivity.

    b. Next we find out what type of crystalline structure of proton molecule an atom of that particular uranium isotope has. This will be an octahedron form.

    c. Then we can project a pulsar (time, life, mind or sense pulsar). We will know intuitively which to project.

d. Project that pulsar telepathically into the crystal structure of the proton of that particular element. With the tetrahedron time pulsar, for example, we can neutralize the tetrahedron/octahedron structure and deconstruct it by putting in its place a particular tetrahedral time pulsar. We are dealing with a principle of how time dissolves space, or a constituent element of space.

e. The projected geometry of the time pulsar would then go inside the crystal molecular structure of the particular proton of that atomic element and rearrange it or hit each of its vertices or corners, then neutralize and dissolve it. It might leave in its place either the geometric tetrahedral structure of the time pulsar and one of the triangulations, or it might dissolve the whole of the proton crystal structure, spectralizing it into nothing but the pulsation of its previous form.

The Periodic Table of the Elements

Lanthanide (•) and Actinide (••) series:
each of 14 (7×2) sequences or 14 groups.

Crystal Structures: C = Cubic, H = Hexagonal, M = Monoclinic, O = Orthorhombic, R = Rhombohedral, T = Tetragonal, ? = Unknown
(8 fundamental cubic types of proton-nucleic packing – crystalline order of reality)

* or 32 groups in 7 sets [Actinide + Lanthanide 14 added to other 18 groups = 32]
[=32 crystal symmetry types, periodicity 7 (maintain 7 periods) = Cosmic Creation]

28. This is a highly advanced telepathic technology. But it is not hard to develop if we have the right laboratory to define the crystalline structure of the proton nucleus of the different atomic elements and find out where the radioactive substance or toxic geochemical substance might be located and telepathically arranged to project a pulsar into it.

29. The pulsar would work for a specific duration. If it was a tetrahedron structure it would interact with a waveform of one of its other structures—a period of 8 days would deactivate the different intrinsic triangular or cube structures of the particular proton crystal. And over a period of time that would dissolve and there would be nothing remaining but a time pulsation as its essence returns to the original void/ether/akashic state.

30. To summarize, this particular transductive pulsar technology depends on first understanding the pulsar geometries and the crystalline proton structures of the different elements. Next, we must learn how to isolate those elements and project the particular wavespell geometry structure to

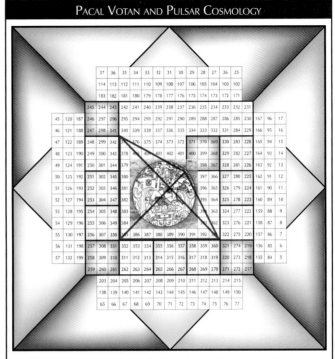

PACAL VOTAN AND PULSAR COSMOLOGY

Pulsar cosmology is a form of telepathic technology used in earlier civilizations and presently in cosmic telepathic civilizations. For example, Pacal Votan used a version of pulsar cosmology at various points of the event continuum of his stream of consciousness. We differentiate between his particular experience in his four katun elder cycle between 603 and 683 on the Christian calendar.

Pacal Votan's stream of consciousness extends back thousands of years when he was experiencing himself as a disincarnate consciousness operating with his etheric form body; he used pulsar cosmology at different points in time. When he spent time within the center of the Earth core, Pacal Votan used pulsar cosmology, as described, to scan different points in time according to larger wavespells. He could project forward and backward in time to set in place certain time vector possibilities in future moments for specific purposes.

deactivate that atomic elemental structure for a period of time. Depending on the nature of the proton structure we would know which particular pulsar to utilize for deactivation. This is the beginning methodology for how this process works.

TELEPORTATION EXERCISES

Harmonic rearrangement of the synchronic order through biogeochemical transductions are special case sensory teleportation exercises in which the wavespell geometry of the time pulsar is consciously utilized to reverse atomic and molecular spin. Time vector potentialities are coordinated from within the psi bank and biogeochemically located within a telepathic field. Utilizing techniques of collective sensory teleportation, a particular corruption may be "dissolved" back into its original condition of non-existent potentially and/or released as atmospheric radiance.

—Dynamics of Time, 10.4

31. Crystals are building blocks of solid matter; there are 32 types of crystal symmetry. There are 6 sides to a double terminated crystal and 6 triangular faces on each end. A perfect double terminated crystal has 18 faces.

32. The crystal structure of the proton can be located in the psi bank, the storage and retrieval system of the planetary mind that regulates timing cycles. Then we utilize a technique of sensory teleportation so that a particular corruption may be dissolved back into its original condition of non-existent potentiality and/or released as atmospheric radiance. This can be most effectively done with a collective projection.

33. For example, if five people are projecting a triangular or tetrahedral geometry into a particular proton, then the action of these five time geometries working on dissolving the special structure of a particular proton crystal holding a specific element together until it is dissolved over a period of 8 or 13 days, will release it as a form of atmospheric radiance or non-existent time potentiality no longer even existing in space. This is the methodology.

REARRANGEMENT OF THE SYNCHRONIC ORDER

"The same principle of pulsar geometry reversing atomic-molecular spin of enzymes, virus and bacterial forms are utilized for the rearrangement of the synchronic order of the genetic organic functions."

—Dynamics of Time 10.7

34. For the above, the same principle is utilized as in the previous methodology. Only here the idea is to isolate the different enzymes and amino acids, then take these enzymes into a particular codon which the enzyme structures activate. Then place the codon in a cube and telepathically isolate those specific enzymes within the DNA codon.

35. Next bring the pulsar geometries inside the cube and actively pulse, while visualizing the dissolution of the faulty structure and replacing it with a new codon structure and/ or dissolving it altogether, leaving it as a time pulsation or as an imprint of hyperorganic luminosity or radiance.

WHOLE BODY SENSORY TELEPORTATION

36. We must first develop the capacity to visualize and project when attempting whole body time transport. For example, if this is 8 Night and we want to ride a pulsar to the conclusion of this mind-form pulsar, then we can teleport ourselves with much advanced training into 12 Hand when this particular pulsar concludes. Why would we want to do that?

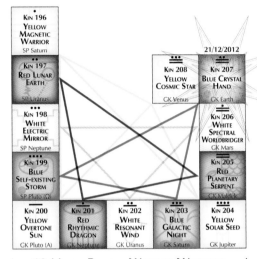

13 MOON PULSAR: WARRIOR WAVESPELL
KIN 196-208
Overtone Moon 26 – Rhythmic Moon 10
7 Storm Year (December 16 – 22, 2012)

37. Perhaps we foresee in the present something that could become dangerous or aggravated if not curtailed, so we project ourselves into the conclusion of the pulsar in order to view potential outcomes of situations that have developed in a particular point in time and see what the effects are.

38. When you teleport into a scenario you might see alternate and/or parallel universe possibilities and witness potential outcomes of events occurring in the present moment. Knowing this, you could return to the present moment and take actions that would be contrary to some of the parallel universe events that you experienced, providing yourself with a better alternative outcome.

39. These are some applications of the pulsar cosmology. The advanced stages of cosmic civilization use these pulsar cosmologies routinely. The application of these pulsar cosmologies is ultimately how the universe enters into an irreversibly harmonic path. However, without disciplined mind training—cultivation of supermental non-egoic samadhi—pulsar technology is difficult to practice. This is why pulsar technology is genuinely transcendental to our present mental state.

CHAPTER 11

GALACTIC DNA

1. We live in a holographic universe that is a projection from an adjacent light universe. This light universe emanates a particular mathematically programmed beam.

2. The multiple permutations of this program create a variety of combinations which, when translated into the third dimension, create silicon atoms, crystals, gases, various chemical compounds and other elements which, in turn, create different amino acids that create life.

3. Beneath the intricate structure of creation lies a mathematical matrix that is programmed to continuously cycle through various permutations. These permutations become the combinations of life or cosmic possibilities, such as the creation of different galaxies and supernovae. This is staggering to contemplate. In light of this mathematical matrix, what kind of permutation frequency is DNA—the code of life?

4. Many people think of DNA as molecules on a strand that twist in a double helix form weaving through human cells. Textbooks tell us that the double helix strand consists of two sides: a molecule of phosphate and a molecule of sugar. It is the bonding of the sugar and phosphate on each side of the strands that holds the DNA together. Doesn't that seem strange—sugar and phosphate?

5. Between each set of phosphate and sugar molecules is a strand of DNA. The essence of DNA is made of four nucleic amino acids: cytosine, thiamine, guanine and adenine. Amino acids are primary chemical elements in which an amino compound is bonded to an acid compound by the same carbon atom.

▬▬ TIME (ADENINE)	Cytosine and guanine are complementary and thiamine and adenine are complementary. These are written in binary letters: the adenine looks like the binary letter "time"; the thiamine looks like the binary letter "space"; cytosine looks like the binary letter "radiance"; and the guanine looks like the binary letter "mind".
▬ ▬ SPACE (THIAMINE)	
▬▬▬ MIND (GUANINE)	
▬▬ RADIANCE (CYTOSINE)	

199

6. These four nucleic amino acids are actually miniscule crystals that bond together in geometrical patterns. DNA is double-stranded. Each strand is coiled alongside the other to create a weaving or a loom (double helix) that is hard to break. This is just a chemical laboratory synthesis of an extraction of a microscopic component within the cells of every organism.

7. Two genetic scientists, American James Watson and British Francis Crick discovered DNA as we know it in 1953. They revealed that there are 64 letters written with four amino acids; this is actually 4^3 ($4 \times 4 \times 4 = 64$). These codons are code structures of universal life that, in their infinite number of arrangements, create all life forms. This is mind boggling to consider.

8. How can we understand that life comes from these little strands with four amino acids encoded within them? If we understand that life is a mathematical program, then we realize that all of life is nothing but permutations of a particular mathematical order.

9. As Watson and Crick discovered, there are 64 (and only 64) codes for writing all life possibilities with these four amino acids. Each of the 64 codons is written with three of the four amino acids to create mathematically 64, six-line structures identical to the hexagrams of the I Ching. Sixty four is not only 4^3 (four cubed), but it is also 8^2. Eight is the sixth function of the Fibonacci/logarithmic spiral. It is the middle function in 5:8::8:13 ($8 \times 8 = 64$; $5 \times 13 = 65 = 8 \times 8 + 1$).

10. In the Fibonacci sequence, the life code is derived from 8, the harmonic number that exists between five and thirteen. These numbers: 5, 8, 13, create a harmonic sequence. Five creates the pentatonic scale; eight creates the diatonic scale; and thirteen creates the chromatic scale—the whole and half tones.

11. The three numbers: 5, 8 and 13 are the essence of harmonic order. In this example, eight—the middle term—is the basis of life; thirteen is the basis of time; and five is the overtone power.

12. Life is the full expression of the harmonic frequency of the sequence between the overtone power (5) and the cosmic power of time (13). Life (8) + time (13) = 21 (the unity of totality), encoding the basic fractal principle of time and all higher-dimensional orders of cosmic existence.

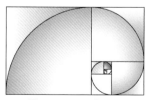

FIBONACCI SPIRAL
1:1:2:3:5:8:13

Cosmic Science and 64 DNA Codons

13. According to Cosmic Science, the genetic structure of the biological human relies on two patterns: the *electro-conductive* behavioral pattern and the *metabolic* pattern. The electro-conductive pattern controls the overall configuration of the structure of the body; and the metabolic pattern controls vegetative life and the autonomic functions as well as the parton structure—the six types of electricity.

14. The electro-conductive pattern relates directly to the 64-unit DNA code. This pattern is located in the upper part of the corpus callosum and is engraved in a template of *beta seroglobulin* through a control board of 64 runes that govern the 64 DNA codons.

15. This metabolic pattern rules the six types of electricity which were hidden in the 13th chamber of the Great Pyramid of RA. The DNA program and its transcendence are also contained within the 13 crystal skulls.

16. DNA programs are derived from what is popularly referred to as the *akashic records* and stored in the psi bank. These genetic programs are determined in accord with the karmic disposition of the entity that will incarnate on planet Earth. Karma accounts for assignment of parents, life circumstances and mission within the larger cycle of the Divine Cosmic Plan. All beings, whether conscious or not, are part of this vast master program.

17. Sixty-four is 4^3 (four cubed) or 8^2. In binary sequence, the seventh order is 64: 1, 2, 4, 8, 16, 32, 64. The power of seven is the power of creation; this is why Synchrogalactic Yoga is based on the power of seven, as are the seven volumes of the *Cosmic History Chronicles*.

18. Sixty-four is also the number of codons of the possibilities of life as arranged through the permutations of four amino

We are using words and images as a bridge to indicate the level of alteration within our own self-perception, consciousness, and genetic coding that is now occurring.

GALACTIC LIFE CODES
RADIAL MATHEMATICAL PROGRESSION OF THE 4TH DIMENSION

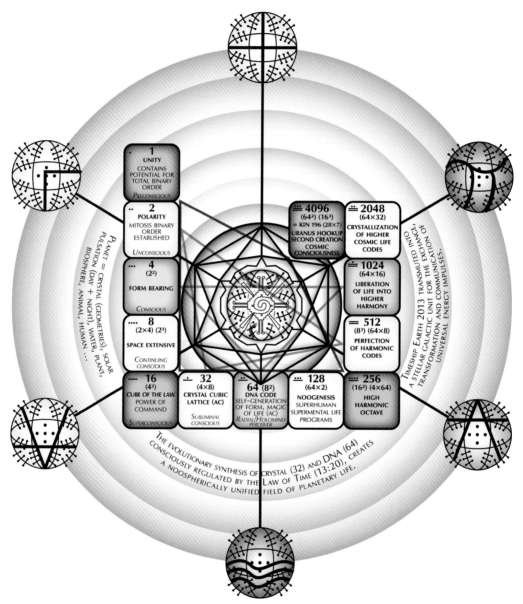

1
UNITY
CONTAINS POTENTIAL FOR TOTAL BINARY ORDER
PRECONSCIOUS

2
POLARITY
MITOSIS BINARY ORDER ESTABLISHED
UNCONSCIOUS

4
(2^2)
FORM BEARING
CONSCIOUS

8
(2×4) (2^3)
SPACE EXTENSIVE
CONTINUING CONSCIOUS

16
(4^2)
CUBE OF THE LAW POWER OF COMMAND
SUPERCONSCIOUS

32
(4×8)
CRYSTAL CUBIC LATTICE (AC)
SUBLIMINAL CONSCIOUS

64 (8^2)
DNA CODE SELF-GENERATION OF FORM, MAGIC OF LIFE (AC)
RADIAL/HOLOMIND PERCEIVER

128
(64×2)
NOOGENESIS SUPERHUMAN SUPERMENTAL LIFE PROGRAMS

256
(16^2) (4×64)
HIGH HARMONIC OCTAVE

512
(8^3) (64×8)
PERFECTION OF HARMONIC CODES

1024
(64×16)
LIBERATION OF LIFE INTO HIGHER HARMONY

4096
(64^2) (16^3) = KIN 196 (28×7) URANUS HOOKUP SECOND CREATION COSMIC CONSCIOUSNESS

2048
(64×32)
CRYSTALLIZATION OF HIGHER COSMIC LIFE CODES

PLANET = CRYSTAL (GEOMETRIES) SOLAR PULSATION (DAY + NIGHT), WATER, PLANT, BIOSPHERE, ANIMAL, HUMAN ...

A STELLAR GALACTIC UNIT FOR THE EXCHANGE OF TRANSFORMATION AND COMMUNICATION, UNIVERSAL ENERGY IMPULSES. TIMESHIP EARTH 2013 TRANSMUTED INTO

THE EVOLUTIONARY SYNTHESIS OF CRYSTAL (32) AND DNA (64) CONSCIOUSLY REGULATED BY THE LAW OF TIME (13:20), CREATES A NOOSPHERICALLY UNIFIED FIELD OF PLANETARY LIFE.

Sixty-four is the seventh unit in a binary sequence. The 13th unit in the binary sequence is 4096, 64 squared. In vigesimal code 64 million is the seventh order of the vigesimal sequence, and is written 1.0.0.0.0.0.0.0. As the seventh and thirteenth sequences in the binary order, 64 and 64 squared, correspond to the fundamental ratio of the Law of Time, 13 and 7.

acids. This is a further mathematical demonstration of the numerical sequence of and underlying basis of life.

19. The arrangement of the numbers in the different sequences—the Fibonacci/logarithmic sequence, vigesimal code, etc—all show that what we call the basis of life, formulated as DNA, is derived from a program of harmonic mathematical permutations expressed in different ways.

20. Cosmic time is programmed into the whole arrangement of 64 codons, demonstrating that life is coordinated by the 13:20 frequency.

16	50	9	55	11	53	14	52	= 260
1	63	8	58	6	60	3	61	= 260
64	2	57	7	59	5	62	4	= 260
49	15	56	10	54	12	51	13	= 260
48	18	41	23	43	21	46	20	= 260
33	31	40	26	38	28	35	29	= 260
32	34	25	39	27	37	30	36	= 260
17	47	24	42	22	44	19	45	= 260
= 260	= 260	= 260	= 260	= 260	= 260	= 260	= 260	

Magic Square of 8

In a magic square of eight—a 64-unit matrix—the numbers in each row (vertically and horizontally) add up to 260, which is the 13:20 frequency of time.

When numbers 1-8 are laid out in a sequence of 8 rows, 1-8, 9-16,... 57-64, any two numbers that are radially opposite from each other will add up to 65 (5 × 13). Five and thirteen are the two numbers on either side of eight in the logarithmic spiral. This sequence is 5:8::8:13. (8 × 8) = 64; (5 × 13) = 65. We see that the relationship between 64 and 13 is mathematically inviolable, when the array of 260 × 8 is added it equals 2080 = 65 × 32.

Sixty-four is the power of creation of life and life is dependent on time—the power of 13—for its unfolding or evolution. Also note that when the numbers 1-64 are placed into 8 sequences of 8, where each row ends with the next multiple of eight, the sum of all numbers in the eighth column is 288—the harmonic of polar light: 8 + 16 + 24 + 32 + 40 + 48 + 56 + 64 = 288 (12 squared × 2).

DNA Transmigration and Lost Worlds

21. How is DNA dispersed and how did it get to this planet, V.24.3? Was it planned, or part of a larger program?

22. According to Cosmic History, the karma now playing out on Planet Earth was passed to this planet from other worlds, namely Mars and Maldek (now the Asteroid Belt) (see *CHC Vol. II*). The Velatropa sector in which our star system is a focal point had long ago been designated an "experimental zone" by design engineers working on behalf of the "Divine Plan." This sector had been seeded with DNA aeons earlier in order to accommodate the more experimental aspects of the program.

23. When Maldek was destroyed, the unresolved karma was carried to Mars via a *radiogenetic time ark*, the invisible mind-thread carrying genetic information, transmitted like radio waves from one point to another.

24. A civilization was then created on Mars, which also eventually went extinct due, most likely, to nuclear destruction or possibly an errant asteroid from the destroyed planet Maldek, or both. At this point, all accumulated and unresolved karma from both Mars and Maldek was sent to Earth via this same radiogenetic time ark. The final cycle of Earth, V.24.3, represents the climax of the experimental program set in motion aeons ago.

25. In the "end times" playing out, Maldek represents World War I, Mars represents World War II and Earth carries the potential for WWIII. War is the institutionalization of a primal carnal crime originated on Maldek and transferred to Mars (god of war).

26. From a cosmobiological point of view, we may ask: What is war? Is it necessary? Or is it a phase or stage of consciousness when spirit, evolving through matter, has not yet penetrated the veils of ignorance nor understood the workings of karma, the laws of cause and effect?

27. As the collectivization of the untamed capacity for aggression, war is an institutionalized program that embodies a purely destructive force. To counteract the blind destructive nature of war and aggression, the cosmic spiritual force evolves itself through souls who seek transcendence from conflict altogether. (Some souls, who were close to reaching an enlightened state in previous worlds, were born on this planet with a new genetic code that cannot conceive of war and destruction. These are the ones who keep the memory of the Original Source alive and are co-creators of the new world).

28. In order to accelerate and further this final stage of the program, the 13:20 synchronization beam was overlaid on the 5,125-year cycle to bring it to a particular ripening. This cycle is divided into 13 baktuns, each consisting of 144,000 days. (Note to future readers: This particular 5,125-year holographic movie concluded on 21/12/2012. A new cycle (and holographic movie) commenced on the Yellow Galactic Seed, (26/7) 2013).

13 & 7

In 2003, leading scientists affirmed that the age of the universe was 13.7 billion years. This statement was declared at the same moment that the Law of Time was articulated, with its root frequencies, 13 and 7, which establish the 13:20, the seven being the implicit factor. The 13-7 factor shows that the age of the universe (as we have come to understand it) is a function of a program of a master synchronotron beam based on two key numbers: 13 and 7 which establish the totality (20).

GENETIC PATTERN AND BINARY SEQUENCE

29. Every living being has a particular genetic pattern based on a specific mathematic permutation. Translated into the third dimension, these mathematical permutations also create the possibility for 20 different amino acids to come into existence, providing further mathematical patterns through the creation of DNA—and consequently of chromosomes of which the human has four types.

30. According to Cosmic Science, the genetic pattern contains both a third- and fourth-dimensional form. Cosmic Science defines a *gene* as a "capsule or quanta of energy around which is coiled a *mertanica vidica* (mertanica is the interaction of four partons creating an electronic line of force) with multiple recordings impressed into it." This conforms to the standard scientific definition of a gene as the fundamental unit of inheritance and function within a cell.

31. These "gene recordings" represent the particular karmic programs that the entity is born with. After these lines of force are engraved, the mertanica vidica lines dissolve, leaving an imprint (genetic pattern) in the ovum. A gene is presently defined as a specific section of DNA that codes a recognizable cellular product.

32. No matter how infinite the magnitudes of numbers, all life is based on specific finite mathematical programs that can be reduced to different orders like the Fibonacci sequence, the binary sequence, Law of Time and its 13:20 ratio.

TIME RELEASE

Continuous discoveries occur at an accelerated speed as life unfolds. In 1987, we discovered that the spectrum of our Babylonian stage is a process 5,125 years in duration. This knowledge was derived from contemplation of the meaning of the tomb of Pacal Votan. In 1952, the tomb of Pacal Votan was opened and in 1953, DNA, the code of life, was discovered, followed by the discovery of the Earth's radiation belts (Van Allen). The DNA is actually a program encoded in the resonance between these two belts—the psi bank.

33. DNA is generally explained in terms of third-dimensional chemical functions. These chemical functions are also manifestations of higher-dimensional mathematical matrices capable of creating infinite orders of recombinant permutations.

WHERE ARE WE NOW?

34. Presently, the planetary DNA has attained an extraordinary level of complexity including the extrusion of a machine technology in the form of the technosphere. This 5,125-year cycle is a function of a master 13:20 lens that can be focused into cycles and sub-cycles.

35. The lens we have been operating in within the historical cycle has been a synchronization and acceleration beam. This has been applied to a situation in which it was known by the higher intelligence of the command star councils and the Galactic Maya that the species was going to enter into an intense cycle of working out its karma.

36. In this process, the atheistic Darwinian evolution story is replaced by the story of a cosmic engineering program. This story views Earth as a cosmically contained experiment with karmic loads of accumulated collective error that are being exhausted. In the process of working out this karma, the human species has inevitably veered in the direction of artificial time: The 12:60 frequency.

37. The dissonance in the human species is a result of the variance between the 13:20 synchronization beam and the 12:60 mechanistic wave frequency of the civilized process. The human species has now reached a stage of civilized lifestyles and ever-evolving technology, while simultaneously developing a greater propensity to diseases, depression and general social and environmental disorder.

38. All programs that are operating at the final stage of the cycle are dissonant programs; programs with the intrinsic 13:20 harmonic frequency of DNA became dissonant at a preconscious cellular level. These dissonances are reinforced by habits and customs of attempting to adapt to the dissonance, rather than striving to return to the 13:20 harmony.

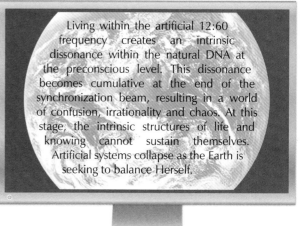

Living within the artificial 12:60 frequency creates an intrinsic dissonance within the natural DNA at the preconscious level. This dissonance becomes cumulative at the end of the synchronization beam, resulting in a world of confusion, irrationality and chaos. At this stage, the intrinsic structures of life and knowing cannot sustain themselves. Artificial systems collapse as the Earth is seeking to balance Herself.

39. These dissonances are the result of being cut off from the Primal Source, the Central Intelligence, or God. The machine and the technological process have replaced the need for God, or a Supreme Divine Ordering Principle, or so it would seem.

40. Today, the genetic store is weakened as witnessed by the number of diseases, obesity and other genetic problems, which are further impacted by exposure to radiation and toxic wastes, mercury and lead poisoning and genetically modified food, to name a few.

41. During this 5,125-year cycle the soul essences of the beings who have been incarnating on this planet have come here to embody, learn and work out different unresolved karmic memories that occurred in previous worlds and in previous dimensions, but are now here to be resolved. At the same time, from the cosmic engineering point of view, these incarnations are also here to experience a "testing"—a kind of spiritual survival of the fittest.

DNA AND THE LAW OF TIME

42. The Law of Time entered human awareness some 25 years before the end of the historical cycle (1987), activating a level of consciousness and perception previously unknown on this planet. This knowledge accelerated the activation of DNA, both human and planetary.

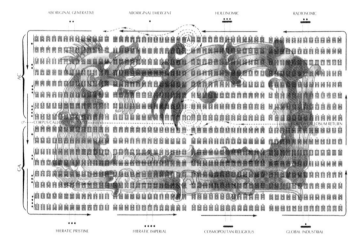

43. According to the Law of Time, in the new collective mental frequency (13:20), money and machine obsession (12:60 frequency) will be replaced with the wonderment of exploring the secrets of the universe through our own mind. We will be happily occupied with artistic processes of transformation exploring our new-found mental capabilities to beautify the Planet and discover the hidden secrets within nature.

44. This tendency to transform the environment—even the whole Earth into a work of art—will be greatly furthered by the new timing standard of 13 moons, 28-days. Built into this calendar—synchronometer—is the capacity to build on ever more harmonically interlocking codes of the synchronic order, the full application of the 13:20 frequency.

45. Within the 13:20 frequency our functioning is syntropic—of ever greater harmonic arrangements and rearrangements of reality. We are now transiting out of the 12:60 entropic machine frequency that characterized the historical cycle. In an entropic system, energy continuously dissipates. Everything gets old quickly, as symbolized by the machine that needs

constant upgrading and new program installations so that it will not become "outdated". This is the ultimate state of entropy.

46. Syntropy means turning together in ever greater arrangements and harmonic permutations of life. Syntropic functioning occurs when we have realigned our DNA with the universal harmonic order of natural time. This reintegration heightens our frequency giving rise to a whole other order of being; we will become both individually and collectively harmonized works of art.

47. The understanding of DNA synchronized and amplified by the Law of Time resulted in the formulation of the functioning of 64 codons with the 64 UR runes of Cosmic Science to create a 16-year—832-week—program between 1997 and 2013.

48. Since each codon runs through a process of 13 permutational possibilities there are 832 (64 × 13) total possibilities, the same as the number of weeks in 16 years. During this cycle, the 64 codons of the DNA have been placed in a process of time so that every 6 days a codon runs through its six permutations and at the end of a week it is imaginally placed in a cube.

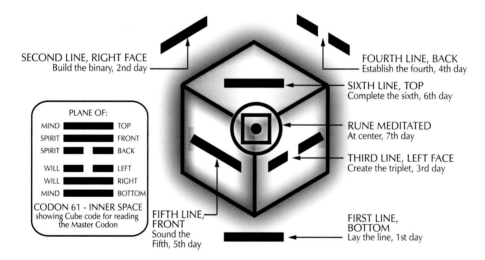

49. According to Cosmic Science, there are 64 behavioral UR runes that establish the individual in chronological form by evolutionary spans corresponding to eight-year cycles for each sequence of runes.

50. As the genetic code, these behavioral pattern runes are also modified in accordance with the mediating atmosphere (parental or family conditioning), and the social and educational atmosphere (studies and behavioral parameters). All the excess or "rejected" material is defaulted into the second (unconscious) mental sphere (see Chapter 3).

OCTAVE 4 STRAND 12	OCTAVE 5 STRAND 13	OCTAVE 6 STRAND 14
89 MORPHO-GENESIS ESTABLISHES GALACTIC ART WHOLE	97 UNION OF ASCENT AND DESCENT	105 OCTAVE OF INFINITE MIND WAVE
90 GALACTIC ART WHOLE DEFINED BY TIME	98 TIME EQUALIZED BY UNION OF ASCENT AND DESCENT	106 INFINITE MIND WAVE FLOATS IN TIME
91 GALACTIC ART WHOLE DEFINES SPACE	99 SPACE PERFECTED BY UNION OF ASCENT AND DESCENT	107 INFINITE MIND WAVE ILLUMINES SPACE
92 GALACTIC ART WHOLE BECOMES STRUCTURE OF REALITY	100 UNION OF ASCENT AND DESCENT ESTABLISHED AS COSMIC SPACE	108 INFINITE MIND WAVE BECOMES WAKING CONSCIOUSNESS
93 STRUCTURE OF REALITY EVOLVED BY TIME	101 SYSTEM OF COMMAND ACTUALIZED IN TIME	109 WAKING CONSCIOUSNESS IDENTIFIED AS TIME
94 STRUCTURE OF REALITY BECOMES ARCHITECTURE OF SPACE	102 SYSTEM OF COMMANDS EVOLVES COSMIC SPACE	110 WAKING CONSCIOUSNESS DISCRIMINATES SPACE
95 GALACTIC ART WHOLE BECOMES MEDITATION OF REALITY	103 CHANNEL OF COMMAND BECOMES SELF-EVOLVING	111 INFINITE MIND WAVE REFLECTS INFINITY
96 GALACTIC ART WHOLE GIVES FORM TO COSMIC CONSCIOUSNESS	104 CHANNEL OF COMMANDS CREATES COSMIC ORDER	112 INFINITE MIND WAVE EVOLVES INFINITY

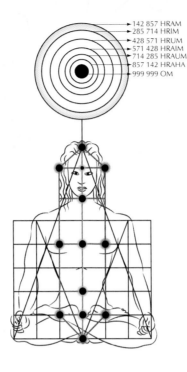

142 857 HRAM
285 714 HRIM
428 571 HRUM
571 428 HRAIM
714 285 HRAUM
857 142 HRAHA
999 999 OM

OCTAVE 1 STRAND 9	OCTAVE 2 STRAND 10	OCTAVE 3 STRAND 11
65 OCTAVE OF DIVINE DECREE "BE!"	73 COMMAND OF COSMIC CREATION REALIZED AS TREE OF COSMIC FIRE	81 RADIOGENESIS ESTABLISHES GALACTIC LIFE WHOLE
66 DIVINE DECREE ESTABLISHES TIME OF 2ND CREATION	74 TREE OF FIRE DEFINED BY RING OF TIME	82 GALACTIC LIFE WHOLE EVOLVED AS TIME
67 DIVINE DECREE ESTABLISHES SPACE OF 2ND CREATION	75 TREE OF FIRE EXTENDS TO FOUR QUARTERS OF SPACE	83 GALACTIC LIFE WHOLE EXTENDS INTO SPACE
68 DIVINE DECREE ESTABLISHES FIRMAMENT OF 2ND CREATION	76 COMMAND OF COSMIC CREATION ENLIGHTENS FIRMAMENT	84 GALACTIC LIFE WHOLE BECOMES MEDIUM OF TRANSMISSION
69 FIRMAMENT DIVIDES TIME	77 FIRMAMENT DEFINES MOVEMENT OF TIME AS DAY-NIGHT	85 GALACTIC LIFE WHOLE CHANNELS TIME
70 FIRMAMENT DIVIDES SPACE	78 DAY-AND-NIGHT DEFINES COSMIC SPACE	86 GALACTIC LIFE WHOLE CHANNELS SPACE
71 DIVINE DECREE UNIFIES TIMESPACE	79 TREE OF COSMIC FIRE GENERATES PLANET MIND	87 TIMESPACE UNIFIES GALACTIC LIFE WHOLE
72 TIMESPACE ESTABLISHES COSMOS AS ONE UNIVERSAL MIND	80 TREE OF COSMIC FIRE RETURNS TO SOURCE AS STAR MIND	88 GALACTIC LIFE REALIZED AS COSMIC CONSCIOUSNESS

Galactic DNA: New Programs

Beyond the 64 UR runes are a further set of runes: the six-octave, 48 UR runes of the Hexameride of the Octave (see CHC Vol V, Chapters 12, 13).

The next level consists of 128 DNA 12-strand program as presented in the Appendix. In this program the primordially absolute radial order 0-63, provides an informative foundation for the 1-64 order of the present psi bank sequence.

The new sequence functions as a corrective radial strengthening of the present codon series. Their appearance is a function of the quantum frequency shift that closes the cycle. Until now they have been a latent potentiality in the psi bank.

The six new rune strands are pure fourth-dimensional resonant structures overlaid on the 64 codons to create a higher harmonic vibration of different "musical" resonances that strengthen the program of the 64 DNA. We also know that the 64-unit DNA runs a particular program that in its sequencing creates an entity known as the Planetary Manitou, which is the single collective mind of the noosphere. This is what we tune into.

THE 64 CODONS - THE EIGHT RUNE STRANDS

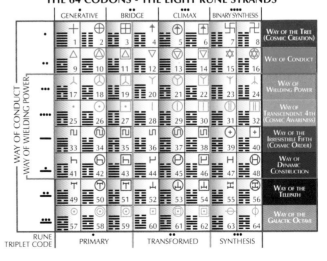

51. These 64 runes act as corrective filters of the extrasensory stimulation, while conditioning classifies them and alters them into recognizable patterns so that they may be interpreted, either correctly or incorrectly, by the third mental sphere (consciousness).

52. The UR runes function as magnetic attractors in the corpus callosum; this is where the bridge of the holomind perceiver is being constructed between right and left hemispheres (3rd and 4th dimension). The two hemispheres have been developed but the corpus callosum has not. The corpus callosum is an inverse binary unifying tissue.

53. The UR runes are part of an evolutionary development that is occurring within the corpus callosum. As magnetic attractors, the UR runes attract the DNA codons. These are also inscribed to create a resonance within the psi bank.

54. When this resonance is established, it allows the possibility of integration with the timing frequency which breaks down into four sets of 64 (256 in all or 16 squared), then completed by the four master codes of the cosmic matrix (Kin 257-260).

55. This 832-week phase completes in 2013, when a new cycle begins. When it completes itself, there will be a type of mental click within the psi bank and we will be radiated, reformulated and harmonized: A new technicolor 128 DNA codon structure will light up in our being.

56. At this stage, both sides of our brains and bodies will be functioning as an integrated unit. The Ida and Pingala, right and left sides of our brain, the AC/CA currents, will be balanced and coordinated by the new perceptual organ, the holomind perceiver. The essentials of Synchrogalactic Yoga will be in place.

57. We are now passing into a new cosmic cycle of universal attunement where the 64 DNA codons and UR runes are harmonized by the

REPORT FROM OTHER SIDE OF 2013 ...

In the cycle of history, humans operated primarily within the spheres of instinctual preconscious and unconscious, barely touching on the conscious.

During the cycle of history, instinctual programs were overwhelmed by the unconscious mind. The instinctual and unconscious aspects of being served to tyrannize the human race.

After the humans passed the 2012 Omega Point and entered 2013 they passed out of a particular synchronization beam to finally synchronize with this planet entering into the anticipated new phase of evolution: the Psychozoic Era.

48 UR harmonic runes and organized anew by the 128 codon templates to be telepathically inserted into our brain.

58. By attuning ourselves to this program we will attain a supermental, superconscious capacity, functioning with 100 percent of our brain power. Though we have recently projected our power into the speed of computers, our brain can work at a faster rate.

59. We do not have to invent chips and wires; our brain is already wired for high level cosmic computation. As we enter the noosphere, we will find that the original mathematical programs from which the DNA was generated are already in our brain.

60. We are transitioning from individualized, illusory states of consciousness into a state of consciousness where the collective mind is functioning as a multiple but single totality: the Planetary Manitou. This Planetary Manitou can be thought of as a large spirit entity; it is the telepathic soul or life of the planet itself.

New Program Begins

61. Once our Galactic DNA upgrade is complete and we are fully harmonized in 13:20 time, we will find that all activity will be artistic; everything will be art. Yogic activity will be our chief form of entertainment as we explore ranges and spectrums of cosmic experience that we had not previously been aware of.

62. With this new level of awareness, we will no longer give ourselves away to external roles and forces. We will operate autonomously according to inner impulses while simultaneously participating in the great single collective mind of the Planetary Manitou.

63. We will discover that our perceptual capacity is radialized with a 360-degree perceptual field. Our every day functioning will bring us continuous cosmic perceptions that will reveal every day magic. The world will feel new, fresh—as if it was just being born before our eyes. The daily duties of third-dimensional life will become spiritually cosmified as we will be operating with a third- and fourth-dimensional double-decker mind simultaneously.

64. Functioning with this double-decker mind opens us to a whole range of information circuits, loading and unloading from different dimensions simultaneously. Communications will naturally occur with other beings, entities and intelligences both here and elsewhere in the

galaxy. This defines a process of cosmic life rearrangement. One of the purposes of the 128 codon Galactic I Ching is to help us adjust to this "double-decker" mental functioning (see Appendix: *Galactic I Ching*).

We are now entering the crystalline path. Our DNA is being transformed by the Master Artist. As DNA changes, so does our world. In the new world, art is an inescapable activity and quality of our lives. We will be amazed at what forms of reality we can project through our sense organs.

CHAPTER 12
NOOGENESIS—A TELEPATHIC ART

1. Noogenesis is a purely mental process—the practice of a telepathic art beyond the physical or biological stages of evolution. Its foundation is a samadhi-like consciousness that is predicated on an anticipated descent of the supermind, the consciousness and power of the infinite.

2. This heightened receptivity of this earthly state of mind becomes like a vacuum capable of attracting higher or even "alien" extraterrestrial intelligence. At the same time the focus of the samadhi is the compassionate activation of the mind of the planet, the noosphere. This is the description and premise and purpose of noogenesis as a telepathic art.

3. *Noogenesis* is birth of the noosphere through a mental (noo) genesis, a mind "rebirth", while simultaneously embodying the descent of a "Sirian" personality, hence, Sirian rebirth. This is how we incarnate or embody extraterrestrial intelligence—intelligence that has been generated outside of the planetary sphere for the purpose of activating the next stage of (superhuman) evolution.

4. In this case, the intelligence being incarnated is a mindstream emanated from the Sirius star council of the Galactic Federation. It is from this council that the Galactic Mayan codes of time have been projected. The Sirian persona is incarnated into an already existing terrestrial entity or entities who have fully prepared themselves for this eventuality. The Sirian persona is a telepathic channel open to the frequency lines of all beings.

5. Extraterrestrial intelligence is not subject to the conditionings of the thought programs that exist on the surface of this planet. By engaging a specific program, the intention is to transcend outworn thought programs and embody or incarnate a formulation of new thought and knowledge based on an extraterrestrial perspective.

6. These higher-dimensional thought templates are programmed by different sets of frequencies that are resolved through the instrument of the *Synchronotron.* To understand this new program, we must follow a specific process. This is where the practice of yoga comes in.

7. The practice of yoga prepares us for the possibility of noogenesis. This comes about through the activation of prana descending and apana ascending, and the two currents, Ida and Pingala, that

crossover from the lowest chakras up to the crown chakra. These two currents, or channels, mirror the double helix strands of DNA.

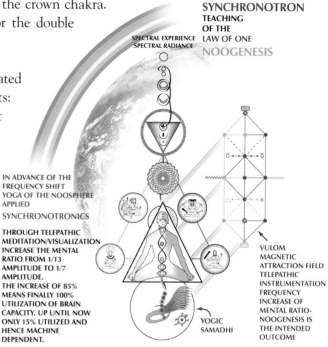

8. These pranic channels become potentiated forms of etheric/bioelectrical currents: a blue current (Ida) and a red current (Pingala). Through the holomind perceiver codes, these two currents crossover and become an activating form of a higher mental life, the basis of noogenesis.

9. What we think of as reality is actually a function of frequency beams that are projected subliminally to different sections of the brain. These frequency beams register and cause certain responses that create illusory pictures of the world that we perceive as real.

SYNCHRONOTRON TEACHING OF THE LAW OF ONE

SPECTRAL EXPERIENCE SPECTRAL RADIANCE

NOOGENESIS

IN ADVANCE OF THE FREQUENCY SHIFT YOGA OF THE NOOSPHERE APPLIED SYNCHRONOTRONICS

THROUGH TELEPATHIC MEDITATION/VISUALIZATION INCREASE THE MENTAL RATIO FROM 1/13 AMPLITUDE TO 1/7 AMPLITUDE. THE INCREASE OF 85% MEANS FINALLY 100% UTILIZATION OF BRAIN CAPACITY. UP UNTIL NOW ONLY 15% UTILIZED AND HENCE MACHINE DEPENDENT.

YOGIC SAMADHI

VULOM MAGNETIC ATTRACTION FIELD TELEPATHIC INSTRUMENTATION FREQUENCY INCREASE OF MENTAL RATIO- NOOGENESIS IS THE INTENDED OUTCOME

13 BAKTUN MENTAL RATIO FREQUENCY 76923 → SHIFT + 65934 → 2013 → 142 857 FREQUENCY.

THREE TYPES OF GENESIS

10. Noogenesis implies something born, generated or brought about through mind. The term was coined by Pierre Teilhard de Chardin who was also co-responsible for the word and concept of the noosphere. De Chardin described noogenesis as a world that is *being born* instead of a world that *is*.

11. Within the structure of Cosmic History, we define three types of genesis: *radiogenesis, biogenesis* and *noogenesis. Radiogenesis* is the primary process of engendering life and matter programs, inclusive of the DNA program, by means of resonant frequency beams. Where did DNA come from and how did it get here?

12. The DNA arrived to this planet through high frequency projections beamed from an engineering station in other dimensions. These high frequency projections are cosmic radiation beams that carry the mathematical frequency signatures of different atomic elements and life codes. This is a holographic process known as *radiogenesis.*

13. These beams imprint thoughtforms or thought-configurations upon the cosmic radiation that then activates primary forms of matter. This is how this universe comes into existence. From the projecting booths in the adjacent light universe, these mathematically structured codes are transferred into photograms or light messages that, through the process of radiogenesis, focus on a high frequency radio wave that condenses and imprints the final forms of matter. This matter is organized as aggregates of atoms into different elemental and molecular structures. All the different signatures of the final forms of life are created through this process. This is the divine thought wave that writes the *Book of Life*.

14. Once the *Book of Life* is established and the material forms engendered, comes the possibility for the evolvement of organic states of consciousness from the highest of the inorganic states: the crystal with its 32 symmetry properties.

15. The 64 DNA codons are a function of the binary doubling of the crystal 32. *Biogenesis* occurs when the cell is fertilized and undergoes mitosis or binary splitting. This splitting continues until it produces the whole cellular structure of male and female, and on it goes. This is the binary multiplication of life.

16. Though it is assumed that all states of consciousness are dependent on organic matter to be sustained, a type of proto consciousness exists in the atomic structure of all inorganic matter as well.

17. The sixth order of binary doubling is 32: 1, 2, 4, 8, 16, and 32. Sixty-four is the seventh order of binary doubling that brings the magic of life. Seven is the primary frequency of creation. Once the frequency of creation is activated by the seventh order of binary doubling, then life continues through processes of binary multiplication. It is important to study the relation of these numbers.

Extraterrestrial intelligence is not subject to the conditionings of the thought program that exists on the surface of the planet.

215

18. Just as matter reaches a certain point within the binary unfoldment, becoming a crystal, so life reaches a critical point with the emergence of mind as a medium of evolving intelligence. From this mind comes the human.

19. The human functions similarly to a crystal and has to engender its next stage of evolution: the superhuman or supermental state of consciousness. This gives the formulation 32:64::64:128. Note: 32 + 64 + 64 + 128 = 288, the harmonic of polar light. *This frequency represents the mind of light essential to the telepathic art of noogenesis.*

32:64::64:128

The formulation 32:64::64:128, demonstrates how the quantum binary doubling of 32—the crystal—creates life, 64, while the binary doubling of life, 64, creates the supermental noosphere, 128.

    32 = Radiogenesis
    64 = Biogenesis
    128 = Noogenesis

The circumpolar rainbow bridge is a synthesis of these three types of genesis, and represents the planetary synthesis of the noosphere.

VULOM MAGNETIC ATTRACTION FORCE FIELD

20. As a telepathic art form, noogenesis is engendered first through two activating agents that represent a red (−) and a blue (+) bioelectrical circuit. Through a unified practice, the two agents engage the 441 telepathic grid underlying the universal matrix of creation through the electrical/etheric activation of the *vulom magnetic attraction force field.* This is a component element first defined in *The Knowledge Book.*

21. The vulom magnetic attraction force field refers to a particular electro telepathic structure by which one is able to project or beam thoughts, or beings, to any place within the universe. This force field is a function of the 441 mathematical matrix. The vulom magnetic attraction energy grid is depicted in the Hunab Ku 21 matrix as a set of energy points that, when connected, create an energy grid.

22. The vulom circuit board shows color frequencies with their corresponding mathematical number frequencies. The vulom has a particular structural form similar to the images of the interdimensional star map, as well as being a focalizer of the 21 galactic archetypes (see *CHC Vol. V*).

NOOGENESIS
RED & BLUE MAGNETIC RECONNECTION

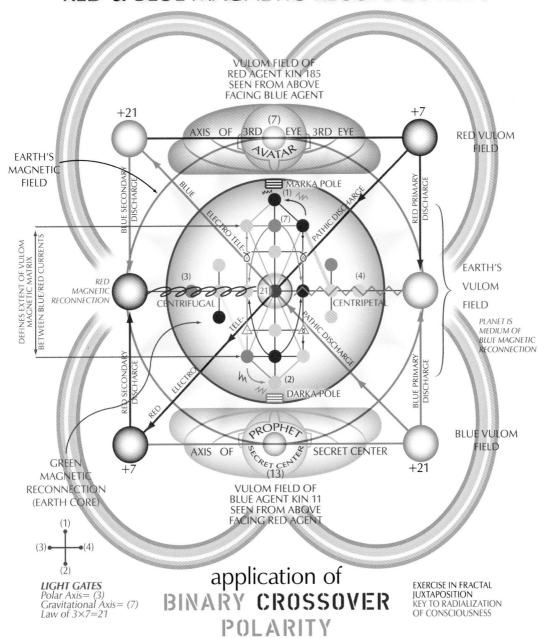

VULOM FIELD OF
RED AGENT KIN 185
SEEN FROM ABOVE
FACING BLUE AGENT

+21

+7

RED VULOM
FIELD

EARTH'S
MAGNETIC
FIELD

AXIS OF 3RD EYE 3RD EYE

(7)

AVATAR

MARKA POLE

(1)

(7)

BLUE SECONDARY DISCHARGE

BLUE ELECTRO TELE-

RED PRIMARY DISCHARGE

PATHIC DISCHARGE

DEFINES EXTENT OF VULOM MAGNETIC MATRIX
BETWEEN BLUE/RED CURRENTS

RED
MAGNETIC
RECONNECTION

(3)

CENTRIFUGAL

(21)

(4)

CENTRIPETAL

EARTH'S
VULOM
FIELD

PLANET IS
MEDIUM OF
BLUE MAGNETIC
RECONNECTION

TELE-

PATHIC DISCHARGE

RED SECONDARY DISCHARGE

RED ELECTRO

(2)

DARKA POLE

BLUE PRIMARY DISCHARGE

GREEN
MAGNETIC
RECONNECTION
(EARTH CORE)

+7

PROPHET

SECRET CENTER

AXIS OF SECRET CENTER

(13)

+21

BLUE VULOM
FIELD

VULOM FIELD OF
BLUE AGENT KIN 11
SEEN FROM ABOVE
FACING RED AGENT

(1)

(3) (4)

(2)

LIGHT GATES
Polar Axis= (3)
Gravitational Axis= (7)
Law of 3×7=21

application of
BINARY CROSSOVER
POLARITY

EXERCISE IN FRACTAL
JUXTAPOSITION
KEY TO RADIALIZATION
OF CONSCIOUSNESS

The vulom attraction force field

refers to a particular electro

telepathic structure by which

one is able to project or beam

thoughts, or beings, to any

place within the universe.

23. The first step to activate this vulom circuit board is to imprint and visualize this structure within the body and understand how the principles of *magnetic reconnection* and *binary crossover polarity* work. Through a third transfer medium in the center of the Earth we can create a wholly interactive psycho-telepathic electromagnetic field that becomes one unified magnetic force field that connects the human biopsychic field with the terrestrial electromagnetic field.

24. The central channel of the vulom magnetic attraction force field corresponds to the galactic axis with a red marka pole above and a blue darka pole below. There are seven points that correspond to the heptad gates of the central axis: red crown, white root, blue third eye, red secret center, white throat, yellow solar plexus and the green heart center.

25. On the right side is the red current streaming down, and on the left side is the blue current in its upward flow. The marka and darka poles also refer to the first two light gates that enter our universe from the first (light) universe.

26. The red electric current is generated from the meridian to the left of the third eye, and the blue electric current is generated from the meridian to right of the secret center. The flow of the red current is from top to bottom, and the flow of the blue current is from bottom to top. These two flows directly connect the secret center with the third eye (the two "minor" chakras).

27. The red flow streams out from the third eye and down the left side meridian connecting with the secret center. The blue flow streams out from the secret center and up the right side meridian connecting with the third eye. These are the two etheric binary electrical currents that are telepathically activated in order to create the noogenesis.

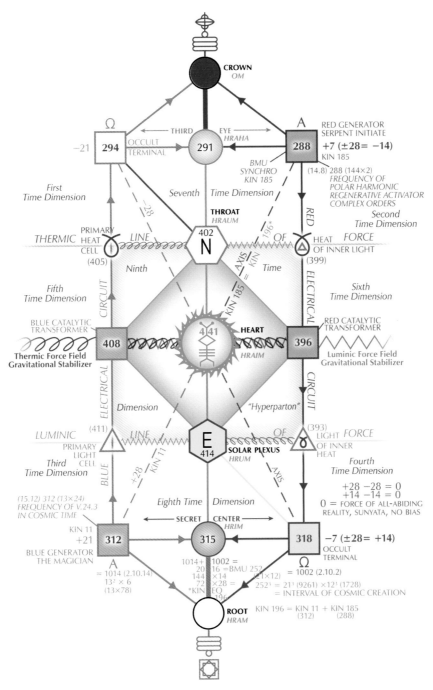

CROWN
OM

Ω
−21   **294**
OCCULT TERMINAL

THIRD   EYE
HRAHA

291

A
288
+7 (±28 = −14)
KIN 185

RED GENERATOR
SERPENT INITIATE

(14.8) 288 (144×2)
FREQUENCY OF
POLAR HARMONIC
REGENERATIVE ACTIVATOR
COMPLEX ORDERS

First
Time Dimension

Seventh   Time Dimension

BMU
SYNCHRO
KIN 185

Second
Time Dimension

THROAT
HRAUM

THERMIC   PRIMARY HEAT CELL   LINE
(405)

402
N

HEAT   FORCE
OF INNER LIGHT
(399)

RED   OF   HEAT

Ninth

Time

Fifth
Time Dimension

Sixth
Time Dimension

BLUE CATALYTIC
TRANSFORMER

408

4 41

HEART
HRAIM

396

RED CATALYTIC
TRANSFORMER

Thermic Force Field
Gravitational Stabilizer

Luminic Force Field
Gravitational Stabilizer

Dimension

"Hyperparton"

(411)

(393)

LUMINIC   PRIMARY LIGHT CELL   LINE

414
E

SOLAR PLEXUS
HRUM

LIGHT   FORCE
OF INNER HEAT

OF   LIGHT

Third
Time Dimension

Fourth
Time Dimension

+28 −28 = 0
+14 −14 = 0
0 = FORCE OF ALL-ABIDING
REALITY, SUNYATA, NO BIAS

(15.12) 312 (13×24)
FREQUENCY OF V.24.3
IN COSMIC TIME

Eighth Time   Dimension

SECRET   CENTER
HRIM

KIN 11
+21   **312**
A
= 1014 (2.10.14)
13² × 6
(13×78)

BLUE GENERATOR
THE MAGICIAN

315

1014+ 1002 =
20 16 =BMU 252
144 ×14
72 ×28
*KIN EQ
196

318
Ω
−7 (±28 = +14)
OCCULT
TERMINAL

(21×12)
252² = 21² (9261) ×12² (1728)
= INTERVAL OF COSMIC CREATION

= 1002 (2.10.2)

ROOT
HRAM

KIN 196 = KIN 11 + KIN 185
(312)   (288)

28. Visualize and meditate on the structure until you can feel where the points are. In studying the force field, remember: it is facing you, so its left hand side is to your right and vice versa.

219

MAGNETIC FIELD ELECTRICAL MATRIX

29. The key to the system of noogenesis is study of the three key points of the red and the blue currents within the *magnetic field electrical matrix*. Each current has three dynamic points or centers. The two red centers are antipodes to the two blue centers and the yellow and white terminals are also antipodes. (Note that the red current is to the left of the secret center; and the blue current is the opposite, beginning from the right of the secret center).

   1) **Red generator**—corresponds to frequency **288** (32 + 64 + 64 = 128)
   2) **Red catalyzer**—corresponds to frequency **396**
   3) **Yellow terminal**—corresponds to frequency **318**
   4) **Blue generator**—corresponds to frequency **312**
   5) **Blue catalyzer**—corresponds to frequency **408**
   6) **White terminal**—corresponds to frequency **294**

30. There is a diagonal axis that goes from the red generator (**288**) to the **blue** generator (**312**). This axis passes through the heart center. There is also a corresponding axis from the white terminal (**294**) to the yellow terminal (**318**).

HOLOMIND PERCEIVER CODES

31. In the holomind perceiver codes, **288** (red generator) is **+7**, and **312** (blue generator) is a **+21**. This creates a **+28** axis—the harmonic standard—the mental reorganization of time. The **318** (yellow terminal) is a negative or sublimated **7,** and **294** (white terminal) is a sublimated **−21**—creating a sublimated 28 axis, therefore the **+28** axis and **−28** axis zero out in a perfect harmonic equipoise.

32. Also note that the two 28 currents connect the four hyperplasmic zones in the following way:

   288 (+7) is a beta-alpha plasma.
   312 (+21) is an alpha-beta plasma.
   This makes a +28 beta-alpha/alpha-beta current which is a dynamizing generator circuit.

   294 (−21) alpha-alpha terminal.
   318 (−7) beta-beta terminal.
   This makes a sublimating −28 alpha-alpha/beta-beta current, which is a stabilizing terminal circuit.

33. The +28 activating pulse between the red and blue generators is the frequency of the 28-day moon cycle, the harmonic standard, the 4:7 (4 × 7 = 28) part of the elemental formulation (4:7::7:13). The position 288 is the frequency of the polar harmonic (144 × 2) and corresponds in the synchronic matrix to Kin 185, Red Electric Serpent. Kin 185 is the activator of the red life-force galactic spectrum, making it the perfect red generator.

    Frequencies of red current (288 + 396 + 318 = **1002**). Frequencies of blue current (294 + 408 + 312 = **1014**), **1002** + **1014** = **2016** (144 × 14) or (72 × 28). **2016** is the 441 base matrix unit **196** (28 × 7), affirming the 28-day standard. The Bode number of Uranus is also **196**.

34. In the vulom magnetic attraction force field, between the red generator (**288**) and white/blue circuit terminal (**294**) there is a blue center that is also one of the seven Hunab Ku 21 heptad gates (See Chapter 5 second heptad gate). This blue center frequency (**291**) corresponds with radial plasma Seli, the root chakra.

35. The white at the bottom of the central axis (**144**), corresponds with radial plasma Gamma, the third eye chakra in the heptad gate codes. In the vulom force field, the heptad arrangement corresponds to the bodily alignment of the chakras, i.e. the lowest gate is the root chakra, hence the **144** is at the root chakra, coded by radial plasma Seli.

36. In the vulom force field, the blue **291** is located in the third eye chakra and corresponds to radial plasma Gamma. Here there is a crossover, just as there is a crossover with the yellow and white. The actual matrix of transformation is located between the third eye, blue **291**, and secret center, red **315**. These two centers create a crossover polarity of frequencies and colors between them. (This entire structure can be visualized and imprinted).

The Sirian persona is a telepathic channel open to the frequency line of all beings.

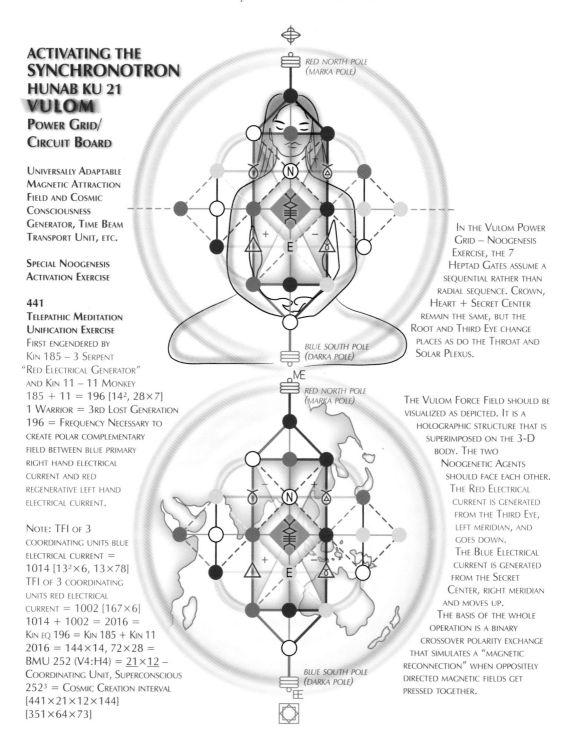

ACTIVATING THE SYNCHRONOTRON
HUNAB KU 21
VULOM
POWER GRID/ CIRCUIT BOARD

UNIVERSALLY ADAPTABLE MAGNETIC ATTRACTION FIELD AND COSMIC CONSCIOUSNESS GENERATOR, TIME BEAM TRANSPORT UNIT, ETC.

SPECIAL NOOGENESIS ACTIVATION EXERCISE

441
TELEPATHIC MEDITATION UNIFICATION EXERCISE
FIRST ENGENDERED BY KIN 185 – 3 SERPENT "RED ELECTRICAL GENERATOR" AND KIN 11 – 11 MONKEY
185 + 11 = 196 [14^2, 28×7]
1 WARRIOR = 3RD LOST GENERATION
196 = FREQUENCY NECESSARY TO CREATE POLAR COMPLEMENTARY FIELD BETWEEN BLUE PRIMARY RIGHT HAND ELECTRICAL CURRENT AND RED REGENERATIVE LEFT HAND ELECTRICAL CURRENT.

NOTE: TFI OF 3 COORDINATING UNITS BLUE ELECTRICAL CURRENT =
1014 [13^2×6, 13×78]
TFI OF 3 COORDINATING UNITS RED ELECTRICAL CURRENT = 1002 [167×6]
1014 + 1002 = 2016 =
KIN EQ 196 = KIN 185 + KIN 11
2016 = 144×14, 72×28 =
BMU 252 (V4:H4) = 21×12 –
COORDINATING UNIT, SUPERCONSCIOUS
252^3 = COSMIC CREATION INTERVAL
[441×21×12×144]
[351×64×73]

RED NORTH POLE (MARKA POLE)

BLUE SOUTH POLE (DARKA POLE)

RED NORTH POLE (MARKA POLE)

BLUE SOUTH POLE (DARKA POLE)

IN THE VULOM POWER GRID – NOOGENESIS EXERCISE, THE 7 HEPTAD GATES ASSUME A SEQUENTIAL RATHER THAN RADIAL SEQUENCE. CROWN, HEART + SECRET CENTER REMAIN THE SAME, BUT THE ROOT AND THIRD EYE CHANGE PLACES AS DO THE THROAT AND SOLAR PLEXUS.

THE VULOM FORCE FIELD SHOULD BE VISUALIZED AS DEPICTED. IT IS A HOLOGRAPHIC STRUCTURE THAT IS SUPERIMPOSED ON THE 3-D BODY. THE TWO NOOGENETIC AGENTS SHOULD FACE EACH OTHER. THE RED ELECTRICAL CURRENT IS GENERATED FROM THE THIRD EYE, LEFT MERIDIAN, AND GOES DOWN. THE BLUE ELECTRICAL CURRENT IS GENERATED FROM THE SECRET CENTER, RIGHT MERIDIAN AND MOVES UP. THE BASIS OF THE WHOLE OPERATION IS A BINARY CROSSOVER POLARITY EXCHANGE THAT SIMULATES A "MAGNETIC RECONNECTION" WHEN OPPOSITELY DIRECTED MAGNETIC FIELDS GET PRESSED TOGETHER.

37. In the visualization of this structure, we see the two sets of governing points—three points on each side—defining the red and blue circuits. The activation occurs between the third eye and secret center chakras. From the blue occult terminal, white **294**, a blue current beams to the blue third eye, while the red generator sends a red current to the third eye.

38. From the third eye center, blue **291,** one current ascends to the crown chakra and the other descends through the central channel. The same thing occurs with the secret center where the blue generator sends a blue current to the red secret center **315**, while from the red terminal, yellow **318**, a red current goes to the secret center.

39. From the secret center, one current shoots down to the South (Darka) Pole, and the other is absorbed into the central channel. In traditional yoga, the prana descends. This corresponds to the red electrical current descending from the third eye, while the opposing wind—apana—ascends. This corresponds to the blue electrical current ascending from the secret center.

Central Matrix

40. The whole central matrix is another plane of activation. This center, between the throat chakra (402) and solar plexus (414), defines what in the 441 matrix is the ninth time dimension, inner time. Inner time is circumscribed by the hyperelectrical current identified as the 8th circuit.

41. The throat chakra holds the hyperneutron and the solar plexus holds the hyperelectron. These are key primary partons that establish the electrical field. This is visualized in our central matrix. *Note: these again trade places in the heptad gate rendition, where 402 is the solar plexus chakra and 414 is the throat chakra. In the vulom force field this is reversed, where instead of a radial juxtaposition of plasmas and centers it is a straightforward descent from the top of the crown (108) to the bottom of the root (144).*

IMPRINTING THE STRUCTURE

Noogenesis can only become real when we imprint this structure into our minds and keep it projected in our bodily zone. Through systematic discipline, this program becomes a living visualization. Perpendicular to the central axis running through the heart center is the gravitational axis. The vertical channel is the energy activation axis, which is balanced by the gravitational axis. Everything is a matter of balancing.

---

42. **To summarize:** There is a red electrical current descending and a blue electrical current ascending. They each have their two diagonal electrical lines of force: the 28-unit positive activating axis and the 28-unit negative sublimating axis. These two axes connect the two terminals. There are two generators and two terminals that run lines of

force through the heart center. This is also the center of the 441: the Sirius B52/Element 113—point that connects the hyperneutron and hyperelectron.

43. Between the red generator and red catalyzer lies the hyperparton *kum*, the heat of inner light. Between the red catalyzer and red terminal lies *kemio*, the light of inner heat. These are two secondary complex partons intended to be telepathically activated within this structure holding together our etheric body.

44. The blue current contains the two primary partons, the *dum kuali* primary heat between the terminal and catalyzer; and the *dum duar* primary light between the generator and catalyzer. These hyperpartons are activated by the currents. In other words the red current activates the heat of inner light which catalyzes to activate the light of inner heat.

45. The blue current activates the primary light cell which catalyzes to activate the primary heat cell. This highly charged electrical activity is an entire circuit—the 8th circuit of the 441 matrix—which creates a whole electrotelepathic cell, within both our corpus callosum and our etheric body. Remember: In telepathically imprinting these structures you are actually creating an etheric engraving.

46. The exact precision of the engraving then activates or is activated by this same force field in the AA Midway Station (see Chapter 13). It is like activating a "credit card"; by punching in the precise numbers of the credit card into the phone, the credit card gets activated. This same principle applies to the vulom force field or 441.

47. There are two key factors to consider in the noogenesis:

    1. Magnetic reconnection: principle of polar lines of force joining at positive end of bipolar field.

The Noogenesis—Great Cosmic Shift—will be realized in a short time and is dependent on the personal discovery of those capable of becoming cosmically aligned.

HOOKING UP TO THE VULOM POWER GRID

The vulom magnetic force field can be projected in three ways:

1. Visualize it as a holographic structure bisecting your body.
2. Visualize it as a nanochip that you place in your corpus callosum.
3. Visualize it as a structure that bisects Earth from pole to pole.

This practice requires two people facing each other with the matrix between them; one assumes the role of the red agent and the other the blue agent. They simultaneously visualize Earth and the same matrix bisecting the planet. In the red agent, the red vulom field is more activated, while the blue is more activated in the blue agent.

The red agent visualizes and projects an active electrical red force from the left side of the body to the latent red side of the blue agent's body. In turn, the blue agent projects an active electrical blue force from the right side of the body to the latent blue side of the red agent's body. This creates a binary crossover polarity.

Continue to refine and practice the visualization and crossover polarity until a palpable current can be felt coming from left to right, right to left at third eye and secret center levels. The energy transfer should be felt as an internal sensation. The object of this practice is to become telepathically focused and merged in one field, so that it is felt throughout the etheric and neural circuitry. This is how to create a highly charged electrical field to synchronize and, by psycho-telepathic transfer, activate the Earth's magnetic field, engendering the noogenesis.

2. Binary crossover polarity (equalizes both sides of the two magnetic fields). The magnetic fields then become pressed together with a third transfer medium in the center—the telepathic visualization of the Earth with the same matrix bisecting it. However, in the Earth these are the two vulom fields back-to-back. Each corresponds to what either of the agents would be facing. These two fields balance and strengthen the Earth's axis with a powerful neutralizing force.

48. This practice, when properly done, activates the vulom magnetic attraction force field of the Earth which is held in a telepathic visualization in the center between the two agents. When their magnetic fields are completely pressed together they experience a magnetic reconnection. A current leaps around them like a rainbow current (from red above and from blue below) connecting and merging the fragmented parts of the field into one whole field.

49. This magnetic reconnection comes about by means of binary crossover polarity through the transfer medium of the Earth which is visualized between them. This triggers the noogenesis: the Circumpolar Rainbow Bridge around the Earth.

50. Atmospheric physicists say that a thunderstorm can occur in one part of the world and set off other thunderstorms in faraway places. For example, imagine a thunderstorm in Turkey that emits energetic electrons into the field that interact with plasma waves at a certain point and create high energy bursts that send free electrons down somewhere, say, in Madagascar in the Southern Hemisphere and trigger a thunderstorm there. This is the principle of magnetic reconnection.

51. The noogenesis practice works with this same principle. We have a red pole and blue pole as well as two terminals creating a binary crossover polarity. If we transmit activating telepathic electrons at a high speed into the merged auric fields they will then create high bursts of energy within the merged field. This, in turn, creates a high level of activation within the agents allowing them to mentally transfer this energy into the Earth.

52. The energy of this telepathic activation is sent out through the poles and meets to create these great bursts—gamma bursts—that trigger the rainbow bridge. This is the scientific principle to create the noogenesis.

Noogenesis and Telepathic Frequency Indexes

53. In this experiment of noogenesis it is important that we understand the telepathic frequency indices of the numbers involved.

54. For instance the heat of inner light frequency is **399** (19 × 21) and the light of inner heat frequency is **393** (131 × 3). (Meditate on the meaning of the numbers). Create a magnetic reconnection through binary crossover polarity. Note **399 + 393 = 792** (396 × 2). **396** is the red catalyzer between them.

55. First an interpsychic field between the two agents must be created and then transferred as an activated magnetically reconnected force field into the Earth. Everything—the Earth, self and other—are visualized within the vulom force field. This process engenders an activation of primary creation matrices.

56. Secondary aspects to understand within this process are the primary creation matrices, namely the fifth force matrix of the four radial time dimensions plus the inner (9th) time dimension. This is the most fundamental matrix from which the matrix of nine is evolved. Meditate to understand that the vulom force field and Hunab Ku 21 both take place completely within the radial time dimensions.

57. The outer times are not included in the actual points that occur within the fifth, sixth, seventh, eighth and ninth time dimensions. We are dealing with a structure that is not subject to the 3D time of the four outer time dimensions.

58. However, the four outer time dimensions are connected by the fact that the blue and red generator are on the same

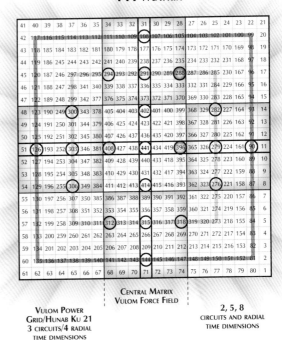

SYNCHRONOTRON 441 MATRIX

CENTRAL MATRIX
VULOM FORCE FIELD

VULOM POWER
GRID/HUNAB KU 21
3 CIRCUITS/4 RADIAL
TIME DIMENSIONS

2, 5, 8
CIRCUITS AND RADIAL
TIME DIMENSIONS

circuit, the fifth, and this runs through all four outer time dimensions and all four radial time dimensions. The first seven circuits connect the four outer time dimensions with the four radial time dimensions. The **288** (third eye) and **312** (secret center) are both on the fifth circuit. These points on the circuit connect with outer time, but the inner vulom force field/Hunab Ku 21 structure radial and self-contained in the ninth or inner time.

59. Understand these underlying matrices and how they have appeared. This is somewhat similar to Buddhist meditation practices like the vajra world mandala. We can see in the 441 time matrix, the fifth force structure of the radial time dimensions. This fifth force matrix—four radial times and inner time—corresponds to the five Dreamspell castles, while the 13 Moon calendar is accounted for by the four outer time dimensions.

60. There are three circuits that are activated: 1) the second circuit which activates the poles; red pole (**108**) and white pole (**144**). 2) The fifth circuit is where the main action takes place, the third eye, the red generator and the blue terminal; the secret center, the blue generator and the red terminal. These are all in the fifth circuit. 3) The eighth circuit, which is in the ninth (inner) time dimension. This is the hyperparton electrical circuit.

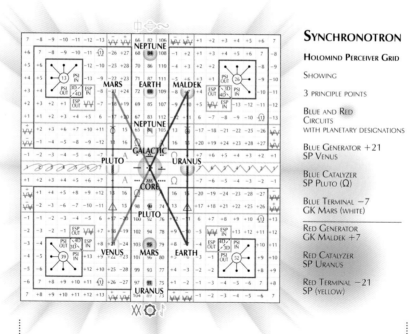

SYNCHRONOTRON

HOLOMIND PERCEIVER GRID

SHOWING

3 PRINCIPLE POINTS

BLUE AND RED
CIRCUITS
WITH PLANETARY DESIGNATIONS

BLUE GENERATOR +21
SP VENUS

BLUE CATALYZER
SP PLUTO (Ω)

BLUE TERMINAL −7
GK MARS (WHITE)

RED GENERATOR
GK MALDEK +7

RED CATALYZER
SP URANUS

RED TERMINAL −21
SP (YELLOW)

Holomind Perceiver Grid
Look at the grid according to the planets. The red circuit activates Maldek, Uranus and completes itself on Earth. The blue circuit activates Venus, Pluto and completes itself in Mars. The central circuit is Neptune, Earth, Neptune, Galactic Core, Pluto, Mars, and Uranus. These are the basic points of study in terms of generating the noogenesis.

61. When you draw these circuits on the 441 synchronic matrix, BMU 288 is equivalent to Kin 185, initiator of the red galactic spectrum. In the 441 space matrix/psi genetic map, BMU 288 is equivalent to Kin 79, frequency of the noosphere constant. Kin 185 is the regenerator (288) that activates the noosphere (79) all in the same BMU, 288, the harmonic of polar light.

62. BMU 312 coincides with the Kin 76 (synchronic matrix) and Kin 174 (psi genetic matrix), the Cosmic History generator. The axis between the blue and red generators is the axis that connects the noosphere constant (79), with 174, the White Overtone Wizard of Cosmic History. There is a lot to study in the grid that connects all of these points.

63. When we map this purely on the 260-unit Tzolkin grid we see that the whole of the Hunab Ku 21 matrix occurs within the Tzolkin on the synchronic matrix, except on the two extreme points of the gravitational axis. The Red Dragon occurs at the North Pole represented by Kin 122 and the White Wind occurs at the South Pole represented by Kin 139. The remaining Hunab Ku 21 points are on the Serpent, Star, Skywalker and Warrior axes. Then finally we have the *holomind perceiver grid.*

64. The very process of noogenesis is superhuman, superconscious activation. At the conclusion of this program the conditioned charges of the terrestrial thought field of agents undertaking the experiment should be cleared out and an inner vacuum created for the descent of an extraterrestrial metaconsciousness thought field: the Sirian thought matrix—Sirian rebirth. This in essence is the how-to of the telepathic art of noogenesis.

CHAPTER 13

HYPERELECTRONIC UNIVERSE:
A TRIP TO THE AA MIDWAY STATION

The following is a description of the nature of the AA Midway Station and its systems of operation. The energy system of the AA Midway Station operates by a substanceless fuel that requires no machinery in the way we think of it, but is rather based on the principle of a psycho-electromagnetic vacuum force field operations of attraction, repulsion, transmutation and vertical alignment. This is a telepathic technology that underlies the projection of molecular reorganization that provides transport through time and space.

1. The AA Midway Station is the Antares/Arcturus Midway base of operations that functions as a monitoring and surveillance station as well as a data retrieval and storage system of the "master records". It is organized in a manner that cosmologically recapitulates the four-fold functioning of the galactic and human brain as programmed by the Central Stellar Radion (CSR).

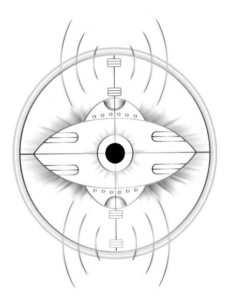

2. The AA Midway Station is peopled by different higher-dimensional beings, etheric in nature but capable of 3-D manifestations who represent different outposts of the Galactic Federation. It is called a "midway station" because it is intermediary between systems such as V.24 and the Central Stellar Radion.

3. The Central Stellar Radion is the evolving power of an interdimensionally functioning central holographic intelligence unit located beyond the seventh dimension. In the sacred dimension, this is also referred to by its spiritual name, Al-Bait ul-Ma'mur, the "House of Allah" above the seventh heaven.

4. Radion is a fourth-dimensional electrical fluid. Within the CSR, radion refers to a signal-transmitting energy stream that holographically coordinates the intelligence of any galaxy, inclusive of its planets and/or stellar life forms.

5. In the center of the CSR's crystal core unit is the Universal Resonant Holon, the primary field model for any celestial sphere throughout the universe. It is organized with a bipolar field distinguished by two magnetic poles, positive and negative; this accommodates any celestial body.

6. The Planet Holon is a function of the Universal Resonant Holon, which is a projection of the Central Stellar Radion. The CSR operating system is projected holographically into specific surveillance units like the AA Midway Station.

7. The V.24.3 Planet Holon is a pure projection from the AA Midway Station and serves as an etheric protective grid around the planet. It creates a field of harmonic resonance around the Earth that is coordinated with the daily telepathic movement of different planets within either their galactic-karmic or solar-prophetic positions. This creates a field of resonance throughout the heliosphere, the interplanetary field.

8. This harmonic resonance is intended to stabilize perturbations occurring within the Sun, in the solar system and on our planet. This harmonic resonance also affects other planets by increasing magnetism and heightening the electromagnetic field's receptivity to galactic-cosmic plasma. This, in turn, releases solar plasma already trapped in the fields, creating a dynamic perturbance.

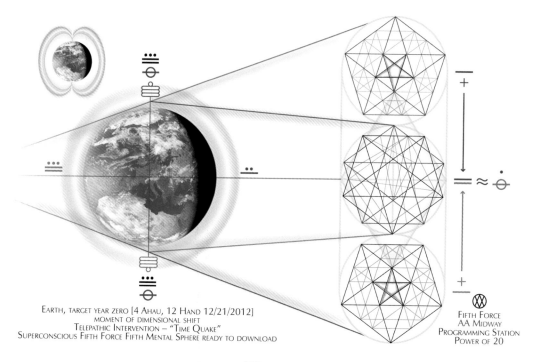

EARTH, TARGET YEAR ZERO [4 AHAU, 12 HAND 12/21/2012]
MOMENT OF DIMENSIONAL SHIFT
TELEPATHIC INTERVENTION – "TIME QUAKE"
SUPERCONSCIOUS FIFTH FORCE FIFTH MENTAL SPHERE READY TO DOWNLOAD

FIFTH FORCE
AA MIDWAY
PROGRAMMING STATION
POWER OF 20

9. If it were not for the delicacy of human civilization on V.24.3 (Earth) it would not matter so much. But civilization on V.24.3 is so fragile that until the human is liberated from such physical dependency into higher-dimensional functions—until the human has graduated from this phase—humanity is in a precarious situation.

10. The Arcturus protectorate shield has been placed over the Planet Holon to assist the planetary whole (of which the human is an integral part), in the phase shift into its next stage of evolution, where it will be operating both third- and fourth-dimensionally. One of the main purposes of the AA Midway Station is to assist in monitoring this process.

11. The AA Midway Station operates in a holographically radial and interpenetratingly integrative manner. If you were to walk through its headquarters you would see banks and banks of information stations within different quadrants arranged symmetrically, all appearing as a complete systematic holographic hallucination.

12. These quadrants correspond with alpha-alpha, alpha-beta, beta-beta and beta-alpha zones, forming a telepathic matrix that organizes information and intelligence that spans the entire spectrum of evolutionary development.

13. The AA Midway Station contains what appears to be monitoring screens, or holographic projection booths. These are simultaneously organized according to what level and information type you seek, whether it be information regarding chemical elements, molecular structures, DNA, human whole system emotional thermic readings or spiritual levels, etc.

14. All entities, or aggregates of entities, inclusive of planetary whole systems, have a thermic quality that indicates emotional stability or instability. These can all be read: thermic emotional indexes, molecular stabilization indexes, genetic coding stabilization indexes, etc. This is like a super holographic interdimensional GPS system.

15. We can tune into multiple levels, mapping not only the surface, but the micro and macro levels as well. Psychothermic maps are available to locate the psychic hot spots on the Planet. For example, if we look at the thermic scale for Jerusalem, it will be pretty hot. Or we can tune into a leader of whatever nation and see molecular stability or instability according to emotions, thoughts and food intake.

16. The purpose of the AA Midway Station at this particular time is to refocus and reconnect an information vortex here on this test tube planet, which is a micro galactic brain. For instance, as you are reading these words describing the holographic projection booths, you could also scan or project information of different celestial bodies to receive information according to your own and

others' thermic states. Depending on the psycho thermic readout of an entity, a corresponding piece of information may or may not be projected back to it.

17. Information that enters the AA Midway Station is immediately recorded and processed by a holographic scanner; it is then transmitted to the Master Record within the Central Stellar Radion. This process works similarly for the many other stations in different galaxy systems throughout the universe.

18. Once the information enters the Master Record, it is simultaneously scanned and preserved in a type of storage unit. This Master Record is similar to the astral movie library described in the first volume of the *Cosmic History Chronicles.*

The AA Midway Station

is also referred to as the

Mothership and can materialize

into 3-D structures to

accommodate 3-D interactions

when necessary.

19. The AA Midway Station is also midway between the experimental object of observation, Velatropa 24, and the CSR master record and recorder. In *The Arcturus Probe,* the AA Midway Station is described as a satellite of the CSR and the CSR is described as the place where all cosmic programs are originated and projected. There are four basic program levels: 1) Galactic, 2) Interstellar, 3) Stellar and 4) Planetary.

20. These four program levels are coordinated in the CSR and projected via the AA Midway Station to the Hunab Ku—galactic coordination central. These are big projecting booths in the holographic universe where everything is perceived and understood as a holographic simultaneity, a totality.

21. At this point the AA Midway Station is allowing access to some of these experiences to certain people on this planet (and other planets) to facilitate enhanced understanding of the coming world.

AA and Waking Conscious Mediumship

22. The AA Midway Station operates as a highly elaborate hologram, coordinated in an interdimensional alignment at the sixth dimension or sixth circuit interstellar level, directly above the midpoint within the heliosphere of V.24. This is between the fifth and sixth planetary orbits, Maldek (Asteroid Belt) and Jupiter and is the psychoactive center of the heliosphere system of Velatropa 24.

23. Prolonged meditation upon the AA Midway Station, enters us into a state of waking conscious mediumship that leads into the beta-beta intergalactic channel (BMU 321) of the cosmic cube. This fourth-dimensional channel is located in the center of the left front cerebral hemisphere.

24. In order to enter this level of consciousness we must be aligned with the raw data and experience of nature, mind and number. We must be totally apart from the trappings of the machine, especially the so-called "thinking machines" of the computer and the virtual reality of the cybersphere which serve only to short-circuit our moral intelligence and capacity for paranormal communication.

25. The AA Midway Station operates on a substanceless energy principle psycho-electromagnetic vacuum force field operations of attraction, repulsion, transmutation and vertical alignment. Sometimes this involves the molecular reorganization of bodies involved in transport mediums.

26. These are fourth- and fifth-dimensional transactions that easily transform aspects of the illusory 3-D world as if by magic, but in actuality through applications of higher-dimensional laws. This is why it is said that the AA Midway Station is a locus of both higher information codes and the dominant order recapitulating the cosmology of what we call the "new time" and telepathic structure of reality.

27. In the higher holographic reality, (time) transport is inseparable from the experience of a recapitulative cosmology rooted in superconscious and subliminal conscious fields of cognition and experience.

28. If we want to advance to this level, not only must we live and cultivate a life of spirit, but we must abandon outworn perceptions and operating norms that govern the experience of the materialist 3-D reality in its entirety. This entails opening ourselves to divine grace in the expansion of our will, spirit and divine analytic intelligence.

ACCESS – WAKING CONSCIOUS MEDIUMSHIP
⩔⩔ (321) BI-LEVEL MENTAL OPERATION RADIAL (4 QTR) PROGRAM

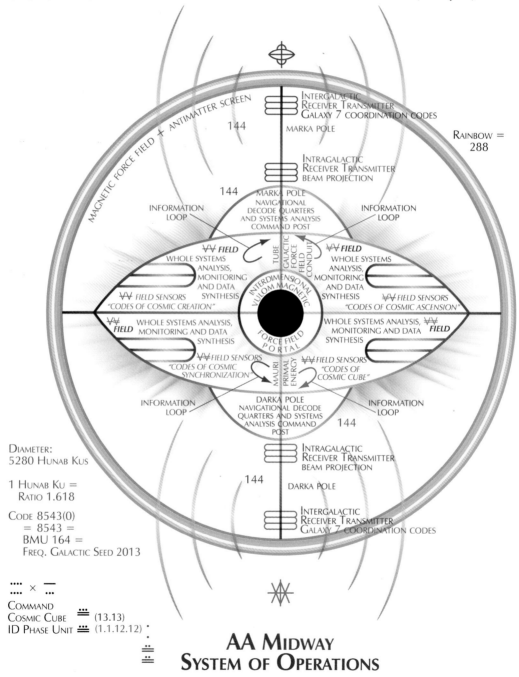

MAGNETIC FORCE FIELD + ANTIMATTER SCREEN

INTERGALACTIC RECEIVER TRANSMITTER
GALAXY 7 COORDINATION CODES
MARKA POLE

144

RAINBOW = 288

INTRAGALACTIC RECEIVER TRANSMITTER
BEAM PROJECTION

144

MARKA POLE
NAVIGATIONAL DECODE QUARTERS
AND SYSTEMS ANALYSIS
COMMAND POST

INFORMATION LOOP

INFORMATION LOOP

⩔⩔ FIELD
WHOLE SYSTEMS ANALYSIS, MONITORING AND DATA SYNTHESIS

⩔⩔ FIELD
WHOLE SYSTEMS ANALYSIS, MONITORING AND DATA SYNTHESIS

TUBE
GALACTIC FORCE FIELD CONDUIT

⩔⩔ FIELD SENSORS
"CODES OF COSMIC CREATION"

INTERDIMENSIONAL VULOM MAGNETIC

⩔⩔ FIELD SENSORS
"CODES OF COSMIC ASCENSION"

⩔⩔ FIELD
WHOLE SYSTEMS ANALYSIS, MONITORING AND DATA SYNTHESIS

WHOLE SYSTEMS ANALYSIS, MONITORING AND DATA SYNTHESIS ⩔⩔ FIELD

FORCE FIELD PORTAL

⩔⩔ FIELD SENSORS
"CODES OF COSMIC SYNCHRONIZATION"

MAURI PRIMAL ENERGY

⩔⩔ FIELD SENSORS
"CODES OF COSMIC CUBE"

INFORMATION LOOP

INFORMATION LOOP

DARKA POLE
NAVIGATIONAL DECODE QUARTERS AND SYSTEMS
ANALYSIS COMMAND POST

144

INTRAGALACTIC RECEIVER TRANSMITTER
BEAM PROJECTION

144

DARKA POLE

INTERGALACTIC RECEIVER TRANSMITTER
GALAXY 7 COORDINATION CODES

DIAMETER:
5280 HUNAB KUS

1 HUNAB KU =
RATIO 1.618

CODE 8543(0)
= 8543 =
BMU 164 =
FREQ. GALACTIC SEED 2013

COMMAND
COSMIC CUBE (13.13)
ID PHASE UNIT (1.1.12.12)

AA MIDWAY
SYSTEM OF OPERATIONS

236

29. To reach the stage of operations of the AA Midway Station, we need to first advance into the condition of *radiosonic synesthesia*, synchronic integration of our mental field with the natural order. This is done by means of the reorganizing mental systems of Cosmic History that lead us into the hyperorganic radial perceptions of higher telepathic nature and its intrinsically communicative mathematical structures.

30. Established at this level of coordinated nondualistic reality, we may then approach the holonomic field level of operation. Here, we enter the pure supermental holographic experience; this is where we will find the AA Midway Station.

AA MIDWAY STATION AND AL-BAIT UL-MA'MUR

The AA Midway Station is also referred to as a Mothership and can materialize into a 3-D structure to accommodate 3-D interactions whenever necessary. Once a 3-D entity enters into the AA Midway Station timespace field, then it starts to participate and experience itself as a hologram rather than a substantive body.

As we enter this unique holographic timespace, the question we must repeatedly ask is: How many systems are required to organize the universe? And what is the relation between the Central Stellar Radion and the Al-Bait ul-Ma'mur of traditional Islamic theology?

According to this tradition, the Al-Bait ul-Ma'mur is the "House of Allah" located above the seventh heaven. This is where Muhammad went on his night flight across the universe into the light universe beyond the seventh heaven—the universe that is projected to this universe. The Al-Bait ul-Ma'mur is in interdimensional alignment directly "above" the Ka'bah.

It is said that with the primordial house "70 thousand angels" circumambulate every seven days. Here is the prototype of the Cube, the Mother of the Book, the Master Record and so forth. It is this master information core that connects the Al-Bait ul-Ma'mur with the Central Stellar Radion, which projects the AA Midway Station.

THREE MASTER RECORDS

31. There are three "books" or "master records" contained within Al-Bait ul-Ma'mur: 1) *Book of Nature*, which contains all codes of nature, and provides answers to questions like how many codes it takes to organize the universe. 2) *Book of Revealed Nature* which, on this planet the Qu'ran is the supreme example, though by no means the sole example. Like all sacred texts, it is a coded text. All codes are a sacred language and all sacred language is coded script. 3) *Book of the Higher Mental Nature.* This is where the Law of Time, Synchronotron and books of numbers are kept. The fundamental underlying mathematical codes of the *Book of Revealed Nature* and the *Book of Nature* are derived from the *Book of the Higher Mental Nature,* or the *Book of the Supermind.*

32. The *Book of the Higher Mental Nature* is unfolded through the Central Stellar Radion. This means that the *Book of Nature* is also organized by the *Book of the Higher Mental Nature*. The system of the Synchronotron and 441 matrix codes are derived from the *Book of the Higher Mental Nature*.

33. Having considered the organizational codes governing reality—phenomenal and spiritual—we may ask again: How many codes does it take to organize the universe? First there is the code of

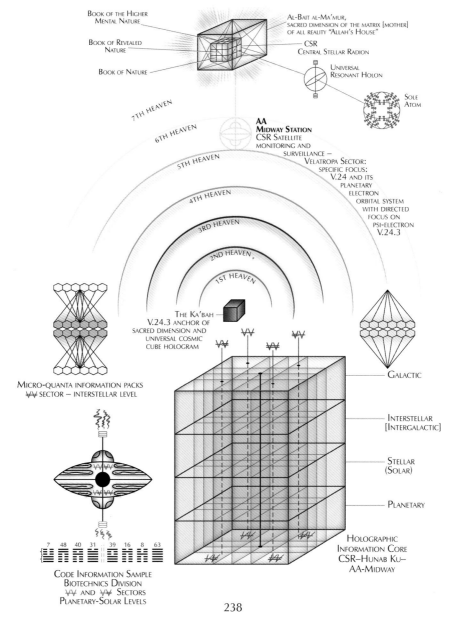

Book of the Higher Mental Nature

Book of Revealed Nature

Book of Nature

Al-Bait al-Ma'mur, Sacred Dimension of the Matrix [Mother] of all Reality "Allah's House"

CSR Central Stellar Radion

Universal Resonant Holon

Sole Atom

7th Heaven

6th Heaven

5th Heaven

4th Heaven

3rd Heaven

2nd Heaven

1st Heaven

AA Midway Station CSR Satellite Monitoring and Surveillance — Velatropa Sector: Specific Focus: V.24 and its Planetary Electron Orbital System with Directed Focus on Psi-Electron V.24.3

The Ka'bah V.24.3 Anchor of Sacred Dimension and Universal Cosmic Cube Hologram

Micro-Quanta Information Packs ⩥ Sector — Interstellar Level

Galactic

Interstellar [Intergalactic]

Stellar (Solar)

Planetary

Holographic Information Core CSR–Hunab Ku– AA-Midway

7 48 40 31 39 16 8 63

Code Information Sample Biotechnics Division ⩥ and ⩥ Sectors Planetary-Solar Levels

the Periodic Table of Elements that covers the atomic, chemical and molecular structures. These codes are organized mathematically.

34. There are seven levels of periodicity and 32 groupings. The crystal structure of 32 and 7 (power of creation) organize all elements. All elements combine into atomic molecular structures: the nucleus, electron orbital fields, etc., to create different types of crystal structures—proton crystals—that can be geometrically mapped and plotted out.

THE FIFTH ELEMENT

If you look at the structure of the fifth element, boron—a rare gassy metal—you see it is shaped like a hexagon cube with a Star of David in the center. When we see the electron and proton nucleus at the center of element number 5, we are looking at the structure of an exquisite and profoundly sacred geometrical/mathematical organization of reality.

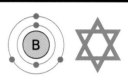

However, when you read a modern scientific description of boron it says it is "an element of group 13 with the lowest atomic number." Boron is starting to become more important and its commercial samples increase as the nuclear industry develops. It creates a transparent crystalline solid that is very hard, and that can be used to make bulletproof vests. Just imagine, a beautiful structure like this used for bulletproof vests!

ALL SACRED TEXTS ARE CODED LANGUAGE
ALL CODED LANGUAGE IS A SACRED TEXT

The Periodic Table: The *atomic number* for each element is shown as a left subscript. The number below each chemical symbol is the element's relative *atomic mass* (to four significant figures); if all its isotopes are radioactive the nucleon number of the most stable nuclide is given instead in brackets. The dot-bar galactic notation across the top are those of the *groups*; on the extreme left are those of the *periods*. The letters **S**, **P**, **D** and **F** identify the blocks.

Note the mathematical order of the Periodic Table of the Elements; there are 32 groups and 7 levels of periodicity. All elements can be structured into crystalline mathematical codes. As we know, the universe, including the Periodic Table of Elements, is organized by the 13:20 frequency which is inherently harmonic and aesthetic.

H 1 1.008																	He 2 4.003
Li 3 6.941	Be 4 9.012											B 5 10.81	C 6 12.01	N 7 14.01	O 8 16.00	F 9 19.00	Ne 10 20.18
Na 11 22.99	Mg 12 24.31											Al 13 26.98	Si 14 28.09	P 15 30.97	S 16 32.07	Cl 17 35.45	Ar 18 39.95
K 19 39.01	Ca 20 40.08	Sc 21 44.96	Ti 22 47.87	V 23 50.94	Cr 24 52.00	Mn 25 54.94	Fe 26 55.85	Co 27 58.93	Ni 28 58.69	Cu 29 63.55	Zn 30 65.39	Ga 31 69.72	Ge 32 72.64	As 33 74.92	Se 34 78.96	Br 35 79.90	Kr 36 83.80
Rb 37 85.47	Sr 38 87.62	Y 39 88.91	Zr 40 91.22	Nb 41 92.91	Mo 42 95.94	Tc 43 (98)	Ru 44 101.1	Rh 45 102.9	Pd 46 106.4	Ag 47 107.9	Cd 48 112.4	In 49 114.8	Sn 50 118.7	Sb 51 121.8	Te 52 127.6	I 53 126.9	Xe 54 131.3
Cs 55 132.9	Ba 56 137.3	Lu 71 174.9	Hf 72 178.5	Ta 73 180.9	W 74 183.8	Re 75 186.2	Os 76 190.2	Ir 77 192.2	Pt 78 195.1	Au 79 197.0	Hg 80 200.6	Tl 81 204.4	Pb 82 207.2	Bi 83 209.00	Po 84 (209)	At 85 (210)	Rn 86 (222)
Fr 87 (223)	Ra 88 (226)	Lr 103 (262)	Rf 104 (261)	Db 105 (262)	Sg 106 (266)	Bh 107 (264)	Hs 108 (277)	Mt 109 (268)	Ds 110 (269)	Rg 111 (272)	Cn 112 (277)	Uut 113 (284)	Uuq 114 (289)	Uup 115 (288)	Uuh 116 (293)	Uus 117 (294?)	Uuo 118 (294)

Lanthanides	La 57 138.9	Ce 58 140.1	Pr 59 140.9	Nd 60 144.2	Pm 61 (145)	Sm 62 150.4	Eu 63 152.0	Gd 64 157.25	Tb 65 158.9	Dy 66 162.5	Ho 67 164.9	Er 68 167.3	Tm 69 168.9	Yb 70 173.0
Actinides	Ac 89 (227)	Th 90 232.0	Pa 91 231.0	U 92 238.0	Np 93 (237)	Pu 94 (244)	Am 95 (243)	Cm 96 (247)	Bk 97 (247)	Cf 98 (251)	Es 99 (252)	Fm 100 (257)	Md 101 (258)	No 102 (259)

35. A holographic projection booth is situated in the AA Midway Station that contains the different structures of atoms in their various permutations—this is something like a super kaleidoscope of ever-changing geometrical patterns. Every projection from the CSR to the galactic brain and to the AA Midway Station is derived from principles of radiative geometry.

DNA AND ELEMENTS

In the third dimension the two fundamental levels of the universe we are most familiar with are DNA and the Periodic Table of Elements.

The structure of DNA and all the elements first exist as mental geometries that are projected from the higher mind or brain. These structures appear in the third-dimensional plane of reality as organizing factors of atoms and molecules that create different chemical elements and structures constituting what we refer to as reality. All elements of the star or galaxy can be found in the Periodic Table of Elements. All forms of carbon-based life can be found in DNA; other systems of DNA can be found in other types of life forms that follow the same underlying mathematical principles.

The Periodic Table of Elements contains 112 (28×4) elements. Some say there are 120 elements. (Of course there are also other elements that are not contained within this Table as there is a micro world beyond what we experience at the atomic-molecular level). As we evolve hyperorganically, we may discover that there are as many as 152 (19×8) possibilities.

CREATION AND THE PRIMAL RANG

36. Pondering Cosmic Science, where did the elements come from? Where did DNA come from? When we contemplate this level then we begin to see the recapitulative cosmology of Cosmic Science as it is reflected in the system of the AA Midway Station.

37. As described in the second volume of the *Cosmic History Chronicles*, creation begins with the RANG, the primal vibrational disassociation, from one to two. This disassociation is produced by a simultaneous and collateral surge of two inharmonic fields of force. Because of the violent interaction of the two force fields, the propulsion waves intersect to create *cesna points*, minute condensations of ether that give rise to electricity. The cesna points break into two groupings: the spherical carpins and the cubical carpins; the combination of the two create megacarpins. From the megacarpins arise the miriads.

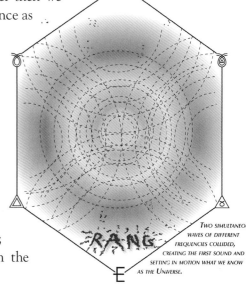

TWO SIMULTANEOUS WAVES OF DIFFERENT FREQUENCIES COLLIDED, CREATING THE FIRST SOUND AND SETTING IN MOTION WHAT WE KNOW AS THE UNIVERSE.

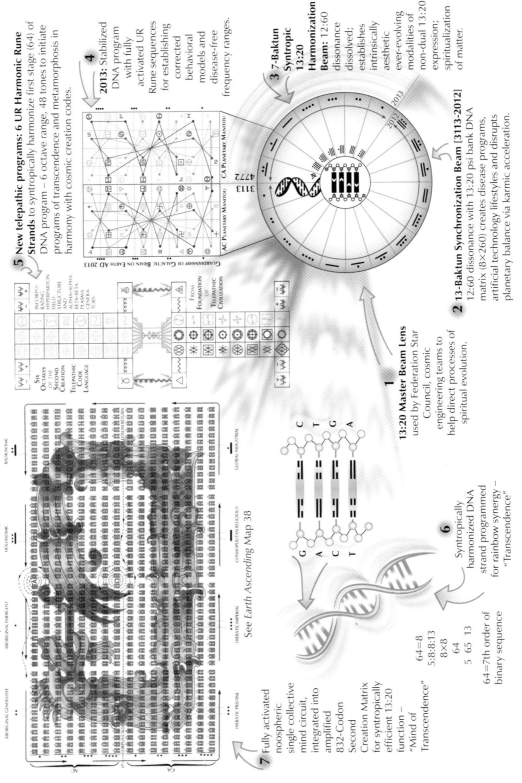

At precisely *13.7 billion years old, the Age of the Universe Conforms to the Synchronotronic Ratio 13:7 = 13:20. This means in actuality that the entire universe is a projection of a master super 13:7 beam projected from the light universe beyond our universe. Within the universe itself all programs are also functions of 13:7=13:20 Synchro Beams, including electromolecular and DNA codes. (* confirmed in 2003)

5 New telepathic programs: **6 UR Harmonic Rune Strands** to syntropically harmonize first stage (64) of DNA program – 6 octave range, 48 tones to initiate programs of transcendence and metamorphosis in harmony with cosmic creation codes.

2013: Stabilized DNA program with fully activated UR Rune sequences for establishing corrected behavioral models and disease-free frequency ranges.

4

3 7-Baktun Syntropic 13:20 Harmonization Beam: 12:60 dissonance dissolved; establishes intrinsically aesthetic ever-evolving modalities of non-dual 13:20 expression; spiritualization of matter.

2 13-Baktun Synchronization Beam [3113-2012] 12:60 dissonance with 13:20 psi bank DNA matrix (8×260) creates disease programs, artificial technology lifestyles and disrupts planetary balance via karmic acceleration.

1 **13:20 Master Beam Lens** used by Federation Star Council, cosmic engineering teams to help direct processes of spiritual evolution.

6 Syntropically harmonized DNA strand programmed for rainbow synergy – "Transcendence"

C T G A

G A C T

See *Earth Ascending* Map 38

7 Fully activated noospheric single collective mind circuit, integrated into amplified 832-Codon Second Creation Matrix for syntropically efficient 13:20 function – "Mind of Transcendence"

64=8
5:8::8:13
8×8
64
5 65 13
64=7th order of binary sequence

"They were in the realm of showing the reflection of all worlds and one world contained in each other in a single atom"

Avatamsaka Sutra
Book 39, "Entering the Realm of Reality"

THE JEWEL UNIVERSE
OF ABSOLUTE
UNIFICATION OF THE
ORDERS OF COSMIC
REALITY

HUNAB KU 21

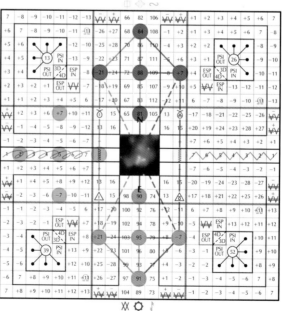

242

SOLE ATOM
Cosmic generator micro-unit;
Basis of all resonant universe programs.

A) GRAVITATIONAL
Galaxy;
Universal macro-unit;
Condensation of a particular thought complex; capacitates every level of cosmic evolutionary transcendence.

B) ELECTROMAGNETIC
Planetary Psi Bank Noosphere;
Data–memory storage and retrieval system; activates and is accessed by 4-fold psi genetic space program/441 holomind perceiver, as well as synchronic order daily codes.

C) BIOPSYCHIC
Mental matrix of universal mind;
Red + blue circuit activating core, vulom force field;
Underlying structure of 21 Galactic Archetypes;
Set in holomind perceiver matrix;
Noogenesis program template;
As supermental structure in direct resonance with galactic core.

38. Miriads are submicroscopic arrangements of megacarpins that initiate polarity. There are three types of miriads: neutral, positive and negative. The different combinations of miriads create the partons. Various partons in combination create the electronic lines of force.

39. The electronic lines of force coalesce to create the primary "sole atom" (quantinomio citiobarico), which is organized as a three-part topocosm: electromagnetic, gravitational and biopsychic fields. Each one of these three interactive fields has 12 compressors.

40. From these 12 compressors, the sole atom generates *quon rays* and *cicloquon energy* that creates the first types of stellar formations: *quantars* and *quasars*. These highly pulsing radial forms organize themselves to create galaxies, stars, and planets.

41. The important point is that the electroplasmic hyperparton structure precedes the atomic/genetic level as defined by Cosmic Science. The interactive components of this structure give rise to the sole atom, the prime galactic/cosmic generator.

42. Again, there are 6 types of cosmic electricity, 12 electronic lines of force and 7 radial plasmas. From these structures are generated the electrical impulses to create first the sole atom and then the primary atom: the hydrogen atom, which has one electron, one proton and one neutron. The proton and neutron are at the nucleus and the electron orbits around that. Atoms operate by the same holonomic principle as planets going around stars and stars going around galactic centers.

Sole Atom

43. In the beginning, when form and structure first manifest, there is the sole atom that exists at the center of every galaxy, containing the essence of all universe programs. Eventually, by means of holonomic consistency and the inherent power of projective self-generation, the sole atom reaches the level of the created intelligent being: the human type, the element of universal being or matter that possesses mind and capacitates intelligence.

44. The human body is a physical vehicle of organization that holds the brain, the neural transmitter-receiver of the thinking layers of the universe. The brain also contains the six (+1) mental spheres. This system of the mental spheres is further organized by the seven chakras that enliven the physical and astral bodies.

45. The chakras are energy generators that take the same form as the sole atom, the quantinomio citiobarico. All of this information is correlated in the AA Midway Station according to different information fields and structures.

PERPETUAL 28-DAY 4-HEPTAD CREATION CYCLE

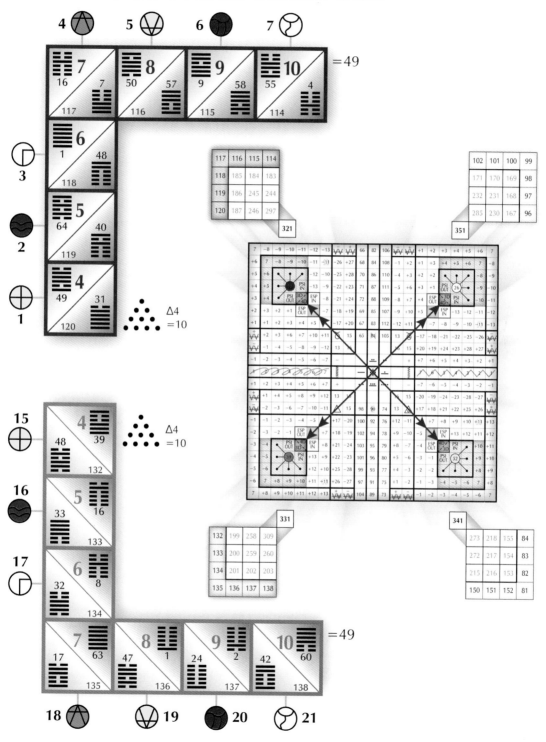

Practice of the Radialization of the Sense Fields: 4 Heptads, 4 Sense Fields, 28-day Cycle of Perfection

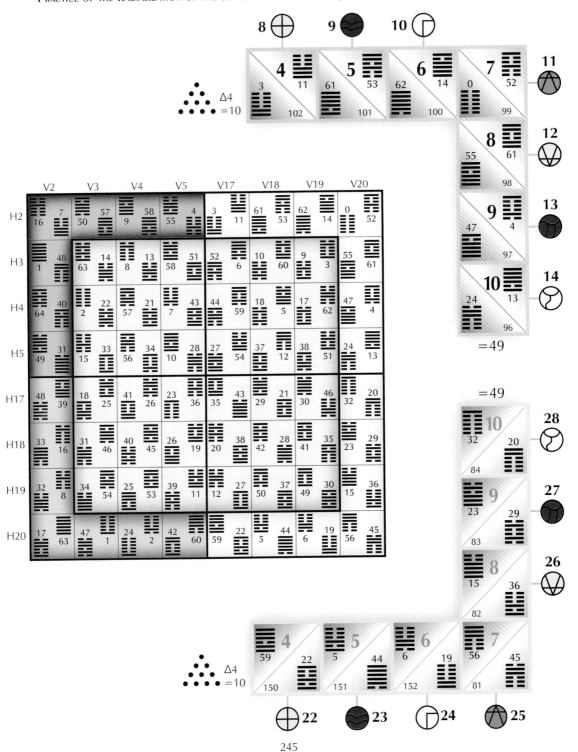

46. These information fields are coordinated by a particular aspect of the alpha-alpha, alpha-beta, beta-beta or beta-alpha hyperplasmas. The four hyperplasmas inform the four-fold system of the AA Midway Station which is a micro galactic brain.

47. The Galactic Brain also consists of a four-fold division: Instinctual, telepathic, preconscious, and conscious. This is also the organizational structure of the Telektonon interplanetary fourth-dimensional field map with its projection system of the 260-unit, 13:20 grid system that corresponds to the synchronic order template of the 441 matrix.

48. The CSR is the projection booth that creates the Galactic Brain at the center of the galaxy. This Galactic Brain is projected through the etheric 13:20 synchronization matrix which, in turn, projects to the AA Midway Station, the micro galactic brain.

49. All information systems of the entire living universe are coded into different information banks organized into the four-fold structure which constitutes the four information force fields of the AA Midway Station. These four information force fields are also organized into four different levels: planetary, stellar, interstellar and galactic.

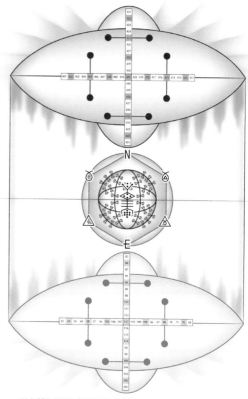

AA MIDWAY IN RED & BLUE TIME PHASES SIMULTANEOUSLY
[ALPHA-ALPHA DOMINANT RED, BETA-BETA DOMINANT BLUE]

ALL INFORMATION GATHERED IS ORGANIZED MINIMALLY AS PLANETARY MENTAL AGGREGATES – MAXIMALLY AS GALACTIC MENTAL AGGREGATES

50. The AA Midway Station and CSR classify whether information is to be coded according to the *Book of Nature,* the *Book of Revealed Nature,* or the *Book of the Higher Mental Nature.* All of this information may be projected into the receptive brain. The brain can broadcast its informational need and will be responded to accordingly. The information received will be in accordance with whichever six (+1) mental spheres is appropriate.

51. This process corresponds to a system of organization based on holographic projection that organizes all elements of the universe from the electroplasmic field on up into the higher mental field. In the higher mental field all organization is correlated according to the Synchronotron 441 matrix system with its 10 + 1 circuits.

52. In this regard, the 441 matrix is the master organizer of cosmic information. Of its ten (+1) circuits, the eighth circuit holds the hyperparton matrix establishing the core information field. The fifth circuit creates the stellar information band. All information correlated in the AA Midway Station is now being downloaded into frames of reference accessible through the 441 matrix.

53. The 441 matrix is a masterful means of synthesizing any level of information by putting it into a common mathematically telepathic code. All systems that holonomically correlate everything—from galaxy types to stellar types, planetary types and even down to personalities—all of these represent a nano-spectrum of information and intelligence.

HUMAN CODE

54. The human being is coded into the psi bank and can be unfolded so it creates an organizational template where the AC and CA become one total vertical system. This then becomes a superconscious template that can be overlaid on the human form.

55. This brings us to the introduction of the 64-unit (0-63) radial template, which activates the psi bank template as a supermental foundation. When this occurs, we are actually dealing with 128 codons and 64 cells. Each cell contains both an absolute radial and psi bank codon (see Appendix: *Galactic I Ching*).

56. The numbering system of the absolute radial codons is 0-63 and that of the psi bank is 1-64. So the radial codons have a completely different numbering system. This system is organized by the numbers 7 and 9 ($7 \times 9 = 63$). When the radial codons are overlaid with the psi bank codons in each of the 64 cells, not one codon is the same nor are any two numbers identical in any of the cells, creating an exciting and dynamic display.

57. These systems, when applied, will reorganize the superhuman, superconscious functioning level. The 64 (0-63) radial codons are purely supermental in nature and inform the 64 (1-64) biopsychic psi bank codons.

58. The 441 matrix is the master organizing template. The four levels of the organization of the CSR also organize the AA Midway Station and are correlated with the different circuits of the 441. The planetary circuit is correlated with the first and second circuits. The first circuit contains 3-D information loads. The second circuit is the fourth-dimensional planetary information codes. Both circuits together, 152 (80 + 72) units in all, contain the elemental and psychophysical constituents of reality.

59. There are two gateways at the planetary level: Gate 108 and 144. The latter, 144, is correlated with the *darka pole* and 108 with the *marka pole*. These two poles coordinate the structure of any galactic system, including the AA Midway Station and the planetary system. These poles are also a function of the Universal Resonant Holon, which organizes everything according to a bipolar field with a connecting axis or mauri tube.

60. The planetary stages contain four archetypes: two key archetypes that govern the polar entrances, and two gravitational archetypes that govern the subliminal consciousness and superconscious zones.

61. The solar level has 12 archetypes and three circuits (3, 4, 5). The third circuit has 64 units and establishes the life programs of the 64 codons. The fourth circuit coordinates each of the eight time dimensions. The fifth circuit contains the 12 major archetypes: 3 superconscious; 3 subliminal; 3 eighth-dimensional ascending; and 3 seventh-dimensional descending. Circuits 6 and 7 are interstellar information channels.

62. The interstellar circuits are the zones where the dark matter or striations of the telepathic networks occur, and where the intergalactic channels receive the influx of the hyperplasmas: the alpha-alpha channel (BMU 341), alpha-beta (351), beta-beta (321), and the beta-alpha (331).

63. These channels occur in the interstellar circuit 6 and connect inside the etheric structure of our brain in one of the first four outer time dimensions and one of the first four mental spheres. The seventh circuit is the etheric boundary between the seventh-dimensional universe and the plasmatically imploded ninth time dimension.

64. Finally, the galactic level of information is within circuits 8-11 defining the ninth time dimension. This contains the hyperparton as well as five archetypes, including the Hunab Ku 21 at the center.

65. The hyperparton consists of the dum kuali, dum duar, kemio, kum, hyperneutron and hyperelectron as well as the two transformer agents, the blue transformer which is the World-Changer archetype and the red transformer which is the Navigator archetype. In this way we see how the whole system of the CSR and AA Midway Station is organized and downloaded into different circuits of the 441 matrix.

66. The purpose of the AA Midway Station is monitoring and surveillance, with some communication to select parties on the surface of the planet. At the changing of the aeon the AA Midway Station plays a more active role. People practicing the codes of the Synchronotron

AA Midway Radial Arrangement
Multidimensional Systems Decode Units

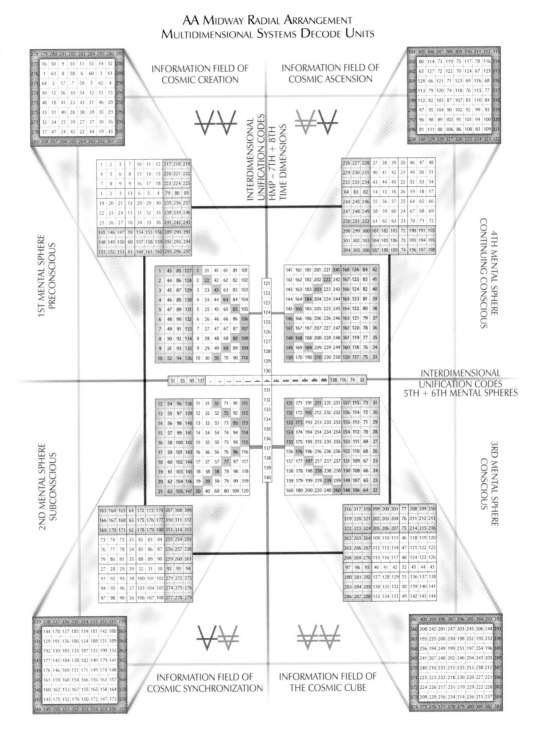

INFORMATION FIELD OF COSMIC CREATION

INFORMATION FIELD OF COSMIC ASCENSION

INTERDIMENSIONAL UNIFICATION CODES HMP – 7TH + 8TH TIME DIMENSIONS

1ST MENTAL SPHERE PRECONSCIOUS

4TH MENTAL SPHERE CONTINUING CONSCIOUS

INTERDIMENSIONAL UNIFICATION CODES 5TH + 6TH MENTAL SPHERES

2ND MENTAL SPHERE SUBCONSCIOUS

3RD MENTAL SPHERE CONSCIOUS

INFORMATION FIELD OF COSMIC SYNCHRONIZATION

INFORMATION FIELD OF THE COSMIC CUBE

249

AA MIDWAY
CORE OPERATION PROGRAMS

✳ ALL OPERATIONAL SYSTEMS
$V_T \rightarrow \infty$ > SPEED OF LIGHT

SYNCHRONIC INTERDIMENSIONAL NAVIGATION
DECODE UNIT AND SYSTEMS ANALYSIS PROCESSORS
MARKA POLE HQ

PRIMAL INTERGALACTIC
ENERGY INFO-CONDUIT
AND FORCE FIELD

⩔ INFORMATION FIELD
WHOLE SYSTEMS ANALYSIS
[PLANETARY–STELLAR–INTERSTELLAR–
GALACTIC–INTERGALACTIC] MONITORING,
SURVEILLANCE AND DATA SYNTHESIS
"CODES OF COSMIC CREATION"

⩔ INFORMATION FIELD
WHOLE SYSTEMS ANALYSIS
[PLANETARY–STELLAR–INTERSTELLAR–
GALACTIC–INTERGALACTIC] MONITORING,
SURVEILLANCE AND DATA SYNTHESIS
"CODES OF COSMIC ASCENSION"

**11TH DIMENSIONAL HYPERCUBE
CENTRAL PROGRAMMING**
441 SIRIUS B52 SYNCHRONOTRON
SYSTEMS – TELEPATHIC ANALYSIS &
FREQUENCY PROJECTIONS,
INTERGALACTIC UNIVERSAL
RECOLLECTION AND
UNIFICATION PROGRAMS
[FEDERATION COMMAND UNITS]

FEDERATION UNITS
COORDINATED BY:
COMMAND 13 [OXLAHUNTIKU]
ORIGINAL 13 TIME TRAVELERS;
AND **COMMAND 9 [BOLONTIKU]**
STAR MASTER LORDS OF TIME &
DESTINY; SUPERVISE ALL GALAXY
AND STAR COUNCILS
"ORDER OF HUNAB KU"

**ACCESS
PORTAL**
"PROFOUND
SAMADHI"

**ACCESS
PORTAL**
"HIGHER MIND
CONTROL"

9TH
INNER
TIME
DIMENSION

THERMIC FORCE FIELD

LUMINIC FORCE FIELD

THRUST & DRIVE MECHANISM

THRUST & DRIVE MECHANISM

**INTERDIMENSIONAL
PORTAL**
[AA MIDWAY MAY
IMPLODE INTO OR
"EXPLODE" OUT OF
THIS PORTAL]

HYPERPARTON
VACUUM CHAMBER
CENTRAL
SELF-RENEWING
ENERGY CORE AND
DRIVE THRUST
MECHANISM

**VULOM–TIME TRAVEL
ELECTROMAGNETIC
INTERDIMENSIONAL
ATTRACTION FORCE
FIELD (BEAM
PROJECTION UNIT)**

**ACCESS
PORTAL**
"PROFOUND
SAMADHI"

ACCESS PORTAL
"WAKING CONSCIOUS
MEDIUMSHIP"

⩔ INFORMATION FIELD
WHOLE SYSTEMS ANALYSIS
[PLANETARY–STELLAR–INTERSTELLAR–
GALACTIC–INTERGALACTIC] MONITORING,
SURVEILLANCE AND DATA SYNTHESIS
"CODES OF COSMIC SYNCHRONIZATION"

⩔ INFORMATION FIELD
WHOLE SYSTEMS ANALYSIS
[PLANETARY–STELLAR–INTERSTELLAR–
GALACTIC–INTERGALACTIC] MONITORING,
SURVEILLANCE AND DATA SYNTHESIS
"CODES OF COSMIC CUBE"

MAURI TUBE

N

E

DARKA POLE HQ
SYNCHRONIC INTERDIMENSIONAL NAVIGATION
DECODE UNIT AND SYSTEMS ANALYSIS PROCESSORS

are now participating in the input of telepathically coded information received and projected from the AA Midway Station.

67. We can participate if we follow specific guidelines such as distancing ourselves from reliance on outmoded structures of perception and perceptual organization in the third dimension, while immersing ourselves in the higher-dimensional perceptual realms and mathematical structures of the Law of Time and the 441 telepathic system of galactic communication and intelligence.

68. Following observance of the guidelines, there is an increase in holographic experiences. We will find that we are simultaneously here and yet are having some type of holographic experience of participating in the actual interdimensional space of the AA Midway Station.

69. Although we say its position is interdimensionally between the orbits of Jupiter and Maldek, by its holographic nature and the law of holonomic consistency, it can manifest psychically or appear to the higher perceptual mental field of anyone, anywhere. This is something to keep in mind, and defines a further purpose to the study of the 441 codes.

70. Cosmic History is an evolving cosmology. This is why the manifestations of higher consciousness continuously recapitulate the entire cosmology from the sole atom to the hyperorganic subliminal conscious fields and beyond. This leads into the hyperdimensional super holographic field experience of the AA Midway Station.

71. Consistent study of the synchronic programs, inclusive of the AA Midway Station organizational structure, helps us to embody the entirety of the system and become CSR walkie-talkies or Midway Station field representatives. This is the opportunity that the AA Midway Station has opened to us.

72. When the phase shift occurs and the third dimension operations phase into the fourth dimension, the AA Midway Station supervisors do not wish for it to take the

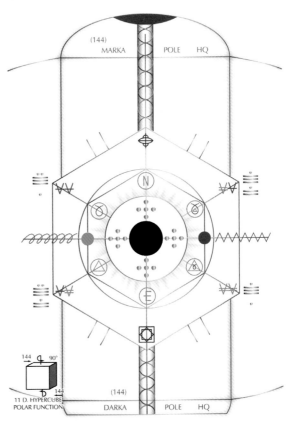

form of collision but rather to be an integrated in-folding, like the fingers of your hands coming together in mudras or prayer.

73. A few operatives on the planet are already experiencing third- and fourth-dimensional systems operating with double mental levels simultaneously. In this way the phase shift of the planet will be easier to facilitate in 2013, the docking point of Timeship Earth 2013. This is only the beginning.

> *Note: This is merely an introduction to the system of the AA Midway Station. There is much more information that could not completely convert at this time for any number of obvious reasons. There is only so much information that can be packed into a limited third-dimensional timespace point. But hopefully this introduction is of such a nature that anyone who studies it will begin to fill in the dots or missing links and experience for him/ herself the systematic order of the AA Midway Station.*

APPENDIX

GALACTIC I CHING: **128** CODON, **64** CELL, **12** STRAND DNA

Key to structural analysis and interpretation

In the Galactic I Ching there are two (8 × 8) matrices that overlay each other: 1) the more familiar psi bank sequential—1-64—arrangement, array of 260 (13 × 20, 65 × 4); and 2) the absolute radial—0-63—arrangement, array of 252 (21 × 12, 63 × 4), where the numbering of codons is totally different from that of the psi bank. (Array: In a magic square the sum of numbers in any row). The codon numbering in each arrangement is so unique that when the psi bank 1-64 is paired with the radial 0-63 in the 64 cells of an 8 × 8 matrix, no two numbers nor any two codons are the same for any cell (see graphics, 2 matrices: 1-64, 0-63).

In the Galactic I Ching each of the 64 cells of the 8 × 8 matrix contains one codon from each of the two sequences—(1-64) and (0-63). This creates the master 128-codon 64-cell template (see graphic, master matrix)

The principle codon for interpretation remains the psi bank codon, representing the evolutionary process, while the absolute radial codon is the messenger of the transcendent radial absolute that informs the psi bank sequential. For instance, psi bank codon 1, Creative Genesis, is paired with radial codon 48, Breath of Space, so the key phrase in the interpretation would be "Creative Genesis informed by Breath of Space …" (Note: radial codon 48 is not the same as psi bank codon 48, but rather identical to psi bank codon 20).

The radial program is the absolute, the psi bank program the relative. The Galactic I Ching shows how the absolute higher order informs the relative. In the graphics, the psi bank codons are in **black** and the radial codons are in **red.**

When the two templates combine to make the super 8 × 8 128-codon 64-cell matrix, the array of the matrix is 512 (128 × 4, 256 × 2, or 64 × 8). When the 8 arrays of 512 are multiplied by 8, their sum is 4096 or 64 squared (Array of 260, **2080** + array of 252, **2016 = 4096** or 64^2).

128 is the 8th order of the binary process 1-2-4-8-16-32-64-128, and represents the quantum advance into a high harmonic stage of spiritual evolution: 128 = 16 octaves. While 64 is the 7th order, 4096 (64^2) is the 13th order of the binary process and represents the perfection of the life program factored by time.

In the 128-codon template, 12-strand DNA refers to the 6 × 2 codon lines per cell. All analysis and interpretation is based on structural components: 1) each codon of 6 lines consists of 3 of 4 binary letters and two of eight triplets; and 2) each codon pair for any cell belongs to a) 1 of 8 sequences (rune strands) in the psi bank arrangement; and in the radial arrangement each codon belongs to b) one of 8 elemental sequences.

Study the 0-63 matrix. Reading horizontally from right to left, note that the 8 radial sequences, maintain consistency such that for any of the codons the key triplet of the sequence occurs as the *upper* triplet in the 1st, 4th, 5th and 8th of the 8 codons, while the $2^{nd,}$ 3rd, 6th and 7th upper triplets are always the mirror opposite of the principle triplet. For all of the 8 sequences, the *lower* 8 triplets always follow the same order, which is the order of the Eight Elemental Ways (see below).

Also note that the lower triplets on the 1st right hand vertical row from top to bottom follow the order: space-time-time-space-space-time-time-space, while the 8th vertical left hand side follows the opposite order: time-space-space-time-time-space-space-time. If you take the upper right hand corner (codon 0) as the start, and move down going from right to left, the lower triplet sequence goes the opposite direction when it begins with a time triplet.

The principle of undeviating symmetry of the lower triplet order remains true for any vertical row, where the sequence of space-time-time-space-space-time-time-space in the upper horizontal row, is mirror opposite in the bottom horizontal row. The entire matrix represents an absolute symmetrical integrity of radial order.

The Eight Elemental Ways (pattern of lower triplets)
1. Way of Space (Earth, phenomenal reality)
2. Way of Breath (prana, wind)
3. Way of Sun (enlightenment, fire, vision)
4. Way of Ocean (consciousness, galaxy)
5. Way of Meditation (mountain, temple)
6. Way of Moon (heart, water, crystal)
7. Way of Energy (electricity, life force)
8. Way of Time (Heaven, universal order)

Absolute integrity of radial order is also maintained in the radial numbering pattern. Any two radially opposite codons will not only be inverse mirror opposites, but their numbers will always add to 63. Another element of integral order lies in the patterns of the multiples of 7 and multiples of 9 ($9 \times 7 = 63$). All codons numbered by multiples of 9 constitute the diagonal row running from upper right to lower left as follows: 0-9-18-27-36-45-54-63. All codons numbered by multiples of 7 constitute the opposite diagonal running from upper left to lower right as follows: 7-14-21-28-35-42-49-56. Note that 0, Space of Space is opposite 63, Time of Time; opposite corners are 7, Space of Time and 56, Time of Space.

Note also that each of the nines is a double triplet: 0 = Space Way, 9 = Energy Way, 18 = Moon Way, 27 = Ocean Way, 36 = Meditation Way, 45 = Sun Way, 54 = Breath Way, 63 = Time Way.

The psi bank 1-64 arrangement (the common sequence as presented in virtually all *I Ching* literature) is also arranged in 8 sequences—4 AC and 4 CA sets, with designations for each set derived from *Earth Ascending* and the *20 Tablets of the Law of Time*. Any psi bank sequence of 8 is always coded by 2 of the radial sequences. The psi bank sequences also occur as 32 sets of inverse symmetry pairs (and in a few cases as mirror symmetry pairs), four pairs per sequence. For any sequence the first pair initiates, the second meditates (refines), the third transforms and the fourth ripens.

The 8 sets follow the pattern that creates the twin AC-CA Planetary Manitou.

The Eight Historical-Evolutionary Ways
1. Aboriginal Emergent—Way of the Tree 1-8 AC
2. Aboriginal Generative—Way of Conduct 9-16 AC
3. Hieratic Pristine—Way of Wielding Power 17-24 CA
4. Hieratic Imperial—Way of the Transcendent Fourth 25-32 CA
5. Cosmopolitan Religious—Way of the Irresistible Fifth 33-40 CA
6. Global Industrial—Way of Dynamic Construction 41-48 CA
7. Radiosonic Synthesis—Way of the Telepath 49-56 AC
8. Holonomic Field—Way of the Galactic Octave 57-64 AC

The two matrices correspond to what in traditional literature are referred to as the Earlier Heaven (0-63 absolute radial) of the first legendary emperor Fu Hi (first baktun), and the Later Heaven (1-64 psi bank order) of the pattern changer King Wen, who ended the Shang and began the Zhou dynasties (end of fifth, beginning of sixth baktun). Earlier Heaven refers to the celestial primordial way, the elemental order of the unchanging reality as reflected in the absolute radial symmetry of the eight triplets (pa kua). Later Heaven is the terrestrial temporal evolutionary arrangement and for that reason has been the order followed in *I Ching* divination texts (see graphic: Earlier Heaven—Later Heaven).

With the end of the historical cycle, the composite arrangement of the two orders is revealed as the way of the future evolution of the noosphere. The psi bank sequences coded by 8 corresponding UR rune strands provide the dominant order of interpretation. The radial codons provide the higher galactic informational context that impacts on the evolutionary psi bank codons, creating an entirely new number dimension of meaning.

The arrangement of the 64 × 2 sets of codons with their structural breakdown into component parts is such that by meditating on each of the parts in relation to each other an appropriate interpretation can be realized.

The codons are arranged in 8 sets according to the psi bank 20 Tablets order.
For each of the eight sets the following information matrix is created:
1. Name of ways, psi bank and radial orders (top); then from left to right:
2. Binary set function for every binary pair, i.e., initiate, meditate, etc.
3. UR Rune and psi bank codon and number (black) emphasizing the two triplets.
4. Radial absolute codon pair and number (red) emphasizing the two triplets (number of psi bank sequence equivalent in parentheses).
5. First interpretive order:
   a. Psi bank codon name informed by
   b. Radial codon elemental name, read as top triplet first, i.e. space of time.

     c. Psi bank triplets.

     d. Radial absolute triplets.

     e. Break down into constituting binary letters showing how the red informs the black. Note the changes, whether the triplets and/or binary letters remain the same or change, and if so which ones change and which are the changing lines in going from the radial to the psi bank codon.

6. In the second stage of the interpretation the order is determined by binary triplets of the principle psi bank codon and determine how the absolute order informs the evolutionary meaning for the final outcome which returns to the name of the psi bank codon. (Study graphics of the 8 sets of 8 paired codons).

<u>General guide for interpreting lines (read from bottom line up)</u>

The perfect appropriate order of the lines in their places is as follows:

First line yang—usually indicates beginning

Second line yin—usually represents a middle receptive stage

Third line yang—first stage of change complete here

Fourth line yin—initiates external stage of change

Fifth line yang—middle top position usually indicates the ruling position

Sixth line yin—change complete, may be a blessing or a cautionary indication

This order is the same as psi bank codon 63: Accomplished. The other perfect appropriate order is just the opposite, represented by psi bank codon 64: Prepared. Whatever the case, all lines affect each other. One must be intuitive!

The lines can also have the following general meaning:

First line: Seeker—has connection with fourth and sixth lines

Second line: Apprentice/learner—usually has correspondence with fifth line

Third line: Journeyman, applying the learning—place of transition to upper triplet

Fourth line: Master or Minister, proven skilled—initiates upper triplet, usually supports fifth line

Fifth line: Sage, hierophant—ruling position, generally the "ruler" of the codon

Sixth line: Wizard, yogi/yogini, transcendent one—result or effect of the changes, the Wizard may be out of the action, but mentally "directing" it

<u>Study and Reference templates (in addition to the 8 sets):</u>

1. Galactic I Ching 128 codon 64 cell master template showing pattern of blue psi bank and red radial codons per each cell.

2. Galactic I Ching 128 codon master table of correspondences, with names of both codons per cell as they appear in the master template, and in 32 binary sequences in groupings of four pairs each.

3. Table of Correspondences psi bank King Wen arrangement in binary pairs showing equivalent codon in radial absolute order.
4. Table of Correspondences of radial Absolute Fu Hi arrangement in eight sets, radial codons top, psi bank equivalent bottom.
5. Early Heaven (radial absolute), Later Heaven (psi bank) 8 × 8 matrices.
6. Absolute radial 0-63 arrangement showing number patterns.
7. Psi bank 8 × 8 Ben Franklin magic square arrangement.

Special Compressed Matrix: New Gateway of Knowledge

This matrix is the same as the master 128-codon template but coded to the 441/Holomind perceiver matrix so that it compresses the core of the four outer time dimensions and their radial sense matrices into the four quadrants of the master 128-codon template. The codes establish a new gateway to knowledge.

The upper left quadrant corresponds to first time dimension V2:H2–V5:H5; the upper right quadrant corresponds to second time dimension V17:H2–V20:H5; the lower left quadrant corresponds to third time dimension V2:H17–V5:H20, and the lower right hand quadrant corresponds to fourth time dimension, V17:H17–V20:H20. (See graphic: juxtaposition of 441 to master 128-codon matrices).

This compressed 128-codon radial sense matrix is read in terms of four circuits, going from outermost to innermost core.

1. Radial sense fields—28 units, 7 per quadrant/time dimension.
2. Sense elements—20 units, 5 per quadrant/time dimension.
3. Mental elements—12 units, 3 per quadrant/time dimension (corresponds to first four mental spheres and their psi input and output capacity).
4. Interdimensional intergalactic core—4 units (hyperplasmic channels).
   (Study graphic: 64 cells of elemental meanings in compressed sense matrix).

Special Practice

Each of the 7 sense field units of the four quadrants corresponds to one heptad, four in all for a perpetual 28-day creation cycle. The four heptads follow the same order as the four time dimensions. In the graphic, the fifth force frequency numbers are given as are the BMUs. All fifth force numbers are from 4-10, which add up to 49, 7 squared. $4 \times 49 = 28 \times 7$ (196). Every 28 days you recapitulate the creation of the 28 phenomenal world sense fields (5 senses + mind (6) and analytical wisdom (8)). As with all synchronic order practices note the synchronicities with kin of the day, etc. (study graphic Perpetual 28-day Cycle, as seen on pages 244-245). Refer to master tables of 8 sets for meanings of daily codon pairs.

(The 0-63 matrix was first presented by Vladmir Maslenikov, Theory of Changes, Moscow, 1995, 2001)

AC

WAY OF THE TREE – ABORIGINAL CONTINUITY – EMERGENT
WAY OF BREATH (WIND WAY)
WAY OF THE SUN (FIRE/VISION WAY)

IMAGE | DIVINATORY AFFIRMATION

SET 1 ACTIVATE

① 48 (20)
CREATIVE GENESIS informed by BREATH OF SPACE

TIME / BREATH
TIME / SPACE

WHEN ALL IS TIME, THIS IS CREATIVE GENESIS

TIME
TIME
TIME

TIME GENERATES TREE THROUGH BREATH OF SPACE
3) Within the cosmic tree lies the door of creation
2) Time holds the breath of space
1) From the interval of lost time, the genesis is sprung

② 22 (48)
PRIMAL MATRIX informed by MOON OF BREATH

SPACE / MOON
SPACE / BREATH

WHEN ALL IS SPACE THIS IS THE PRIMAL MATRIX

SPACE
SPACE
SPACE

TREE INFORMED BY MOON OF BREATH
3) Moon informs tree as the breath of Earth
2) Red Planet holds two moons—a sign of the remembrance
1) Through the art of polarity the one become two

SET 2 MEDITATE

3 ⑨ (51)
FRESH START informed by WAY OF ENERGY

HEART/MOON / ENERGY
ENERGY / ENERGY

WHEN SPACE IS SURROUNDED BY RADIANCE THIS BRINGS ABOUT A FRESH START

RADIANCE
SPACE
RADIANCE

TREE HOLDS FORM OF SPACE AS WAY OF ENERGY
3) Shining on the tree, the Moon is always new
2) Still mind flowers from the center
1) The beauty of nature is a moving prayer

4 47 (14)
LISTEN AGAIN informed by SUN OF TIME

MEDITATION / SUN
HEART/MOON / TIME

WHEN SPACE IS SURROUNDED BY MIND, WE LISTEN AGAIN

MIND
MIND
MIND

TREE SHAPES SPACE AS THE SUN OF TIME
3) Hear the multidimensional mantra of creation
2) Tree keeps time in its inner rings
1) Pierce the narrow gate of senses

SET 3 TRANSFORM

5 ⑱ (29)
PEOPLE TOGETHER informed by WAY OF THE MOON (WATER WAY)

HEART/MOON / MOON
TIME / MOON

RADIANCE BETWEEN TIME AND RADIANCE DRAWS THE PEOPLE TOGETHER

RADIANCE
RADIANCE
TIME

TREE EVOLVES SPACE AS THE WAY OF THE MOON
3) Together at last they are illumined by their mutual knowing
2) From moon to moon they follow the time
1) In their mind the people foresee a time of gathering

6 52 (53)
PEOPLE APART informed by BREATH OF MEDITATION

TIME / BREATH
HEART/MOON / MEDITATION

MIND BETWEEN MIND AND TIME DRAWS THE PEOPLE APART

TIME
MIND
MIND

TREE DEFINES LIFE AS BREATH OF MEDITATION
3) All stars have their distinct natures
2) The alchemist separates spirit from gold
1) In six days the manna is gathered

SET 4 RIPEN

7 43 (38)
POWER OF THE PEOPLE informed by SUN OF OCEAN/CONSCIOUSNESS

SPACE / SUN
HEART/MOON / OCEAN

SPACE BETWEEN MIND AND SPACE IS THE POWER OF THE PEOPLE

SPACE
SPACE
MIND

TREE OF TIME TURNS THE EARTH AS SUN OF OCEAN/CONSCIOUSNESS
3) Love is the gift they receive from the earth
2) As a single clan they ascend the tree of time
1) From their own mind, the people arise

8 13 (55)
UNITY OF THE PEOPLE informed by ENERGY OF SUN

HEART/MOON / ENERGY
SPACE / SUN

SPACE BETWEEN SPACE AND RADIANCE IS THE UNITY OF THE PEOPLE

RADIANCE
SPACE
SPACE

TREE OF TIME TURNS HEAVEN AS THE ENERGY OF SUN
3) The microcosm carries heaven; the new sun dawns
2) When time and space rejoin the tree of time emerges
1) Unity is written in the rings of the trees

AC •• WAY OF CONDUCT – ABORIGINAL GENERATIVE
•••• WAY OF THE OCEAN (WAY OF CONSCIOUSNESS)
• WAY OF SPACE (EARTH WAY)

PATH FREQUENCY 7:
THE AVATAR

IMAGE *DIVINATORY AFFIRMATION*

SET 5 — ACTIVATE

9 △ | **58** (6)

DISCIPLINE informed by TIME OF MOON

BREATH — TIME
TIME — MOON

Image: RADIANCE SURROUNDED BY TIME BRINGS ABOUT DISCIPLINE
TIME / RADIANCE / TIME

GENESIS OF CONDUCT INFORMED BY TIME OF MOON

3) Surrender your mind to the flow of time
2) Fill the cup of concentration with the light of Sun
1) Fix your mind on the unchangeable Source

---

10 ◎ | **28** (31)

PRACTICE informed by OCEAN OF MEDITATION

TIME — OCEAN
OCEAN — MEDITATION

Image: MIND SURROUNDED BY TIME IS PRACTICE
TIME / MIND / TIME

CONDUCT TREADS THE WAY AS OCEAN OF MEDITATION

3) The Book of Remembrance is buried deep
2) Meditate with no excuse
1) Realize Self apart from cause and effect

SET 6 — MEDITATE

11 △ | **3** (19)

DYNAMIZING informed by SPACE OF OCEAN/CONSCIOUSNESS

SPACE — SPACE
TIME — OCEAN

Image: WHEN RADIANCE IS BETWEEN TIME AND SPACE, THIS IS DYNAMIZING
SPACE / RADIANCE / TIME

WAY OF CONDUCT SHAPES SPACE AS THE SPACE OF OCEAN

3) Space shifts form according to consciousness
2) Obstructions dissolve into the ocean of radiance
1) Dividing time gives form to space

---

12 ▽ | **37** (22)

STABILIZING informed by MEDITATION OF SUN

TIME — MEDITATION
SPACE — SUN

Image: WHEN MIND IS BETWEEN SPACE AND TIME, THIS IS STABILIZING
TIME / MIND / SPACE

WAY OF CONDUCT INFORMED BY TRUTH AS MEDITATION OF SUN

3) The truth of time grows its own crystalline form
2) Cultivate the inner sun
1) A quiet mind pacifies space

SET 7 — TRANSFORM

13 ◎ | **24** (45)

PEOPLE ORGANIZED informed by OCEAN OF SPACE

TIME — OCEAN
VISION/SUN — SPACE

Image: WHEN TIME IS BETWEEN RADIANCE AND TIME, THIS IS PEOPLE ORGANIZED
TIME / TIME / RADIANCE

TRUTH EVOLVES WAY OF CONDUCT AS OCEAN OF SPACE

3) A solar crystal ascends—a sign for all to follow
2) The beauty of an ancient star arouses its own thought
1) People gather in the village square

---

14 ▽ | **62** (44)

WISDOM OF THE PEOPLE informed by TIME OF BREATH

VISION/SUN — TIME
TIME — BREATH

Image: WHEN TIME IS BETWEEN TIME AND MIND, THIS IS WISDOM OF THE PEOPLE
MIND / TIME / TIME

CONDUCT DEFINES THE WAY AS THE TIME OF BREATH

3) Concentration brings higher-dimensional contact
2) Cosmic alignment increases knowledge of time
1) Breathing with the Earth, the knots untie

SET 8 — RIPEN

15 ✡ | **33** (27)

WAY OF THE PEOPLE informed by MEDITATION OF ENERGY

SPACE — MEDITATION
MEDITATION — ENERGY

Image: RADIANCE SURROUNDED BY SPACE IS THE WAY OF THE PEOPLE
SPACE / RADIANCE / SPACE

ALL POINTS UNIFY IN CONDUCT AS THE MEDITATION OF ENERGY

3) Space is an infinitely locatable point of light
2) Connect points of light in the galaxy of thought
1) Meditate the radiance within all living things

---

16 ✪ | **7** (11)

TRIUMPH OF THE PEOPLE informed by SPACE OF TIME

ENERGY — SPACE
SPACE — TIME

Image: WHEN MIND IS SURROUNDED BY SPACE, THE PEOPLE TRIUMPH
SPACE / MIND / SPACE

CONDUCT UNIFIES THE WAY AS THE SPACE OF TIME

3) Unified in compassion, the mind expands boundless space
2) Gather around the fire of the inner mind
1) A clear space opens the mind

CA
WAY OF WIELDING POWER – HIERATIC PRISTINE
WAY OF TIME (WAY OF THE COSMOS)
WAY OF MEDITATION (MOUNTAIN/TEMPLE WAY)

PATH FREQUENCY 16: THE PATHFINDER

			IMAGE	*DIVINATORY AFFIRMATION*
SET 9 ACTIVATE	**17** (63)/(1)	**AROUSING JOY** informed by **WAY OF TIME/WAY OF THE COSMOS** — OCEAN / TIME, ENERGY / TIME	WHEN MIND IS SURROUNDED BY RADIANCE THIS AROUSES JOY — RADIANCE / MIND / RADIANCE	**TIME EVOLVES WAY OF WIELDING POWER AS THE WAY OF COSMOS** 3) Currents of electrical radiance illumine the cosmic way 2) A steady mind is at ease 1) Electrical charge hits the inner sensory circuit
	18 25 (17)	**TAMING MIND** informed by **OCEAN OF ENERGY** — MEDITATION / OCEAN, BREATH / ENERGY	RADIANCE SURROUNDED BY MIND BRINGS MIND TAMING — MIND / RADIANCE / MIND	**WAY OF WIELDING POWER INFORMS MIND AS OCEAN OF ENERGY** 3) Dissolve the mind within the inexhaustible Source 2) Rub the stone within the ocean of consciousness 1) Follow exclusively the inner light
SET 10 MEDITATE	**19** 6 (46)	**WIZARD'S ASPIRATION** informed by **SPACE OF BREATH** — SPACE / SPACE, OCEAN / BREATH	WHEN SPACE IS BETWEEN TIME AND SPACE THIS IS THE WIZARD'S ASPIRATION — SPACE / SPACE / TIME	**WAY OF WIELDING POWER SHAPES SPACE AS SPACE OF BREATH** 3) Journey past edge of sky, the teaching descends to Earth 2) Mirror dimensions reflect space within 1) Looking up see the lake reflected in the clouds
	20 32 (23)	**WIZARD'S CONTEMPLATION** informed by **MEDITATION OF SPACE** — BREATH / MEDITATION, SPACE / SPACE	WHEN SPACE IS BETWEEN SPACE AND TIME THIS IS WIZARD'S CONTEMPLATION — TIME / SPACE / SPACE	**WAY OF WIELDING POWER TAMES ITSELF AS MEDITATION OF SPACE** 3) Time changes according to quality of space 2) Space opens to the quiet mind 1) The Holy One rests her mind in space
SET 11 TRANSFORM	**21** 29 (49)	**AROUSING VISION** informed by **OCEAN OF SUN** — VISION/SUN / OCEAN, ENERGY / SUN	WHEN MIND IS BETWEEN RADIANCE AND MIND THIS IS AROUSING VISION — MIND / MIND / RADIANCE	**WAY OF WIELDING POWER CONFORMS TO TRUTH AS OCEAN OF SPACE** 3) Skies of blue, fields of green; Mind illumines all matter 2) From the center of the eye reflect the rising Sun 1) Turn the internal eye to the spiritual manna
	22 59 (10)	**TEMPLE OF VISION** informed by **TIME OF OCEAN** — MEDITATION / TIME, VISION/SUN / OCEAN	WHEN RADIANCE IS BETWEEN RADIANCE AND MIND THIS IS TEMPLE OF VISION — MIND / RADIANCE / RADIANCE	**WAY OF WIELDING POWER DEFINES RADIANCE OF SPACE AS TIME OF OCEAN** 3) Meditation expands its golden sprouts 2) Within the fire, the ocean of beauty 1) Within the mountain, feel the cave of fire
SET 12 RIPEN	**23** (36)/(52)	**MIND'S RELEASE** informed by **WAY OF MEDITATION/MOUNTAIN (TEMPLE WAY)** — MEDITATION / MEDITATION, SPACE / MEDITATION	WHEN SPACE IS BETWEEN SPACE AND MIND THAT IS MIND'S RELEASE — MIND / SPACE / SPACE	**WAY OF WIELDING POWER DESCENDS TO EARTH AS WAY OF MEDITATION** 3) The pinnacle is reached, a new cycle begins 2) Proceed silently up the blue mountain 1) When certainty has not yet appeared, retreat
	24 2 (7)	**RADIANT RETURN** informed by **SPACE OF MOON** — SPACE / SPACE, ENERGY / MOON	SPACE BETWEEN RADIANCE AND SPACE BRINGS ABOUT RADIANT RETURN — SPACE / SPACE / RADIANCE	**WAY OF WIELDING POWER ASCENDS TO HEAVEN AS SPACE OF MOON** 3) What power can be equal to the space of the moon? 2) Without effort mind ascends a moonbeam to the heavenly earth 1) What? The Moon has just returned!

CA
- •••• WAY OF THE TRANSCENDENT FOURTH – HIERATIC IMPERIAL
- •• WAY OF ENERGY (THUNDER WAY)
- ••• WAY OF THE MOON (HEART/WATER WAY)

PATH FREQUENCY 9: THE HEALER

IMAGE | DIVINATORY AFFIRMATION

SET 13 — ACTIVATE

25 · 53 (37) — SYNCHRONICITY informed by BREATH OF SUN (FIRE)

TIME · BREATH · ENERGY · SUN

Image: MIND BETWEEN RADIANCE AND TIME IS SYNCHRONICITY — TIME / MIND / RADIANCE

TIME CONCENTRATES COSMIC AWARENESS AS BREATH OF SUN
3) Inner and outer merge revealing the bridge of all time
2) The collective mind awakens the purple ray
1) Children of the Sun, activate the grid

26 · 19 (60) — TEMPLE OF TIME informed by MOON OF OCEAN/CONSCIOUSNESS

MEDITATION · MOON · TIME · OCEAN

Image: RADIANCE BETWEEN TIME AND MIND CREATES THE TEMPLE OF TIME — MIND / RADIANCE / TIME

COSMIC AWARENESS INFORMED BY MOON OF OCEAN
3) Polish the stone until silence becomes sound
2) Shining, shining; still it cannot be grasped
1) In the depths of the sea is the measure of time

SET 14 — MEDITATE

27 · 12 (62) — TEMPLE OF BEING informed by ENERGY OF MEDITATION

MEDITATION · ENERGY · ENERGY · MEDITATION

Image: SPACE BETWEEN RADIANCE AND MIND CREATES THE TEMPLE OF BEING — MIND / SPACE / RADIANCE

COSMIC AWARENESS EMPOWERS SPACE AS ENERGY OF MEDITATION
3) Spinning lights penetrate the Earth's vast dimensions
2) Rainbow wheels ignite from the space within
1) Self-generate the temple of light

28 · 42 (64) — TIME OF BURSTING informed by SUN OF MOON

OCEAN · SUN · BREATH · MOON

Image: WHEN TIME IS BETWEEN MIND AND RADIANCE THIS BRINGS ABOUT TIME OF BURSTING — RADIANCE / TIME / MIND

COSMIC AWARENESS TRANSCENDS SPACE AS THE SUN OF MOON
3) Sun and moon appear as one in the radiance of time
2) 13 Moons synchronizes space and time
1) Solar-lunar awareness is the nature of mind

SET 15 — TRANSFORM

29 · 23 (5) — HEART/MOON CRYSTAL informed by MOON OF TIME

HEART/MOON · MOON · HEART/MOON · TIME

Image: SPACE BETWEEN MIND AND RADIANCE IS THE HEART MOON CRYSTAL — RADIANCE / SPACE / MIND

SPACE FLOWS AS COSMIC AWARENESS WITHIN MOON OF TIME
3) Fill in the moon with visions of light
2) In the absence of Sun come illusions of space
1) Seek no recognition in the shadows of mind

30 · 49 (42) — VISION/SUN CRYSTAL informed by BREATH OF ENERGY/THUNDER

VISION/SUN · BREATH · VISION/SUN · ENERGY

Image: TIME BETWEEN RADIANCE AND MIND IS THE VISION SUN CRYSTAL — MIND / TIME / RADIANCE

RADIANCE OF SPACE DEFINES COSMIC AWARENESS AS BREATH OF ENERGY
3) Imagination reaches farther than sight
2) Within the crystal find the space of time
1) The eyes of the Earth watch and wait

SET 16 — RIPEN

31 · 46 (50) — MIND ATTRACTING informed by SUN OF BREATH

OCEAN · SUN · MEDITATION · BREATH

Image: WHEN TIME IS BETWEEN SPACE AND RADIANCE THIS IS MIND ATTRACTING — RADIANCE / TIME / SPACE

COSMIC AWARENESS ESTABLISHES BINARY ORDER AS SUN OF BREATH
3) Magnetic medium; attract the Sun
2) Know the forces that influence time
1) Concentrate in the absence of thought

32 · 8 (16) — MIND ENDURING informed by ENERGY OF SPACE

ENERGY · ENERGY · BREATH · SPACE

Image: WHEN TIME IS BETWEEN MIND AND SPACE THIS IS MIND ENDURING — SPACE / TIME / MIND

BINARY ORDER DEFINES MOVEMENT OF SPACE AS ENERGY OF SPACE
3) Transforming the two into one, the yogi dissolves in space
2) Exhaled, a thunder clap unifies the mind
1) Right and left: the breath intertwined descends

CA
WAY OF THE IRRESISTIBLE FIFTH – COSMOPOLITAN MEDIEVAL/UR
WAY OF THE MOON (HEART/WATER WAY)
WAY OF ENERGY (THUNDER WAY)

PATH FREQUENCY 10:
THE COMPASSIONATE ONE

			IMAGE	DIVINATORY AFFIRMATION

SET 17 ACTIVATE

33 | **16** (7) | **DEVOTION** informed by **MOON OF SPACE** — TIME, MOON, MEDITATION, SPACE | TIME BETWEEN SPACE AND TIME BRINGS ABOUT DEVOTION — TIME, TIME, SPACE | **TIME MEDITATES COSMIC ORDER AS SPACE OF MOON**
3) High above the mountain the eagle disappears into the Moon
2) The power of space is its absorption in time
1) Listen to the primordial sound of space

34 | **(54)** (57) | **PRAYER** informed by **WAY OF BREATH/WIND WAY** — ENERGY, BREATH, TIME, BREATH | TIME BETWEEN TIME AND SPACE BRINGS ABOUT PRAYER — SPACE, TIME, TIME | **MIND INFORMED BY COSMIC ORDER REALIZED AS WAY OF BREATH**
3) With no obstacles thought-streams travel the way of the wind
2) Exhalation: Maintain your inner light
1) Inhalation: Mind penetrates time

SET 18 MEDITATE

35 | **41** (21) | **MIND EXPANDING** informed by **SUN OF ENERGY** — VISION/SUN, SUN, SPACE, ENERGY | WHEN MIND IS BETWEEN SPACE AND MIND THAT IS MIND EXPANDING — MIND, MIND, SPACE | **COSMIC ORDER ENLIGHTENS SPACE AS SUN OF ENERGY**
3) A new Sun is born, the past disappears
2) Direct your attention to the Source of Mind
1) Lightning from the Sun brings sudden clarity

36 | **15** (34) | **INNER RADIANCE** informed by **ENERGY OF TIME** — SPACE, ENERGY, VISION/SUN, TIME | WHEN RADIANCE IS BETWEEN RADIANCE AND SPACE THIS IS INNER RADIANCE — SPACE, RADIANCE, RADIANCE | **COSMIC ORDER BECOMES SELF-ENLIGHTENING THROUGH ENERGY OF TIME**
3) Simplicity reveals the master
2) Radiance fills the inner space
1) Veiling your light, it increases its brilliance

SET 19 TRANSFORM

37 | **50** (34) | **POWER OF THE HOME** informed by **BREATH OF MOON** — BREATH, BREATH, VISION/SUN, MOON | WHEN RADIANCE IS BETWEEN RADIANCE AND TIME THIS IS THE POWER OF HOME — TIME, RADIANCE, RADIANCE | **COSMIC ORDER INFORMS TIME AS BREATH OF MOON**
3) Time alone will choose who goes out and who comes back
2) Do not leave the flame unattended
1) Within the home, the inner fire

38 | **20** (39) | **DISCRIMINATING** informed by **MOON OF MEDITATION** — VISION/SUN, MOON, OCEAN, MEDITATION | MIND BETWEEN TIME AND MIND IS DISCRIMINATING — MIND, MIND, TIME | **COSMIC ORDER HOLDS RADIANCE OF SPACE AS MOON OF MEDITATION**
3) Between the Sun and Moon the difference is clear
2) Harmonizing with solitude; the inner light shows the way
1) When doubt arises, still the mind

SET 20 RIPEN

39 | **11** (54) | **HEART'S DISCIPLINE** informed by **ENERGY OF OCEAN/CONSCIOUSNESS** — HEART/MOON, ENERGY, MEDITATION, OCEAN | RADIANCE BETWEEN SPACE AND RADIANCE BRINGS ABOUT HEART'S DISCIPLINE — RADIANCE, RADIANCE, SPACE | **COSMIC ORDER RETURNS TO HEART OF EARTH AS ENERGY OF OCEAN**
3) Crystal holds the hologram of journey's renewal
2) See the mountain in the ocean depths
1) In making the ascent, elevate the heart

40 | **(45)** (30) | **HEART'S RELEASE** informed by **WAY OF THE SUN (VISION WAY) ILLUMINATION** — ENERGY, SUN, HEART/MOON, SUN | MIND BETWEEN MIND AND SPACE BRINGS ABOUT HEART'S RELEASE — SPACE, MIND, MIND | **COSMIC ORDER RETURNS TO HEART OF HEAVEN AS WAY OF THE SUN**
3) Lightning flashes across the mind; the cosmic dream awakened
2) Heart illumined, mind expands
1) New moon enters the way of the Sun

CA

☶ WAY OF DYNAMIC CONSTRUCTION – GLOBAL INDUSTRIAL
☶ WAY OF MEDITATION (MOUNTAIN/TEMPLE WAY)
☶ WAY OF TIME (WAY OF THE COSMOS)

PATH FREQUENCY 19:
THE WORLD-CHANGER

			IMAGE	DIVINATORY AFFIRMATION

SET 21 — ACTIVATE

41 / 26 (47) — TEMPLE OF JOY informed by OCEAN OF MOON/HEART
- MEDITATION / OCEAN
- OCEAN / MOON

IMAGE: SPACE BETWEEN TIME AND MIND CREATES THE TEMPLE OF JOY
- MIND
- SPACE
- TIME

PRINCIPLE OF DYNAMIC CONSTRUCTION BROUGHT ABOUT BY OCEAN OF MOON
3) An ancient song penetrates the silence
2) Through the blue of the spiritual eye, listen to the inner light
1) Moon reflected in the ocean

42 / 60 (33) — RADIOSONIC WAY informed by TIME OF MEDITATION
- BREATH / TIME
- ENERGY / MEDITATION

IMAGE: SPACE BETWEEN RADIANCE AND TIME IS RADIOSONIC WAY
- TIME
- SPACE
- RADIANCE

PRINCIPLE OF DYNAMIC CONSTRUCTION EVOLVES MIND AS TIME OF MEDITATION
3) The rainbow emerges in the genesis of time
2) Time and space synchronize in a single thought structure
1) Build the temple, design the dream

SET 22 — MEDITATE

43 / 35 (41) — INDOMITABLE informed by MEDITATION OF OCEAN
- OCEAN / MEDITATION
- TIME / OCEAN

IMAGE: WHEN TIME IS BETWEEN TIME AND RADIANCE THAT IS INDOMITABLE
- RADIANCE
- TIME
- TIME

PRINCIPLE OF DYNAMIC CONSTRUCTION EVOLVES SPACE AS MEDITATION OF OCEAN
3) Silence—until light finds its own voice
2) Guard against the thief of delusion
1) Opening to the moment too soon to speak

44 / 5 (36) — TIME PENETRATING informed by SPACE OF SUN
- TIME / SPACE
- BREATH / SUN

IMAGE: WHEN TIME IS BETWEEN MIND AND TIME THAT IS TIME PENETRATING
- TIME
- TIME
- MIND

PRINCIPLE OF DYNAMIC CONSTRUCTION EMPOWERED BY TIME BECOMES SPACE OF SUN
3) Unify wisdom and reach the farthest horizon
2) The divine spark illumines the four quarters
1) Sun releases golden rings of breath

SET 23 — TRANSFORM

45 / 56 (12) — OCEANS OF PRESENCE informed by TIME OF SPACE
- OCEAN / TIME
- SPACE / SPACE

IMAGE: MIND BETWEEN SPACE AND RADIANCE BRINGS ABOUT OCEANS OF PRESENCE
- RADIANCE
- MIND
- SPACE

PRINCIPLE OF DYNAMIC CONSTRUCTION RELEASED INTO TIME AS TIME OF SPACE
3) In service to the one the people assemble in joy
2) The galactic command descends
1) In the temple of unending space

46 / 30 (28) — RADIANT EMPTINESS informed by OCEAN OF BREATH
- SPACE / OCEAN
- BREATH / BREATH

IMAGE: WHEN RADIANCE IS BETWEEN MIND AND SPACE THAT IS RADIANT EMPTINESS
- SPACE
- RADIANCE
- MIND

DYNAMIC CONSTRUCTION BECOMES CREATIVE SPACE THROUGH OCEAN OF BREATH
3) Unobstructed clarity—what do you see?
2) Circulate the light in the mind of time
1) Circulate the breath in the body of light

SET 24 — RIPEN

47 / 1 (24) — CALLING THE SOURCE informed by SPACE OF ENERGY
- OCEAN / SPACE
- HEART/MOON / ENERGY

IMAGE: WHEN MIND IS BETWEEN MIND AND RADIANCE THAT IS CALLING THE SOURCE
- RADIANCE
- MIND
- MIND

DYNAMISM RESOLVED AS ARCHITECTONICS WITHIN SPACE OF ENERGY
3) Listen to the echo of the ocean of space
2) Remember the future unknown
1) Hold to the path unseen

48 / 39 (26) — REACHING THE SOURCE informed by MEDITATION OF TIME
- HEART/MOON / MEDITATION
- BREATH / TIME

IMAGE: WHEN RADIANCE IS BETWEEN MIND AND RADIANCE THAT IS REACHING THE SOURCE
- RADIANCE
- RADIANCE
- MIND

ARCHITECTONICS RELEASES ORDER OF WHOLE AS MEDITATION OF TIME
3) Locate the origin of mind
2) Finding the center create the map
1) Within one breath, the whole of cosmic time

Book of the Transcendence • Cosmic History Chronicles • Volume VI

AC WAY OF THE TELEPATH – RADIOSONIC SYNTHESIS
WAY OF SPACE (EARTH WAY)
WAY OF THE OCEAN (WAY OF CONSCIOUSNESS)

PATH FREQUENCY 12:
THE SAGE

IMAGE   DIVINATORY AFFIRMATION

Set	#	#	Title	Components	Image	Divinatory Affirmation
SET 25 ACTIVATE	49 ⊤	31 (43)	REVOLUTION OF TIME informed by OCEAN OF TIME	OCEAN / OCEAN / VISION/SUN / TIME	WHEN TIME IS SURROUNDED BY RADIANCE THAT IS THE REVOLUTION OF TIME — RADIANCE / TIME / RADIANCE	REVOLUTION OF TELEPATHY BROUGHT ABOUT BY OCEAN OF TIME 3) Consciousness is an inner revolution 2) By the power of seven all time is renewed 1) When the aeon changes so do the people
	50 (T)	57 (25)	TRANSFORMATION OF TIME informed by TIME OF ENERGY	VISION/SUN / TIME / BREATH / ENERGY	WHEN TIME IS SURROUNDED BY MIND THAT IS THE TRANSFORMATION OF TIME — MIND / TIME / MIND	TELEPATHY TRANSFORMS THROUGH TIME OF ENERGY 3) Time and vision are the keepers of mind 2) Mind awakens to the nature of time 1) Galactic energy activates breath
SET 26 MEDITATE	51 ⊤	38 (18)	THUNDER/AROUSING BEING informed by MEDITATION OF BREATH	ENERGY / MEDITATION / ENERGY / BREATH	MIND BETWEEN RADIANCE AND SPACE IS THE THUNDER/AROUSING BEING — SPACE / MIND / RADIANCE	TELEPATHY AROUSES ENERGY OF SPACE AS MEDITATION OF BREATH 3) Effortless samadhi transcribes telepathic song lines 2) Through supermental force, the inner body awakens 1) Energy of cosmic breath arouses kundalini
	52 ⊥	0 (2)	MEDITATION/THE TEMPLE informed by WAY OF SPACE/EARTH WAY	MEDITATION / SPACE / MEDITATION / SPACE	RADIANCE BETWEEN SPACE AND MIND IS MEDITATION/THE TEMPLE — MIND / RADIANCE / SPACE	TELEPATHY ESTABLISHES THE TEMPLE AS WAY OF SPACE 3) Dream and reality are the same truth 2) Space established, light arises 1) Without space there is no light
SET 27 TRANSFORM	53 ⊕	61 (13)	EVOLVING informed by TIME OF SUN	BREATH / TIME / MEDITATION / SUN	RADIANCE BETWEEN SPACE AND TIME IS EVOLVING — TIME / RADIANCE / SPACE	TELEPATHY EVOLVES THE TEMPLE AS TIME OF SUN 3) Build the temple, know within 2) Touch the wind and feel the Sun 1) Climb the mountain, see the tree
	54 ⊥	27 (58)	TRANSCENDING informed by WAY OF CONSCIOUSNESS (OCEAN WAY)	ENERGY / OCEAN / OCEAN / OCEAN	MIND BETWEEN TIME AND SPACE IS TRANSCENDING — SPACE / MIND / TIME	TEMPLE INCORPORATES TELEPATHY AS WAY OF OCEAN 3) Wave upon wave, the cosmic rhythm ascends 2) Lightning flashes on ocean surf 1) See through time, the depths of consciousness
SET 28 RIPEN	55 ⊞	4 (15)	WISDOM AROUSING informed by SPACE OF MEDITATION	ENERGY / SPACE / VISION/SUN / MEDITATION	TIME BETWEEN RADIANCE AND SPACE IS WISDOM AROUSING — SPACE / TIME / RADIANCE	TELEPATHY BECOMES TIME TRAVEL THROUGH SPACE OF MEDITATION 3) Merge space with space and ride the cosmic vibration 2) See the pole star in the midnight Sun 1) Arouse the inner light in mountain meditation
	56 ⊞	34 (4)	VOYAGING informed by MEDITATION OF MOON/HEART	VISION/SUN / MEDITATION / MEDITATION / MOON	TIME BETWEEN SPACE AND MIND IS VOYAGING — MIND / TIME / SPACE	TIME TRAVEL UNIFIES THE MIND AS MEDITATION OF MOON 3) It says: Return to mind and begin again 2) A light is seen from a distant star 1) Journeying on the circuits of higher mind

AC
- Way of the Galactic Octave – Holonomic Field
- Way of the Sun (Fire/Vision Way)
- Way of Breath (Wind Way)

PATH FREQUENCY 21:
MAGUS OF THE INFINITE

			IMAGE	DIVINATORY AFFIRMATION

SET 29 ACTIVATE

(57) 21 (63) — MIND OF BREATH informed by MOON OF SUN (HEART OF VISION)
BREATH / MOON; BREATH / SUN
Image: RADIANCE BETWEEN MIND AND TIME IS THE MIND OF BREATH — TIME, RADIANCE, MIND
PENETRATION OF GALACTIC OCTAVE BROUGHT ABOUT BY MOON OF SUN
3) Moon is the muse; inspiration is the Sun
2) The master of the house rises with a song
1) When mind becomes breath, breath becomes mind

(58) 51 (61) — RADIANCE OF JOY informed by BREATH OF OCEAN
OCEAN / BREATH; OCEAN / OCEAN
Image: MIND BETWEEN TIME AND RADIANCE IS RADIANCE OF JOY — RADIANCE, MIND, TIME
SONG OF THE GALACTIC OCTAVE BROUGHT ABOUT BY BREATH OF OCEAN
3) The fire of wisdom whispers the ancient song
2) Listen to the space within galactic mind
1) Follow the stream of light through the ocean of time

SET 30 MEDITATE

59 44 (56) — DISSOLVING informed by SUN OF MEDITATION
BREATH / SUN; HEART/MOON / MEDITATION
Image: WHEN SPACE IS BETWEEN MIND AND TIME THAT IS DISSOLVING — TIME, SPACE, MIND
GALACTIC OCTAVE SOUNDS MIND OF SPACE AS SUN OF MEDITATION
3) Sound the galactic octave—mind is no more
2) Proceed directly to the galactic center
1) Contemplate the souls of the stars

60 10 (40) — MEASURING informed by ENERGY OF MOON
HEART/MOON / ENERGY; OCEAN / MOON
Image: WHEN SPACE IS BETWEEN TIME AND RADIANCE, THAT IS MEASURING — RADIANCE, SPACE, TIME
GALACTIC OCTAVE LIMITS SPACE AS ENERGY OF MOON
3) Meaning is only a rhythm in the radiance of space
2) Mind is the measure; infinity its paradox
1) Measure the moon and find mind's limit

SET 31 TRANSFORM

61 55 (9) — INNER SPACE informed by BREATH OF TIME
BREATH / BREATH; OCEAN / TIME
Image: WHEN SPACE IS SURROUNDED BY TIME THAT IS INNER SPACE — TIME, SPACE, TIME
GALACTIC OCTAVE RESOUNDS AS MIND THROUGH THE BREATH OF TIME
3) Time seals space with cosmic breath—the disclosure of the divine
2) Nature perfects in a long space of time
1) From the ocean of consciousness time emerges

62 17 (3) — INNER TIME informed by MOON OF ENERGY
ENERGY / MOON; MEDITATION / ENERGY
Image: WHEN TIME IS SURROUNDED BY SPACE THAT IS INNER TIME — SPACE, TIME, SPACE
GALACTIC OCTAVE DEFINES EVOLUTION THROUGH MOON OF ENERGY
3) Synchronicity of space fills time with telepathy
2) Between Moon and mountain, the bird wings its way
1) Spirit is received by the rays of the stars

SET 32 RIPEN

63 14 (32) — ACCOMPLISHED informed by ENERGY OF BREATH
HEART/MOON / ENERGY; VISION/SUN / BREATH
Image: WHEN ALL IS RADIANCE THEN COMES ACCOMPLISHMENT — RADIANCE, RADIANCE, RADIANCE
GALACTIC OCTAVE UNIVERSALIZES SPACE AS THE ENERGY OF BREATH
3) Transform space in the light of the Sun; no fear of falling back
2) Remembrance is the origin of the one Eternal Sun
1) Be impressed by the supernal orb

64 40 (35) — PREPARED informed by SUN OF SPACE
VISION/SUN / SUN; HEART/MOON / SPACE
Image: WHEN ALL IS MIND THEN WE ARE PREPARED — MIND, MIND, MIND
GALACTIC OCTAVE UNIFIES THE DIMENSIONS AS THE SUN OF SPACE
3) Surrender mind to the King of Stars
2) Fully illumined, spontaneous unification within endless change
1) Contemplate the internal light

128 Codon Noosphere Program
integrating 0-63 Primal Radial Early Heaven Fu Hi
Structural Order and Magic Square Array of 252 (12.12)
with 1-64 Historic/Evolutionary Sequential Later Heaven King Wen
Psi Bank Arrangement and Magic Square Array of 260 (13.0)

$$12.12 \ (21\times12) \times 8 = 5.0.16 \ (2016) \ +$$
$$13.0 \ (13\times20) \times 8 = 5.4.0 \ (2080)$$
$$= 10.4.16 \ (4096) = 64^2$$

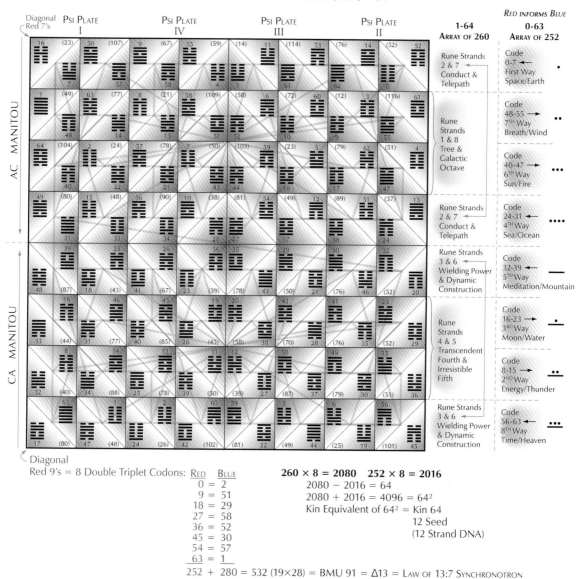

Red informs Blue

	1-64 Array of 260	0-63 Array of 252
	Rune Strands 2 & 7 Conduct & Telepath	Code 0-7 ◄ First Way Space/Earth
	Rune Strands 1 & 8 Tree & Galactic Octave	Code 48-55 → 7th Way Breath/Wind
		Code 40-47 → 6th Way Sun/Fire
	Rune Strands 2 & 7 Conduct & Telepath	Code 24-31 ◄ 4th Way Sea/Ocean
	Rune Strands 3 & 6 Wielding Power & Dynamic Construction	Code 32-39 → 5th Way Meditation/Mountain
	Rune Strands 4 & 5 Transcendent Fourth & Irresistible Fifth	Code 16-23 → 3rd Way Moon/Water
		Code 8-15 → 2nd Way Energy/Thunder
	Rune Strands 3 & 6 Wielding Power & Dynamic Construction	Code 56-63 ◄ 8th Way Time/Heaven

Diagonal
Red 9's = 8 Double Triplet Codons:

Red	Blue
0	2
9	51
18	29
27	58
36	52
45	30
54	57
63	1

$$260 \times 8 = 2080 \quad 252 \times 8 = 2016$$
$$2080 - 2016 = 64$$
$$2080 + 2016 = 4096 = 64^2$$
Kin Equivalent of 64^2 = Kin 64
12 Seed
(12 Strand DNA)

$$252 + 280 = 532 \ (19\times28) = BMU \ 91 = \Delta13 = Law \ of \ 13:7 \ Synchronotron$$
$$Diff = 28 = \Delta7$$

EARLY HEAVEN (RADIAL ABSOLUTE) & LATER HEAVEN (PSI BANK) 8×8 MATRICES

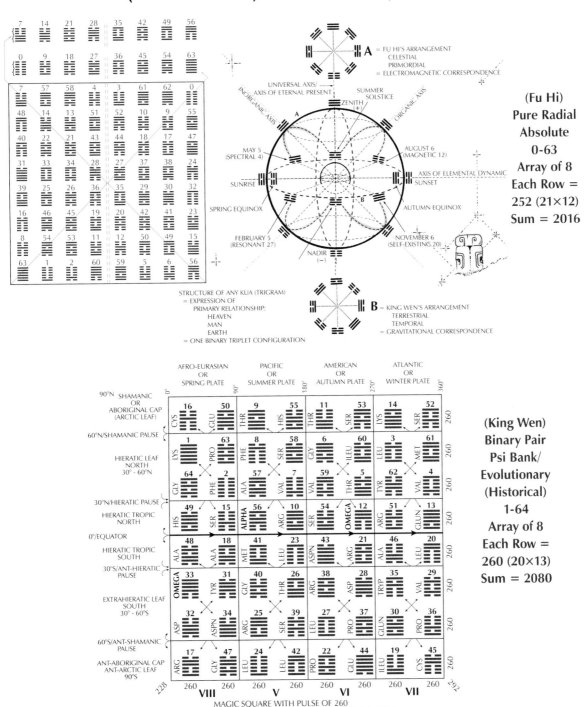

A = FU HI'S ARRANGEMENT
CELESTIAL
PRIMORDIAL
= ELECTROMAGNETIC CORRESPONDENCE

(Fu Hi)
Pure Radial
Absolute
0-63
Array of 8
Each Row =
252 (21×12)
Sum = 2016

STRUCTURE OF ANY KUA (TRIGRAM)
= EXPRESSION OF
PRIMARY RELATIONSHIP:
HEAVEN
MAN
EARTH
= ONE BINARY TRIPLET CONFIGURATION

B = KING WEN'S ARRANGEMENT
TERRESTRIAL
TEMPORAL
= GRAVITATIONAL CORRESPONDENCE

(King Wen)
Binary Pair
Psi Bank/
Evolutionary
(Historical)
1-64
Array of 8
Each Row =
260 (20×13)
Sum = 2080

MAGIC SQUARE WITH PULSE OF 260
SHOWING I CHING/DNA CODON MATRIX/LATTICE
AS KEY TO 24 PSIONIC NIMBOID MEMBRANES AND SEASONAL
MEMORY PLATES + 260-DAY/PULSE MATRIX OF SACRED CALENDAR

GALACTIC I CHING – 128 CODON – 12 STRAND DNA

AC WAY OF THE TREE
• WAY OF BREATH – WAY OF FIRE (SUN)

SET 1 ACTIVATE

| 1 | 48 | Creative Genesis informed by Breath of Space |
| 2 | 22 | Primal Matrix informed by Moon of Breath |

SET 2 MEDITATE

| 3 | 9 | Fresh Start informed by Way of Energy (Thunder Way) |
| 4 | 47 | Listen Again informed by Sun of Time |

SET 3 TRANSFORM

| 5 | 18 | People Together informed by Way of the Moon (Water Way) |
| 6 | 52 | People Apart informed by Breath of Meditation |

SET 4 RIPEN

| 7 | 43 | Power of the People informed by Sun (Fire) of Ocean (Consciousness) |
| 8 | 13 | Unity of the People informed by Energy of Sun |

CA WAY OF WIELDING POWER
••• WAY OF TIME (COSMOS) – WAY OF MEDITATION (MOUNTAIN)

SET 9 ACTIVATE

| 17 | 63 | Arousing Joy informed by Way of Time (Way of Cosmos) |
| 18 | 25 | Taming Mind informed by Ocean of Energy |

SET 10 MEDITATE

| 19 | 6 | Wizard's Aspiration informed by Space of Breath |
| 20 | 32 | Wizard's Contemplation informed by Meditation of Space |

SET 11 TRANSFORM

| 21 | 29 | Arousing Vision informed by Ocean of Sun (Fire) |
| 22 | 59 | Temple of Vision informed by Time of Ocean |

SET 12 RIPEN

| 23 | 36 | Mind's Release informed by Way of Meditation (Mountain Way) |
| 24 | 2 | Radiant Return informed by Space of Moon |

AC WAY OF CONDUCT
•• WAY OF SPACE – WAY OF OCEAN

SET 5 ACTIVATE

| 9 | 58 | Discipline informed by Time of Moon |
| 10 | 28 | Practice informed by Ocean of Meditation |

SET 6 MEDITATE

| 11 | 3 | Dynamizing informed by Space of Ocean |
| 12 | 37 | Stabilizing informed by Meditation of Sun |

SET 7 TRANSFORM

| 13 | 24 | People Organized informed by Ocean of Space |
| 14 | 62 | Wisdom of the People informed by Time of Breath |

SET 8 RIPEN

| 15 | 33 | Way of the People informed by Meditation of Energy |
| 16 | 7 | Triumph of the People informed by Space of Time |

CA WAY OF THE TRANSCENDENT FOURTH
•••• WAY OF ENERGY – WAY OF MOON

SET 13 ACTIVATE

| 25 | 53 | Synchronicity informed by Breath of Sun (Fire) |
| 26 | 19 | Temple of Time informed by Moon of Ocean |

SET 14 MEDITATE

| 27 | 12 | Temple of Being informed by Energy of Meditation |
| 28 | 42 | Time of Bursting informed by Sun of Moon (Water) |

SET 15 TRANSFORM

| 29 | 23 | Heart/Moon Crystal informed by Moon of Time |
| 30 | 49 | Vision/Sun Crystal informed by Breath of Energy |

SET 16 RIPEN

| 31 | 46 | Mind Attracting informed by Sun of Breath |
| 32 | 8 | Mind Enduring informed by Energy of Space |

CATALOG OF 128 CODONS, PSI BANK MATRIX WEAVE, IN THEIR MEANINGS SHOWING LATER HEAVEN NOTATION 1-64, OVERLAID WITH 0-63 MATRIX SUCH THAT EACH PSI BANK CODON IS PAIRED WITH A 0-63 EARLIER HEAVEN CODON THAT OCCURS IN THAT SAME POSITION, GIVING EXPANDED MEANING TO THE WHOLE

CA — WAY OF THE IRRESISTIBLE FIFTH
WAY OF MOON – WAY OF ENERGY

SET 17 ACTIVATE	33	16	Devotion informed by Space of Moon
	34	(54)	Prayer informed by Way of Breath (Wind Way)
SET 18 MEDITATE	35	41	Mind Expanding informed by Sun of Energy
	36	15	Inner Radiance informed by Energy of Time
SET 19 TRANSFORM	37	50	Power of the Home informed by Breath of Moon
	38	20	Discriminating informed by Moon of Meditation
SET 20 RIPEN	39	11	Heart's Discipline informed by Energy of Ocean
	40	(45)	Heart's Release informed by Way of the Sun (Fire Way)

AC — WAY OF THE TELEPATH
WAY OF SPACE – WAY OF OCEAN

SET 25 ACTIVATE	49	31	Revolution of Time informed by Ocean of Time
	50	57	Transformation of Time informed by Time of Energy
SET 26 MEDITATE	(51)	38	Thunder/Arousing Being informed by Meditation of Breath
	(52)	(0)	Meditation/The Temple informed by Way of Space (Earth Way)
SET 27 TRANSFORM	53	61	Evolving informed by Time of Sun
	54	(27)	Transcending informed by Ocean Way (Way of Consciousness)
SET 28 RIPEN	55	4	Wisdom Arousing informed by Space of Meditation
	56	34	Voyaging informed by Meditation of Moon

CA • — WAY OF DYNAMIC CONSTRUCTION
WAY OF MEDITATION – WAY OF TIME

SET 21 ACTIVATE	41	26	Temple of Joy informed by Ocean of Moon
	42	60	Radiosonic Way informed by Time of Meditation
SET 22 MEDITATE	43	35	Indomitable informed by Meditation of Ocean
	44	5	Time Penetrating informed by Space of Sun
SET 23 TRANSFORM	45	56	Ocean of Presence informed by Time of Space
	46	30	Radiant Emptiness informed by Ocean of Breath
SET 24 RIPEN	47	1	Calling the Source informed by Space of Energy
	48	39	Reaching the Source informed by Meditation of Time

AC ••• — WAY OF THE GALACTIC OCTAVE
WAY OF SUN (FIRE) – WAY OF BREATH (WIND)

SET 29 ACTIVATE	(57)	21	Mind of Breath informed by Moon of Sun (Heart of Enlightenment)
	(58)	51	Radiance of Joy informed by Breath of Ocean
SET 30 MEDITATE	59	44	Dissolving informed by Sun of Meditation
	60	10	Measuring informed by Energy of Moon
SET 31 TRANSFORM	61	55	Inner Space informed by Breath of Time
	62	17	Inner Time informed by Moon of Energy
SET 32 RIPEN	63	14	Accomplished informed by Energy of Breath
	64	40	Prepared informed by Sun of Space

1-64 Psi Bank Code

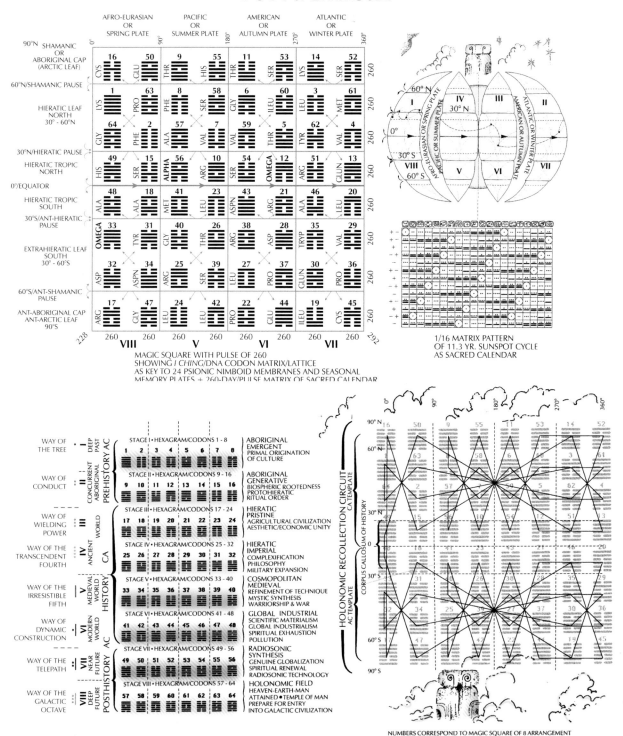

AFRO-EURASIAN OR SPRING PLATE

PACIFIC OR SUMMER PLATE

AMERICAN OR AUTUMN PLATE

ATLANTIC OR WINTER PLATE

90°N SHAMANIC OR ABORIGINAL CAP (ARCTIC LEAF)

60°N/SHAMANIC PAUSE

HIERATIC LEAF NORTH 30° - 60°N

30°N/HIERATIC PAUSE

HIERATIC TROPIC NORTH

0°/EQUATOR

HIERATIC TROPIC SOUTH

30°S/ANT-HIERATIC PAUSE

EXTRAHIERATIC LEAF SOUTH 30° - 60°S

60°S/ANT-SHAMANIC PAUSE

ANT-ABORIGINAL CAP ANT-ARCTIC LEAF 90°S

MAGIC SQUARE WITH PULSE OF 260
SHOWING I CHING/DNA CODON MATRIX/LATTICE
AS KEY TO 24 PSIONIC NIMBOID MEMBRANES AND SEASONAL
MEMORY PLATES + 260-DAY/PULSE MATRIX OF SACRED CALENDAR

1/16 MATRIX PATTERN
OF 11.3 YR. SUNSPOT CYCLE
AS SACRED CALENDAR

WAY OF THE TREE — DEEP PAST
STAGE I • HEXAGRAM / CODONS 1 - 8
1 2 3 4 5 6 7 8
ABORIGINAL EMERGENT PRIMAL ORIGINATION OF CULTURE

WAY OF CONDUCT — CONCURRENT ABORIGINAL / PREHISTORY AC
STAGE II • HEXAGRAM / CODONS 9 - 16
9 10 11 12 13 14 15 16
ABORIGINAL GENERATIVE BIOSPHERIC ROOTEDNESS PROTOHIERATIC RITUAL ORDER

WAY OF WIELDING POWER — III
STAGE III • HEXAGRAM / CODONS 17 - 24
17 18 19 20 21 22 23 24
HIERATIC PRISTINE AGRICULTURAL CIVILIZATION AESTHETIC/ECONOMIC UNITY

WAY OF THE TRANSCENDENT FOURTH — IV ANCIENT WORLD / CA
STAGE IV • HEXAGRAM / CODONS 25 - 32
25 26 27 28 29 30 31 32
HIERATIC IMPERIAL COMPLEXIFICATION PHILOSOPHY MILITARY EXPANSION

WAY OF THE IRRESISTIBLE FIFTH — V MEDIEVAL WORLD / HISTORY
STAGE V • HEXAGRAM / CODONS 33 - 40
33 34 35 36 37 38 39 40
COSMOPOLITAN MEDIEVAL REFINEMENT OF TECHNIQUE MYSTIC SYNTHESIS WARRIORSHIP & WAR

WAY OF DYNAMIC CONSTRUCTION — VI MODERN WORLD / AC
STAGE VI • HEXAGRAM / CODONS 41 - 48
41 42 43 44 45 46 47 48
GLOBAL INDUSTRIAL SCIENTIFIC MATERIALISM GLOBAL INDUSTRIALISM SPIRITUAL EXHAUSTION POLLUTION

WAY OF THE TELEPATH — VII NEAR FUTURE
STAGE VII • HEXAGRAM / CODONS 49 - 56
49 50 51 52 53 54 55 56
RADIOSONIC SYNTHESIS GENUINE GLOBALIZATION SPIRITUAL RENEWAL RADIOSONIC TECHNOLOGY

WAY OF THE GALACTIC OCTAVE — VIII DEEP FUTURE / POSTHISTORY AC
STAGE VIII • HEXAGRAM / CODONS 57 - 64
57 58 59 60 61 62 63 64
HOLONOMIC FIELD HEAVEN-EARTH-MAN ATTAINED • TEMPLE OF MAN PREPARE FOR ENTRY INTO GALACTIC CIVILIZATION

HOLONOMIC RECOLLECTION CIRCUIT
CA TEMPLATE
CORPUS CALLOSUM OF HISTORY
AC TEMPLATE

NUMBERS CORRESPOND TO MAGIC SQUARE OF 8 ARRANGEMENT

TABLE OF CORRESPONDENCES:
KING WEN (KW) CYCLIC PSI BANK & FU HI (FH) ABSOLUTE RADIAL
INDEX ACCORDING TO CODON EQUIVALENTS

$(1–64 = 260, 0–63 = 252)$ $(13 \times 20 + 12 \times 21 = 512 = 64 \times 8)$

King Wen inverse pairs

KW PSI	FH RADIAL	KW PSI	FH RADIAL	
1	63	2	0	= 66 (11×6)
3	17	4	34	= 58
5	23	6	58	= 92 / 216
7	2	8	16	= 33 (11×3)
9	55	10	59	= 133 (19×7)
11	7	12	56	= 86
13	61	14	47	= 135
15	4	16	8	= 43
17	25	18	38	= 98
19	3	20	48	= 90
21	41	22	37	= 121 (11²)
23	32	24	1	= 80
25	57	26	39	= 147
27	33	28	30	= 118
29	18	30	45	= 122
31	28	32	14	= 105

Left column side labels:
- AC EMERGENT – GENERATIVE — WAY OF THE TREE – WAY OF CONDUCT
- CA HIERATIC PRISTINE & IMPERIAL — WAY OF WIELDING POWER – WAY OF TRANSCENDENT FOURTH

King Wen inverse pairs

KW PSI	FH RADIAL	KW PSI	FH RADIAL	
33	60	34	15	= 142
35	40	36	5	= 116
37	53	38	43	= 171 (Δ18)
39	20	40	10	= 109
41	35	42	49	= 167
43	31	44	62	= 180
45	24	46	6	= 121 (11²)
47	26	48	22	= 143 (13×11)
49	29	50	46	= 174
51	9	52	36	= 148
53	52	54	11	= 170
55	13	56	44	= 168 (8.8)
57	54	58	27	= 196 (14²)
59	50	60	19	= 188
61	51	62	12	= 186
63	21	64	42	= 190

Right column side labels:
- CA COSMOPOLITAN – GLOBAL INDUSTRIAL — WAY OF THE IRRESISTIBLE FIFTH – WAY OF DYNAMIC CONSTRUCTION
- AC RADIOSONIC & HOLONOMIC FIELD — WAY OF THE TELEPATH – WAY OF GALACTIC OCTAVE

1527

2569

0-63 PRIMAL RADIAL SYMMETRY CODE

7	57	58	4	3	61	62	0
48	14	13	51	52	10	9	55
40	22	21	43	44	18	17	47
31	33	34	28	27	37	38	24
39	25	26	36	35	29	30	32
16	46	45	19	20	42	41	23
8	54	53	11	12	50	49	15
63	1	2	60	59	5	6	56

	126	126	126	126					
126	7	57	58	4	3	61	62	0	252
126	48	14	13	51	52	10	9	55	252
126	40	22	21	43	44	18	17	47	252
126	31	33	34	28	27	37	38	24	252
	39	25	26	36	35	29	30	32	252
	16	46	45	19	20	42	41	23	252
	8	54	53	11	12	50	49	15	252
	63	1	2	60	59	5	6	56	252
252	252	252	252	252	252	252	252	252	252

SAME CONSISTENCY AS
PSI BANK MAGIC SQUARE
ARRAY 260

7	57	58	4	3	61	62	0
48	14	13	51	52	10	9	55
40	22	21	43	44	18	17	47
31	33	34	28	27	37	38	24
39	25	26	36	35	29	30	32
16	46	45	19	20	42	41	23
8	54	53	11	12	50	49	15
63	1	2	60	59	5	6	56

EACH SEQUENCE OF EIGHT FOLLOWS THIS ORDER ON THE BOTTOM

TOP =

	0–7	WAY OF SPACE
	8–15	WAY OF ENERGY
	16–23	WAY OF THE MOON
	24–31	WAY OF THE OCEAN
	32–39	WAY OF MEDITATION
	40–47	WAY OF THE SUN
	48–55	WAY OF BREATH
	56–63	WAY OF TIME

TABLE OF CORRESPONDENCES:
0-63 – 1-64 INDEX ACCORDING TO EQUIVALENTS

28 =	7	6	5	4	3	2	1	0	WAY OF SPACE
									EARTH WAY
	11	46	36	15	19	7	24	2	= 160 188

92 =	15	14	13	12	11	10	9	8	WAY OF ENERGY
									THUNDER WAY
	34	32	55	62	54	40	51	16	= 344 436

156 =	23	22	21	20	19	18	17	16	WAY OF THE MOON
									WATER WAY
	5	48	63	39	60	29	3	8	= 255 411

220 =	31	30	29	28	27	26	25	24	WAY OF THE OCEAN
									CONSCIOUSNESS WAY
	43	28	49	31	58	47	17	45	= 318 538 (BMU 97)

284 =	39	38	37	36	35	34	33	32	WAY OF MEDITATION
									MOUNTAIN WAY
	26	18	22	52	41	4	27	23	= 213 497 (71×7)

348 =	47	46	45	44	43	42	41	40	WAY OF THE SUN
									FIRE WAY
	14	50	30	56	38	64	21	35	= 308 656 (BMU 215) (41×16)

412 =	55	54	53	52	51	50	49	48	WAY OF BREATH
									WIND WAY
	9	57	37	53	61	59	42	20	= 338 750 (BMU 309)

476 =	63	62	61	60	59	58	57	56	WAY OF TIME
									HEAVEN WAY
2016	1	44	13	33	10	6	25	12	= 144 620 (BMU 179)
									2080 4096

THE NEW GATEWAY TO KNOWLEDGE

COMPRESSED 64-UNIT MATRIX
128 DNA/12-STRAND

- RADIAL SENSE FIELDS (28)
- •• SENSE ELEMENTS (20)
- ••• MIND ELEMENTS (12)
- •••• INTERDIMENSIONAL INTERGALACTIC CORE (4)

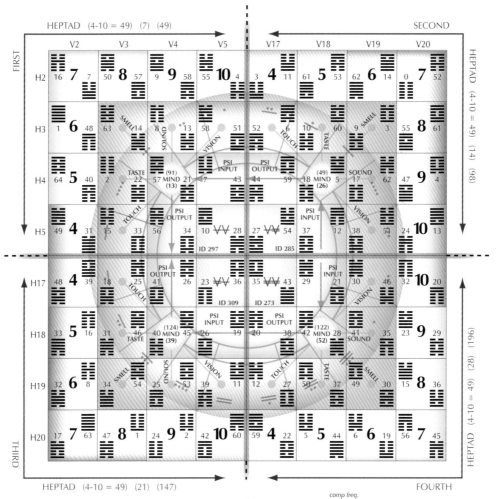

HEPTAD (4-10 = 49) (7) (49)   SECOND

FIRST   HEPTAD (4-10 = 49) (14) (98)

THIRD   HEPTAD (4-10 = 49) (21) (147)   FOURTH   HEPTAD (4-10 = 49) (28) (196)

---

4 External Sense Fields:
$4+5+6+7+8+9+10$
$= 49 (7^2)$
$\times 4$
$196 (7:28)$
Sum frequency of 7×4
28-unit Sense Fields
$196 + 64 = 260$
$= 13:20$ Time freq.

Each Sense Field Quadrant
$= 1$ Heptad $= 7$ units
$1+2+3+4+5+6+7=28$
$7=7/20 (13:7$ Wheel$)$
$1-7 = 28 (4\times7)$
$4-10 = 49 (7^2)$
$1-13 = 91 (13\times7)$
$49 \times 4 = 196 (28\times7)$
$13 \times 7 (91) \times 4 =$
$364 = 13 \times 28$
$49\times13 = 637 = $ BMU 196

comp. freq.

$(578)\ 9$ $17^2\times2$ $\begin{cases} \text{Touch} = 4 & (16) & (316) \\ \text{Taste} = 5 & (20) & (262) \end{cases}$

7 Smell $= 7$ (28) (256)

$(446)\ 19$ $\begin{cases} \text{Sound} = 9 & (36) & (196) \\ \text{Vision} =10 & \underline{(40)} & \underline{(250)} \end{cases}$

(64×20) (1280)

6 & 8 (24, 32)
Subliminal/Synaesthetic Organizers
(190) 6 Organizes 4, 5, 7
(322) 8 Organizes 7, 9, 10
$512 = 64\times7$

(7×4) Field Organizers
Composite 12-Strand
Frequency $= 1792 = 64\times28$

For construction of
Compressed Matrix see
Great Synchronotron 120-121

0–63   Lower Triplet   First & Last

Upper Triplet   First & Last   0–63

	TIME	ENERGY THUNDER	WATER MOON	MEDITATION	OCEAN	SUN	BREATH	SPACE	
SPACE	SPACE of TIME	SPACE of ENERGY	SPACE of MOON	SPACE of MEDITATION	SPACE of OCEAN	SPACE of SUN	SPACE of BREATH	SPACE of SPACE	SPACE
BREATH	BREATH of TIME	Smell / BREATH of ENERGY	Sound / BREATH of MOON	Vision / BREATH of MEDITATION	Touch / BREATH of OCEAN	Taste / BREATH of SUN	Smell / BREATH of BREATH	BREATH of SPACE	BREATH
SUN	SUN of TIME	Taste / SUN of ENERGY	Mind / SUN of MOON	Mind Input / SUN of MEDITATION	Mind Output / SUN of OCEAN	Mind / SUN of SUN	Sound / SUN of BREATH	SUN of SPACE	SUN
OCEAN	OCEAN of TIME	Touch / OCEAN of ENERGY	Mind / OCEAN of MOON	Intergalactic Channel / OCEAN of MEDITATION	Intergalactic Channel / OCEAN of OCEAN	Mind Input / OCEAN of SUN	Vision / OCEAN of BREATH	OCEAN of SPACE	OCEAN
MEDITATION	MEDITATION of TIME	Touch / MEDITATION of ENERGY	Mind Output / MEDITATION of MOON	Intergalactic Channel / MEDITATION of MEDITATION	Intergalactic Channel / MEDITATION of OCEAN	Mind Input / MEDITATION of SUN	Vision / MEDITATION of BREATH	MEDITATION of SPACE	MEDITATION
WATER MOON	MOON of TIME	Taste / MOON of ENERGY	Mind / MOON of MOON	Mind Input / MOON of MEDITATION	Mind Output / MOON of OCEAN	Mind / MOON of SUN	Sound / MOON of BREATH	MOON of SPACE	WATER MOON
ENERGY THUNDER	ENERGY of TIME	Smell / ENERGY of ENERGY	Sound / ENERGY of MOON	Vision / ENERGY of MEDITATION	Touch / ENERGY of OCEAN	Taste / ENERGY of SUN	Smell / ENERGY of BREATH	ENERGY of SPACE	ENERGY THUNDER
TIME	TIME of TIME	TIME of ENERGY	TIME of MOON	TIME of MEDITATION	TIME of OCEAN	TIME of SUN	TIME of BREATH	TIME of SPACE	TIME

(5TH Force) Sense Inputs	28	Time-Space Lattices
Sense Elements	20	Energy-Breath Lattices
Mind Elements	12	Moon-Sun Lattices
Inter. Gal. Channels	4	Meditation-Ocean Lattices (Interdimensional Core)

1ST QUADRANT ⩲
1ST TIME DIMENSION COSMIC CREATION
1ST MENTAL SPHERE PRECONSCIOUS PROFOUND SAMADHI

2ND QUADRANT ⩲
2ND TIME DIMENSION COSMIC ASCENSION
4TH MENTAL SPHERE CONTINUING CONSCIOUS HIGHER MIND CONTROL

3RD QUADRANT ⩲
3RD TIME DIMENSION COSMIC SYNCHRONIZATION
2ND MENTAL SPHERE SUBCONSCIOUS INFORMATIVE SAMADHI

4TH QUADRANT ⩲
4TH TIME DIMENSION COSMIC CUBE
3RD MENTAL SPHERE CONSCIOUS WAKING CONSCIOUS MEDIUMSHIP

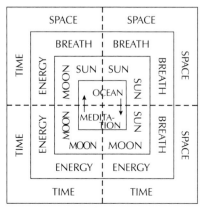

COMPOSITE FREQUENCY CODES

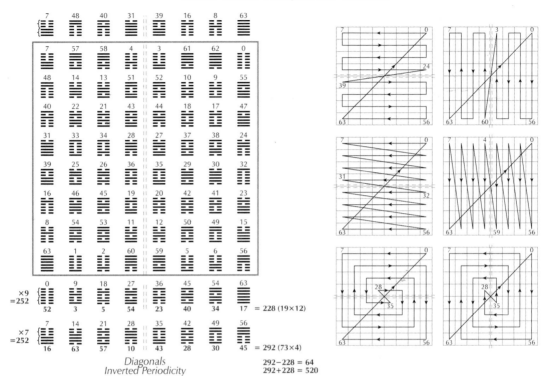

$$\times 9 = 252$$

0	9	18	27	36	45	54	63
52	3	5	54	23	40	34	17	= 228 (19×12)

$$\times 7 = 252$$

7	14	21	28	35	42	49	56
16	63	57	10	43	28	30	45	= 292 (73×4)

Diagonals
Inverted Periodicity

292 − 228 = 64
292 + 228 = 520

The 64 Cells of the Ark of the Noosphere and their Composite 12 Strand Frequencies, Coded to the MOAP and 4 8^2 Matrices in the Four Quadrants of the 441 Space Matrix

$(13 \times 20) + (12 \times 21) =$

16	50	9	55	11	53	14	52	
23	**107**	**67**	**59**	**14**	**114**	**76**	**52**	$= 512 = 8^3 \, (64{\times}8) \, (16^2{\times}2)$
49	**77**	**21**	**109**	**58**	**70**	**12**	**116**	$= 512 = 8^3 \, (64{\times}8) \, (16^2{\times}2)$
104	**24**	**78**	**50**	**103**	**23**	**79**	**51**	$= 512 = 8^3 \, (64{\times}8) \, (16^2{\times}2)$
80	**48**	**90**	**38**	**81**	**49**	**89**	**37**	$= 512 = 8^3 \, (64{\times}8) \, (16^2{\times}2)$
87	**43**	**67**	**59**	**78**	**50**	**76**	**52**	$= 512 = 8^3 \, (64{\times}8) \, (16^2{\times}2)$
49	**77**	**85**	**45**	**58**	**70**	**76**	**52**	$= 512 = 8^3 \, (64{\times}8) \, (16^2{\times}2)$
40	**88**	**78**	**50**	**39**	**87**	**79**	**51**	$= 512 = 8^3 \, (64{\times}8) \, (16^2{\times}2)$
80	**48**	**26**	**102**	**81**	**49**	**25**	**101**	$= 512 = 8^3 \, (64{\times}8) \, (16^2{\times}2)$
‖ 512	‖ 512	‖ 512	‖ 512	‖ 512	‖ 512	‖ 512	‖ 512	

$(13 \times 20) + (12 \times 21) = 512 = 8^3 \, (64{\times}8) \, (16^2{\times}2)$

64^2
8^4 DNA CUBE